95534

O

The *Blackwell Great Minds* series gives readers a strong sense of the fundamental views of the great western thinkers and captures the relevance of these figures to the way we think and live today.

1 **Kant** by Allen W. Wood
2 **Augustine** by Gareth B. Matthews
3 **Descartes** by André Gombay
4 **Charles Darwin** by Michael Ruse
5 **Sartre** by Katherine J. Morris

Forthcoming
Aristotle by Jennifer Whiting
Nietzsche by Richard Schacht
Plato by Paul Woodruff
Spinoza by Don Garrett
Wittgenstein by Hans Sluga
Schopenhauer by Robert Wicks
Heidegger by Taylor Carman
Maimonides by Tamar Rudavsky
Berkeley by Margaret Atherton
Leibniz by Christa Mercer
Shakespeare by David Bevington
Hume by Stephen Buckle
Kierkegaard by M. Jamie Ferreira
Mill by Wendy Donner and Richard Fumerton
Camus by David Sherman
Socrates by George H. Rudebusch
Hobbes by Edwin Curley

blackwell great minds

edited by Steven Nadler

blackwell great minds

sartre

Katherine J. Morris

BLACKWELL PUBLISHING
350 Main Street, Malden, MA 02148-5020, USA
9600 Garsington Road, Oxford OX4 2DQ, UK
550 Swanston Street, Carlton, Victoria 3053, Australia

The right of Katherine J. Morris to be identified as the Author of this Work has been
asserted in accordance with the UK Copyright, Designs, and Patents Act 1988.

First published 2008 by Blackwell Publishing Ltd

1   2008

Library of Congress Cataloging-in-Publication Data

Morris, Katherine J.
   Sartre / Katherine J. Morris.
      p. cm. — (Blackwell great minds)
   Includes bibliographical references and index.
   ISBN-13: 978-0-631-23280-3 (hardcover : alk. paper)
   ISBN-13: 978-0-631-23279-7 (pbk. : alk. paper)   1. Sartre, Jean-Paul, 1905–1980.   I. Title.
   B2430.S34M645 2008
   194—dc22

                                                                              2007035163

A catalogue record for this title is available from the British Library.

Set in 9.5/12pt Trump Mediaeval
by Graphicraft Limited, Hong Kong
Printed and bound in Singapore
by Utopia Press Ptd Ltd

The publisher's policy is to use permanent paper from mills that operate a sustainable
forestry policy, and which has been manufactured from pulp processed using acid-free and
elementary chlorine-free practices. Furthermore, the publisher ensures that the text paper
and cover board used have met acceptable environmental accreditation standards.

For further information on
Blackwell Publishing, visit our website:
www.blackwellpublishing.com

For Phyllis
À la recherche de Bitten perdu

contents

acknowledgements

This book began as a lecture series, given at Oxford over many years; I thank those students who attended those lectures, many of whom I also had the pleasure of getting to know in tutorials. Their questions have fed into this book in innumerable ways. Particular thanks to those former students – Alex Barker, Simon Bruegger, Lucy Ellinas, Navid Pourghazi, and Gabriel Sokoloff – who read and gave their feedback on some draft chapters.

Bill Schroeder made detailed comments on a late draft of the entire book; it was a delight to find in him a critic both sympathetic and astute. Paul Lodge waded though a large part of an earlier draft and I am greatly in his debt for his comments and questions. Annamaria Carusi and Giovanni de Grandis also rescued me from a number of errors both large and small. I am grateful too to Christina Howells and Michael Peckitt for their comments on particular chapters, to Nick Bellorini for his feedback and encouragement throughout the project, and to Mary Dortch for her thoughtful and thought-provoking copy-editing. Tim Horder was the sine qua non of this book.

Bob Solomon – a cherished friend for more than twenty years – provided incisive criticisms of (and even found a few nice things to say about) drafts of Chapters 3 and 4. As I was putting the finishing touches to the manuscript, I was deeply saddened to learn from Kathleen of his sudden death. Bob was a fine scholar and an unsurpassable communicator, and philosophy will be far less fun without him. He would, I'm sure, have told me that my book still has too many cats in it.

I learned about Sartre quite literally at my mother's knee. She it was who taught me, by example, the value of persisting in the effort required to understand him and the fecundity of thinking with him as well as, at times, against him; I owe to her as well my appreciation of Sartre's observations on the lived body. This book was written for her.

introduction

J ean-Paul Sartre, usually cited as the creator of existentialism, is one of those rare intellectuals whose name conjures up definite images in the mind of the person on the Clapham omnibus – be it of the squat, wall-eyed, balding, bespectacled figure, Boyard or pipe in one hand, Pernod in the other, holding forth in a Parisian café, or having his curiously intellectual affairs with beautiful young women and then performing his curiously intellectual dissections of these affairs in letters to his lifelong partner Simone de Beauvoir; the 'committed intellectual', addressing crowds of students on political marches, or smoking a Cuban cigar in Fidel Castro's private apartments; or the playwright and novelist whose main message appears to be that life is meaningless and that 'Hell is other people'.

This powerful public image of the man is apt to raise two somewhat opposing doubts in the minds of academics today. On the one hand, is this man really to be taken seriously *as a philosopher*? On the other, are his philosophical ideas not irredeemably *dated*, 'the height of kitsch' (Lévy 2003: 3), stuck in the overheated atmosphere of post-war Paris?

The first is a concern that is likely to be raised by so-called 'analytic' philosophers. For somewhat obscure historical reasons, philosophers in the twentieth and still to some extent in the twenty-first century are widely classified by English-speaking philosophers into the analytic and the Continental, with Sartre being seen as a paradigmatic Continental philosopher.[1] It has aptly been said that Continental philosophy is analytic philosophy's 'other': it is often deemed not to be philosophy at all, and not even in the way that sociology or biology is 'not philosophy' – these are seen as legitimate activities despite not being philosophy! – but in a way that implies that it is engaged in an enterprise that *ought not to be done*: purporting to be philosophy while being precisely what philosophy *ought not to be* (Glendinning 2002). Continental philosophy is equated with sophistry, with mere rhetoric as opposed to logic, with obscurity rather than clarity, with vagueness rather than precision. It might be added that analytic philosophy plays something of the same role *vis-à-vis* Continental: it is seen as ahistorical, dry, logic-chopping and scientistic. A. N. Whitehead, who, though British, is regarded by some analytic philosophers as veering rather too close to the Continental side, allegedly said of the arch-analytic philosopher Bertrand Russell, 'Bertie thinks I am muddle-headed, but I think he is simple-minded' (Wang 1966: 672), and this nicely encapsulates the respective stereotypes that Continental and analytic philosophers hold of each other.

Yet these stereotypes each contain a grain of truth: Continental philosophy at its worst really *is* muddle-headed and obscurantist, and analytic philosophy at its worst really *is* simplistic and scientistic (cf. Critchley 2001: ch. 3). And there are many features of Sartre's writing that might appear to invite charges like sophistry and obscurantism. Although his philosophical writings contain many brilliant literary passages which are a pleasure to read, they are shot through with a formidable and unfamiliar vocabulary (being-in-itself vs. being-for-itself, transcendence vs. facticity, *négatités*, etc.). In some cases one can give a reasonably concise definition; in other cases the meaning is so multi-layered that it must simply emerge. Sartre's use of locutions like 'human reality' will make well-brought-up analytic philosophers squirm. He has a penchant for expressing himself paradoxically ('man is the being who is what he is not and is not what he is'); for describing things not intrinsically negative in negative-sounding language (e.g., the 'alienation' of my possibilities which the Other brings about); for making statements that border on the hysterical (e.g., the Other 'steals' my world); and for hyperbole (e.g., man is 'always and forever free or he is not free at all'). 'He often attempts three or four ways of conveying a certain impression, which do not necessarily say exactly the same as, and may even contradict, each other' (Warnock 1965: 9).

I am certainly not going to defend his worst excesses. But if the term 'obscurantism' implies writing obscurely for no good reason and with no decent return for the investment necessary to comprehend him, I hope to make a case that Sartre decidedly does not merit this label. First, if Sartre's vision of human beings and the world is full of what Nietzsche somewhere called the rough and uneven contours of things, if it is sometimes unclear and ambiguous, this is often because human reality *itself* is, and there is no merit to ignoring this. And second, many of the stylistic features just canvassed actually play a *methodological* role: the return on our investment is at least in part because of and not despite these features.[2] Rhetoric is not always 'mere rhetoric' or 'empty rhetoric'.[3] Sartre's methodology – what he sees himself as doing, qua philosopher – is indeed different from that of analytic philosophy, and that this is part of what helps to create the perceived chasm between them. But 'different' does not entail 'worse'; there are, for example, certain parallels between Sartre's conception of his own enterprise qua philosopher and the later Wittgenstein's,[4] and Wittgenstein, although clearly doing something different from what most analytic philosophers tell themselves they are doing, is not only not dismissed by them but is on the contrary widely considered to be part of the analytic canon.[5]

The second concern, that Sartre is *passé* and existentialism a 'wasm', is apt to be raised by post-structuralists and postmodernists, both in certain philosophy faculties and within literary criticism, building on the work of more recent French philosophers such as Foucault and Derrida. 'Sartre is often seen as a philosopher of a world that has passed, a child and relic of modernity whose voice rang out amidst the alienations and horrors of the twentieth century but which is now scarcely detectable in the soundwaves of our contemporary postmodern condition' (Fox 2003: 1). He is frequently viewed by such thinkers as a radical individualist, ignoring the social dimension of human reality; as an advocate of extreme freedom, ignoring the economic, political, cultural, biological and historical constraints on human freedom; and as a proponent of a totally lucid self-consciousness, ignoring both the Freudian unconscious and Marx's 'false consciousness'. Even if his language sometimes invites these interpretations, and even if some of them point to blind spots at least in his early work, all of these charges vastly oversimplify his conception of human reality. Additionally, there is both an ahistoricity and a double standard in these charges: ahistoricity, because Foucault and Derrida could not have happened without Sartre;[6] a double standard, because Foucault and Derrida too have their blind spots, some of which they even share with Sartre. For example, Foucault, like Sartre, is largely gender-blind, yet feminists embrace Foucault with enthusiasm, because they see this blindness as a lacuna to be filled as opposed to an irreparable crack in the edifice of his thinking; although there are notable exceptions, including of course Beauvoir, feminists have been slower to accord the same latitude to Sartre.[7]

But a version of the second concern is also apt to be raised by Maurice Merleau-Ponty's many admirers. Although Merleau-Ponty is hardly known outside academia, he was not just a contemporary and friend of Sartre, he was also – Beauvoir excepted – his ablest critic. Merleau-Ponty's fans all too readily take him to have so thoroughly demolished Sartre's thinking that there is nothing left but a pile of rubble. Sartre is accused of ignoring the 'lived body', i.e., our own body as it figures in the everyday stream of life as opposed to the body which is the object of physiological and anatomical investigations; he is accused of what Merleau-Ponty labelled 'intellectualism', in particular of failing to recognize a realm of pre-conceptual experience; he is accused of introducing new dualisms, for instance between 'subject' and 'object', even if not exactly the much-reviled Cartesian mind/body dualism. Merleau-Ponty did point up and help to compensate for some of Sartre's blind spots, for example his seeming unawareness of non-human animals and his blithe neglect, at least in his earlier work, of infants and children – as if we sprang into being like Athena from the head of Zeus, fully conscious, self-conscious and pursuing freely chosen projects.[8] Yet Merleau-Ponty was standing on Sartre's shoulders throughout, including, absolutely centrally, in his celebrated exposition of the lived body; and I prefer to say, not that he *refuted* Sartre but that he often put Sartre's thoughts more clearly, incisively and soberly than Sartre did himself, and took them further. I therefore freely use his formulations to clarify as well as to develop Sartre's own.[9]

In this book I concentrate on Sartre's more straightforwardly philosophical works; nonetheless I will on occasion refer to his literary works, biographies and so on, which continue his philosophical project in interesting ways. I also concentrate on his earlier philosophical works, principally *Being and Nothingness*, rather than later works such as the *Critique of Dialectical Reasoning*. I see more continuities than some do between his earlier and his later work; the facets of his thinking which I particularly want to spotlight are already in place in *Being and Nothingness*; and to indicate in any detail how his thinking developed over time would have made the exposition more lengthy and more complicated than it already is.

I devote more time than is usual to an exploration of Sartre's methodology, of what I take Sartre to be *doing*. This does not entail spending less time than usual on explications of the results of this methodology, because method and results are for him inherently intertwined in a kind of methodological circle:[10] Sartre's starting point is the idea that we philosophers are *human beings* engaged in a project of exploring what it *is* to be a human being. We discover, for example, through reflection on our own conscious acts that human beings are conscious beings, i.e., beings who, *inter alia*, are capable of reflecting on their own conscious acts. Again, we discover that every human enterprise is by its very nature in danger of being subverted by what Sartre calls 'bad faith' (self-deception, illusions, prejudices, etc.) – including the very philosophical enterprise which arrived at this discovery and which is attempting to communicate it.

This suggests that not only is there a kind of circle – though a virtuous circle, I will urge – in Sartre's methodology, but there are two intertwined aspects to it. One – the philosophical method called phenomenology – involves the reflective exploration of what it is to be a human being; the other involves the attempt to overcome the bad faith, prejudices and illusions which are apt to subvert the practice of phenomenology and which may interfere with others' understanding of its results. This second aspect I refer to as 'therapeutic', a term which nods in the direction of the literature on Wittgenstein, since this, I submit, is a central respect in which the phenomenological method and

Wittgenstein's philosophical method come together. Ridding someone of bad faith, including intellectual bad faith, is importantly *unlike* the more familiar philosophical activities of correcting mistakes and fallacies, and requires different tactics. Sartre, like Wittgenstein, is not just aiming to change the way we think, he is aiming to change the way we *live*.

I would be gratified if this book had the side effect of performing a bit of Sartrean therapy on those analytic philosophers who are inclined to see Continental philosophy as mere rhetoric and on the post-structuralists, postmodernists and Merleau-Pontyans who take Sartre to be *passé*.

Sartre has been called 'the philosopher of freedom', and he himself said that '[e]verything that I have tried to write or do in my life was meant to stress the importance of freedom' (quoted in Anderson 1979: 42). This is clearly applicable to the way he conducted his long and highly politically engaged life. It is also plainly true at the level of the content of his philosophy: Sartre holds what appears to be an extreme doctrine of freedom as absolute and responsibility as all-pervasive. That his view of freedom is not as radical as is sometimes suggested, and that it began to *appear* less radical in his later works, does not detract from this point. But, as I will be arguing, his methodology too entails a philosophy of freedom, and this in at least two different senses:[11] he aims to 'free us from our preconceived opinions', to borrow Descartes's phrase, to liberate us from the grip of philosophical bad faith which stands in the way of our acknowledging what we all know to be true from our lived experience as human beings; and in so doing, he frees us to live, as philosophers, in that same world that we, as human beings, inhabit. Those whom philosophy has exiled from the life-world may find this prospect exhilarating.

Indeed, more than that: philosophy's denigration of the life-world has not taken place in a social and cultural vacuum; nor has the phenomenological reaction against it. The notion of a crisis was in the air (and indeed in print) when Husserl, the founder of phenomenology, picked it up in his 1935 lecture 'Philosophy and the crisis of European man'; this lecture formed part of the basis of his great later unfinished work *The Crisis of European Sciences and Transcendental Phenomenology*, and has been published in English, together with 'Philosophy as a rigorous science', under the title *Phenomenology and the Crisis of Philosophy*.[12] Perhaps it was not unnatural for a Jew in Germany at this time to sense a crisis; yet Nazism was only one manifestation of the crisis in question. What concerned Husserl was the danger posed to European culture by the growing predominance – in domains to which it was not appropriate – of a scientific rationality narrowly interpreted as a technical and technological rationality: a frame of mind that was reductive, atomistic, objectivist and scientist. We Anglo-American thinkers are not perhaps so prone to talk in terms of crises, yet many of us will find something resonant in this description. Sartrean phenomenology is not going to save humanity from this threat, but it may serve to remind us of what we are in danger of losing.

notes

1 The distinction is sometimes actually formalized in the institutional structures of faculties and departments in Anglo-American colleges and universities, but even where it is not, there is a tendency to divide philosophy, at least post Kant, into these different traditions. The labels make a slightly nonsensical contrast, the former referring very broadly to a style or a family of styles of doing philosophy, the latter apparently to a geographical region (see Williams 1996; Critchley 2001); moreover, they seem to assume a broad within-group uniformity which is doubtful to say the least. Nonetheless these labels remain in common usage. The proponents of analytic philosophy today are typically Anglo-American or at least Anglophone (e.g., the Britons Bertrand Russell and Gilbert Ryle, the Americans W. V. O. Quine and Donald Davidson), and one often hears analytic philosophy referred to as 'Anglo-American philosophy'; Dummett (1993: 2) is quite right to point out that 'Anglo-Austrian' would respect its historical development rather better, though this would make the contrast with 'Continental' even more nonsensical than it already is. The German Gottlob Frege and the Austrian Ludwig Wittgenstein are often considered honorary non-Continentals, while the British philosophers F. H. Bradley and R. G. Collingwood are held to have a whiff of the Continental about them. There is something other than mere geography behind the labelling.
2 *Pace* Warnock: 'He is interested in presenting a picture of what things are like, in bludgeoning his readers into accepting a certain view of the world, and he does not care very much what weapons he uses to do this' (1965: 10).
3 Indeed rhetoric used to be taught alongside logic as an essential tool for the orator.
4 See K. J. Morris 2007. I am making no historical claims of direct influence between Sartre and Wittgenstein: it is doubtful that Wittgenstein read Sartre, and Sartre confessed that he 'would rather read "thrillers" than Wittgenstein' (W 49) – although this was less an indictment of Wittgenstein than an admission of his weakness for trashy fiction. My only claim here is that there are certain parallels in their philosophical methodologies, parallels which make neither of them happy bedfellows with mainstream analytic philosophers. At the same time, there are a number of thinkers – e.g., Schopenhauer, Nietzsche, Kierkegaard – who influenced both, and this is not, I think, irrelevant.
5 The Oxford 'ordinary-language' philosopher J. L. Austin, himself a star in the analytic firmament (if, unfortunately, slightly dimmed these days), is another. He actually said that his methodology might be called 'linguistic phenomenology', 'only that is rather a mouthful' (1970: 182), phenomenology being the methodology created by Edmund Husserl and further developed by a number of Continental philosophers including Sartre. (See Chapter 1.)

6 This point is increasingly being insisted upon by Sartre scholars; the reading of Sartre which is emerging from this recognition has been dubbed 'the New Sartre'; see Howells 1992, especially her Introduction and Conclusion, and Fox 2003; also Lévy 2003 in places.

7 This is beginning to change; see Murphy 1999.

8 Nor was Merleau-Ponty wholly free of his own blind spots, most notably, to aspects of *Sartre's* thinking, which sometimes resulted in one-sided or unsympathetic readings of the latter's work.

9 There is a whole industry of Sartre-vs.-Merleau-Ponty studies, some of whom take broadly this view. Stewart's (1998a) collection provides a valuable survey of the best examples of this industry; Whitford 1982 is a classic.

10 I might have used the term 'hermeneutic circle', an expression associated with the German phenomenologist Martin Heidegger and his famous pupil Hans Gadamer; but in the present context it seemed better to avoid getting embroiled in debates about the precise meanings of *this* term and whether they fit Sartre.

11 This is another central respect in which Sartre's methodology bears comparison to Wittgenstein's, although this aspect of Wittgenstein's thinking is frequently neglected. Baker 2004, esp. ch. 9, helps to fill this lacuna.

12 Spengler's *Decline of the West* was a contributor to this notion of crisis; Wittgenstein too was influenced by Spengler's deeply pessimistic remarks on culture; see Monk 1990: 299. But there were many other contributors, e.g., Friedrich Nietzsche.

sartre's life

'I began my life', Sartre wrote, 'as I shall no doubt end it: among books' (W 28).

It's not a little daunting to write about the life of a man who wrote his own, brilliant autobiography – *Les Mots* (*Words*); who wrote brilliant biographies of other writers – including *Saint Genet*, a 'preface' to Genet's complete works which ran to more than 500 pages; who wrote brilliantly *about* biography – for example, in Part II.2.i of *Being and Nothingness*; and about whom brilliant biographies have been written – Lévy's, most spectacularly.[1]

It was Sartre's conviction that a biography should reveal the individual's 'fundamental project' (see Chapter 8), and he characterized his own fundamental project as 'being a writer'.[2] 'I existed only to write and if I said: me – that meant the me who wrote' (W 97). His autobiography, which ends at the age of 12, is split into two parts: the first called 'Reading', the second 'Writing'. He describes the moment when he finally learned to read: 'I was wild with delight: those withered voices in their little nature-books, those voices which my grandfather revived with a glance, which he heard and which I did not hear, were mine!' (W 33); 'I had found my religion: nothing seemed to me more important than a book' (W 39).

Sartre wrote his first novel at the age of 7: it was an adventure story called *Pour un papillon* ('For a butterfly'). 'I had borrowed the plot, the characters, the details of their adventures, even the title from a story in pictures which had appeared the previous term' (W 90–1). So wrote Sartre in his autobiography fifty years later – though what 7-year-old child writes original literature of lasting value? We can in retrospect see this childish novel as the first clear note in the melody that was to dominate Sartre's life.

Sartre was a *prodigious* writer in more than one sense of the word. As Leak (2006: 7–8) notes, his works ran to two metres of shelf space on his death, and posthumous publications have expanded this to two and a half. The sheer range of Sartre's literary achievements is extraordinary:

not just philosophy, plays, novels and short stories, not just biography and autobiography, but ten volumes of essays on literary theory, literary criticism, painting, politics, etc., as well as obituaries, published (1947–76) under the sequence title *Situations*; journal articles and newspaper editorials; even film scripts, including that commissioned by John Huston, published posthumously in 1984 as *Le Scénario Freud*. (The film was made in 1962, but Sartre withdrew his name on the grounds that the script had been cut, possibly unsurprisingly since it would have run to eight hours' screen time!) He wrote voluminous diaries at certain periods of his life; his war diaries were published in 1983, again posthumously. He wrote many, many letters, some published posthumously in 1983 as *Lettres au Castor et quelques autres*, Castor ('Beaver') being his pet name for Simone de Beauvoir, his lifelong partner and an almost equally prolific writer.[3] When he wasn't writing, he was talking, often in the context of interviews which were themselves written down, including, most controversially, those with Benny Lévy in the last weeks of Sartre's life.

Sartre was born in Paris on 21 June 1905; his father died not long afterwards, and he and his mother went to live with his grandparents in Meudon in Alsace, then part of Germany. His grandfather, Charles Schweitzer, was a cousin of the Nobel Peace Prize winner Albert Schweitzer. Sartre and his mother moved to Paris in 1911, where Sartre attended *lycée*. His mother remarried in 1917, and they settled in La Rochelle, where Sartre found it hard to fit in. Sartre returned to Paris in 1920; he sat his *baccalauréat* in 1921–2, and entered the École Normale Supérieure, affiliated with the Sorbonne. He failed the *agrégation*[4] the first time around, but passed it a year later, in 1929, with the top marks. Beauvoir, whom he met in his last year there, came second. After military service in 1929–31, he taught philosophy at a *lycée* in Le Havre from 1931 to 1936, a generally unhappy period since he and Beauvoir were separated; he took a year out to study in Berlin; he taught briefly in Laon, then at a *lycée* in Paris. In 1939, he was conscripted; in 1940, he was taken as a prisoner of war; a year later he was released. He joined the Resistance, and he taught for a few more years at a *lycée*.

The remainder of his life lacks those normal bourgeois landmarks of education, employment, marriage and so on, unless one includes his adoption in 1965 of Arlette Elkaim. If anything, the landmarks in his life were *world* events: the Algerian War, the Vietnam War, the Cold War. Throughout this period he wrote, he engaged in numerous affairs ('*contingent* love affairs' which coexisted, uneasily at times, with the '*essential* love' he shared with Beauvoir (see Beauvoir PL 24; see also Chapter 7)), he travelled, he edited journals and newspapers, he got involved in political movements and political protests, he had numerous conversations in Parisian cafés with the other leading lights of the arts, literature, philosophy and politics, he turned down honours (including the Nobel Prize for literature[5]), he gave press conferences and magazine and television interviews, he lectured all over the world, he wrote.

His death, on 15 April 1980, was itself a world event. Originally scheduled for the Friday, his funeral was rescheduled for Saturday to allow more people to attend; and attend they did, more than 50,000 of them. The limousine which carried Beauvoir to the Montparnasse cemetery was mobbed by 'curiosity-seekers and paparazzi' (Bair 1990: 587). Afterwards, the streets of Paris were devoid of cars; small groups gathered in cafés, men and women walked about alone, 'at a loose end' (Lévy 2003: 1). It was more like the funeral of a John F. Kennedy or a Princess Diana than that of a writer and intellectual. His death was front-page news throughout the world; in Japan, a professor who had translated Sartre's works wrote: 'He has embodied the twentieth century, not just with his work, but with his own attitude toward life' (quoted in Cohen-Solal 1987: 521).

What follows is arranged semi-temporally, semi-thematically, each section centring on the philosophical themes and context of key writings.

La Nausée and the Contingency of Existence

Sartre's first published novel is also his most famous: *La Nausée* (1938), published in English as *Nausea* in 1949. He wrote it while teaching in Le Havre, a town thinly disguised in the novel as 'Bouville' or Mudville. It seethes with vitriolic denunciations of the bourgeoisie of Bouville: the concert-goers who 'imagine that the sounds flow into them, sweet, nourishing, and that their sufferings become music, like Werther; they think that beauty is compassionate to them. Mugs' (N 232). And it seethes too with possibly mescaline-enhanced illustrations of the absence of necessary laws in nature,[6] so much more colourful – and so much more *bodily*[7] – than Hume's tepid 'The sun might not rise tomorrow':

> a mother might look at her child's cheek and ask him: 'What's that – a pimple?' and see the flesh puff out a little, split, open, and at the bottom of the split an eye, a laughing eye might appear . . . And someone else might feel something scratching in his mouth. He goes to the mirror, opens his mouth: and his tongue is an enormous, live centipede, rubbing its legs together and scraping his palate. (N 212–13)

Nausea is to say the least a *strange* novel. It is strange in part because nothing really happens in it; strange too because it is a genuinely philosophical novel.[8] It is, as Leak says (2006: 30), a kind of 'metaphysical detective story': the diary of Antoine Roquentin's efforts to discover the source of his uneasy, nauseating sense that 'something has changed'. The experience that finally gives him the answer is recounted in the best-known passage from the book, his encounter with the chestnut tree root in the park:

> In vain to repeat: 'This is a root' – it didn't work any more. I saw clearly that you could not pass from its function as a root, as a breathing pump, *to that*, to this hard and compact skin of a sea lion, to this oily, callous, head-strong look . . . (N 174)

What this encounter reveals is the contingency of the *existence* of things – the unjustifiability, the inexplicability, the 'absurdity', to use one of Sartre's favourite words – and at the same time its sheer brute undeniability: the *thereness* of the root, both its *merely* thereness and its *inescapable* thereness.

What are the origins of this philosophical vision? Sartre discovered phenomenology (see below) during his time at Le Havre, and *Nausea* is sometimes seen as a critique of Husserl's version of phenomenology (e.g., Manser 1966: 4ff.). He began the novel prior to his initial encounter with phenomenology, however; and its core intuition, the intuition of the contingency and the undeniability of the existence of things, certainly predates this encounter, and both his excitement at his discovery of phenomenology and his critique of Husserl's version of it are grounded in this intuition. Its first glimmering, Sartre told Beauvoir, came while he was at the École Normale, when he was struck by 'the contrast between the cinema, where there was no contingency, and the exit into the street, where . . . there was nothing but contingency' (AFS 142). According to his friend the philosopher and sociologist Raymond Aron, Sartre first formulated his ideas on this topic in a paper presented at their professor Léon Brunschvicg's seminar (Lévy 2003: 127),[9] and it was on this subject that he wrote his failed *agrégation* paper (Hayman 1987: 71).

Sartre was well-educated in the greats familiar to today's Anglo-American philosophy students – Plato, Aristotle, Descartes, Leibniz, Spinoza, Kant and so on – as well as some rather less familiar, notably Henri Bergson.[10] The aforementioned Brunschvicg was one of the principal lecturers at the Sorbonne at the time, and although it is not clear that Sartre attended many of his lectures (Hayman 1987: 73), his philosophical outlook was the atmosphere which Sartre and his contemporaries breathed.[11] Brunschvicg, who supervised Beauvoir's thesis on Leibniz (Bair 1990: 128), was an exponent of what was known as 'critical idealism'. Sartre's contemporary Merleau-Ponty describes it as follows:

Brunschvicg transmitted to us the heritage of idealism, as Kant understood it . . . his philosophy in all cases sought to grasp both exterior perception and the constructions of science as creative and constructive activities of the mind . . . his essential contribution consisted precisely in informing us that we must turn toward the mind, toward the subject which constructs science and the perception of the world, but that lengthy descriptions or explications cannot be made of this mind, this subject. (TD 130)

Later Sartre would offer this memorable if not wholly self-explanatory epitome of the Brunschvicgian vision: 'digestive philosophy' (*philosophie alimentaire*), according to which 'the spidery mind trapped things in its web, covered them with a white spit and slowly swallowed them' (IFI 4; cf. BN 187). Arguably even at this early stage in his development, however, he instinctively rebelled against this vision; it seemed to make the existence of things – of the chestnut tree root, for example – *intelligible* and even *justifiable* because constructed by the mind, and by the same token *dubitable*, but finally it seemed to make the exploration of the existence of things philosophically unimportant.

Sartre's Encounter with Phenomenology

Edmund Husserl, the founder of the philosophical methodology called phenomenology, lectured at the Sorbonne in 1929; these lectures became the foundations of his *Cartesian Meditations*. Brunschvicg alerted his students 'to the fact that this was an event of a kind rarely encountered in the history of philosophy' (Jean Hyppolite, quoted in Lévy 2003: 112). And yet Sartre did not attend (Lévy 2003: 112). Different stories are told about his belated encounter with phenomenology; the most famous, recounted by Beauvoir, is this, from 1933:

we spent an evening together at the Bec de Gaz . . . We ordered the speciality of the house, apricot cocktails; Aron said, pointing to his glass, 'You see, my dear fellow, if you are a phenomenologist, you can talk about this cocktail and make philosophy out of it.' Sartre turned pale with emotion at this. Here was just the thing he had been longing to achieve for years – to describe objects just as he saw them, and extract philosophy from the process. (PL 112)[12]

Sartre had always 'wanted to grapple with this living reality, and despised any analysis which limited its dissection to corpses' (Beauvoir PL 30). Aron advised him to read Emmanuel Lévinas's introduction to Husserlian phenomenology; and Sartre himself claims to 'have come to phenomenology through Lévinas' (S 158). This first contact produced in him 'a moment of utter dismay and confusion' because he said to himself 'Oh, he's already discovered all my ideas' (Beauvoir AFS 157).[13] Husserl, unlike Brunschvicg, *seemed* to be saying that it was possible to describe the sheer existence of a chestnut root or an apricot cocktail and still be doing philosophy. Aron, who had just spent a year at the French Institute in Berlin, encouraged Sartre to do the same, to study the works of Husserl.

Husserl saw himself as following the *spirit* of Descartes's philosophizing, a spirit which he characterized as 'radical self-responsibility' and 'the ultimate conceivable freedom from prejudice' (Husserl CM §2).[14] Like Descartes, he wanted philosophy to be absolutely certain: to be, in his terms, a 'rigorous science': 'science' in the sense of the German word *Wissenschaft*, which is broader than the modern use of the term 'science' in English. Phenomenology was to be the name of this rigorous science.[15] The subject-matter to be explored by phenomenology was to be consciousness; but consciousness is *intentional*, that is, it has the 'universal fundamental property' of being '*of* something; as *cogito*, to bear within itself its *cogitatum*' (CM §14); to perceive or imagine or recollect was to perceive, imagine or recollect *something*, what Husserl called the 'intentional object'. Hence this exploration – 'intentional analysis' – was twofold: there are 'descriptions of the intentional object as such', which he labels 'noematic' descriptions, and descriptions of 'the modes of consciousness (for example: perception, recollection, retention)', which he labels 'noetic' descriptions (CM §15).

What seems to have gripped many of Husserl's admirers, including Sartre, was not – to Husserl's chagrin – his own vision of phenomenology as a rigorous science; it was his intentional analyses of these *noemata* and *noeses*. What an *embarras de richesse* the simple perception of a die contained:

> if I take the perceiving of this die as the theme for my description, I see in pure reflection that 'this' die is given continuously as an objective unity in a multiform and changeable multiplicity of manners of appearing, which belong determinately to it . . . they flow away in the unity of a synthesis, such that in them 'one and the same' is intended as appearing. The one identical die appears . . . in the changing modes of the Here and There, over against an always co-intended, though perhaps unheeded, absolute Here (in my co-intended organism) . . . the near-thing, as 'the same', appears now from this 'side', now from that . . . [also] the other manners of appearance (tactual, acoustic, and so forth) . . . (CM §§17–18)

If you can make philosophy out of a die, it is easy to see how you could make philosophy out of an apricot cocktail or a chestnut tree root.

After leaving Le Havre, over the next four years, Sartre published four short phenomenological works: *La Transcendence de l'ego* in 1936, published in English as *The Transcendence of the Ego* in 1962;[16]

L'Imagination, also 1936, published in English as *Imagination* in 1962; *Esquisse d'une théorie des émotions* (1939), published in English under the title *The Emotions: Outline of a Theory* in 1948 and later as *Sketch for a Theory of the Emotions* in 1962, and *L'Imaginaire* (1940), published in English under the title *The Psychology of the Imagination* in 1948. The first is explicitly anti-Husserlian, in particular attacking Husserl's idea that he had discovered a 'transcendental ego' from which 'the world that exists for me . . . derives its whole sense and its existential status' (CM §11). The last three works, on the face of it, look like good Husserlian projects: *L'Imagination* and the *Esquisse* noetic analyses of two important modes of consciousness, *L'Imaginaire* a noematic analysis of the intentional objects of imagination. Yet they too – *L'Imagination* in particular – already contained the seeds of his ultimate disillusionment with Husserl.

As he expressed it later, 'a deeper and deeper gulf was separating me from Husserl. His philosophy evolved ultimately towards idealism, which I could not accept' (WD 184), a form of idealism which Husserl himself called 'transcendental idealism' (CM §41), inviting comparison to Kant and thence to the reviled Brunschvicgian philosophy.[17] Why? Somewhat as Descartes required us to suspend judgement on all our pre-conceived opinions, Husserl required us to 'bracket off' our everyday assumption of the existence of things before describing our experiences of those things (CM §8). If I as a phenomenologist want to describe my perceptual consciousness of a die, part of my description will indicate that the die *claims* existence; but, as a phenomenologist, I must not uncritically accept the truth of that claim. Husserl's *epoche*, as he called this 'bracketing off', was in Sartre's view impossible: Roquentin's encounter with the chestnut tree root showed that. At the same time, the *epoche*, instead of being a temporary procedure, as Descartes's sus-pension of judgement on the existence of external things was, ended up being permanently in play: Husserl's brackets never came off. Thus Husserl's battle-cry 'To the things themselves!' did *not* deliver what Sartre thought it had promised: the ability to make philosophy out of that absurd, unjustifiable but absolutely undeniably existent apricot cocktail. This didn't entail abandoning phenomenology. On the con-trary, it meant developing it in the direction that he felt best preserved what had initially attracted him to it, and that took him, and other phenomenologists, to existentialism (see Chapter 1).

The War, Heidegger, and Resistance

Sartre was a prisoner of war from June 1940 to March 1941. His intern-ment was remarkable for at least two reasons. He lectured on Martin

Heidegger to a group of prisoners, also tutoring one of the priests, Marius Perrin, individually; and he wrote and directed a play, his first play, *Bariona*. It was performed on Christmas Eve in 1940, and not only awoke the dramatist in him (Beauvoir AFS 183) but roused him to the necessity for political activism.

Heidegger was perhaps Husserl's most famous student. His vast treatise *Sein und Zeit* (*Being and Time*) had come out in 1927. Sartre began studying *Sein und Zeit* while he was in Berlin, but

> the effort I'd made to *understand* [Husserl] – in other words, to break my personal prejudices and grasp Husserl's ideas on the basis of his own principles rather than mine – had exhausted me for that particular year. I did begin Heidegger and read fifty pages of him, but the difficulty of his vocabulary put me off. (WD 183)

It may be relevant that Sartre's German wasn't particularly good then – not good enough, anyway, to pursue affairs with German girls (WD 285). He came back to Heidegger, when the time was right for him, just before being taken prisoner (WD 182, 184–7).

BT is a big book, and in its original plan was to be even bigger; the book we know as *Being and Time* is the first two (of three) Divisions of the first of two envisioned Parts. BT aimed to address the question of the meaning of Being. Addressing this question required taking as its starting point the 'vague average understanding' (BT 5) of Being possessed by the Being which is such that 'in its very Being, that Being is an *issue* for it' (BT 12), namely *man*. Heidegger's usual term for man was *Dasein* or 'there-being', reminding us that human beings are *thrown into* the world, at a particular place and time, a place and time not of their choosing. The requisite method for getting at this vague understanding of the meaning of Being was, according to Heidegger, phenomenology. And what we find when it comes to the Being of Dasein is that it 'finds its meaning in temporality' (BT 19); the remainder of the book is devoted to demonstrating this and exploring its implications.

It is impossible to summarize, but a few key points are these: first, the basic state of Dasein is what Heidegger calls *In-der-Welt-sein*: Being-in-the-world; this compound expression 'indicates in the very way we have coined it [that it] stands for a unitary phenomenon' (BT 53); there is no understanding humans without simultaneously understanding the world in which they dwell, or vice versa. Second, 'Dasein's being reveals itself as *care*' (BT 182). To be in-the-world is for the world to have significance for us – we are not mere spectators; our mode of being alongside things in the world is one form of caring, what he calls 'concern'. Another form, what he calls 'solicitude', is our mode of being-with-others. The ontological meaning of care is 'temporality' (BT II§65), since it implies Dasein's 'Being-ahead-of-itself', projecting toward the future: my concern with the hammer is in order to fix the nail, in order to build the house, in order to have shelter . . . Third, Dasein 'in its everydayness' lives inauthentically, it is *'lost* in the "they" [*Das Man*]' (BT 268): 'We take pleasure and enjoy ourselves as *they* take pleasure; we read, see, and judge about literature and art as *they* see and judge . . . we find "shocking" what *they* find shocking' (BT 126–7). Death, the end of Being-in-the-world, is the actualization of Dasein's potentiality-for-Being-a-whole or for Being-its-self; for this potentiality to be authentic, no longer lost in the 'they', requires an authentic Being-towards-death.

So: it is this book which Sartre set himself finally to read, on which he gave a lecture to the prisoners in Stalag XII-D, and on which he tutored one of the priests there.

Meanwhile, he was asked, under the misapprehension that he was already an established playwright (Hayman 1987: 173), to write and direct a play for Christmas. The result, *Bariona*, is a tale of resistance by villagers in Judea against the Roman occupation – transparently a symbol of France under German occupation – with the message of the infant Christ in the neighbouring village of Bethlehem being that 'you are responsible for yourself and your suffering'. It was performed by the prisoners with Sartre in the role of Balthazar.

According to Perrin, '"After Bariona everything changed. It was as if Sartre had introduced a 'virus'. It was as if 'a long period of incubation', during which people had been prevented from rebelling, was coming to an end thanks to him." The men now spoke of nothing but escape' (Lévy 2003: 276–7). But the effect on Sartre himself was even more profound: the stalag 'taught him the meaning of solidarity' (Beauvoir FC 6). More than that: Sartre 'thinks it's time to act . . . He has decided to leave his ivory tower and plunge into the fray' (Perrin, quoted in Cohen-Solal 1987: 157; cf. Lévy 2003: 395).

L'Être et le Néant

L'Être et le Néant, begun in the prison camp, came out in 1943. The title, *Being and Nothingness*, clearly owes something to Heidegger's title *Being and Time*. It also, however, pays homage to René Descartes, whose *Meditations* (1641) are the starting point of so much French philosophy. In *Meditation IV*, Descartes describes human beings as situated 'between God and nothingness, or between supreme being and non-being'. Sartre's allusion to this is anything but accidental; this is the Meditation where Descartes expresses his vision of freedom as 'not restricted in any way', which deeply influenced Sartre (see Chapter 8). A regular theme of commentators is the degree to which Sartre is Cartesian, i.e., committed to Descartes's views, in other respects.

The overall shape of *L'Être et le Néant*, and to some degree its content, also owed something to *Sein und Zeit*. Instead of a narrow, focused study of a particular mode of consciousness or its objects, this 'essay on phenomenological ontology', as its subtitle has it, describes human reality – what Heidegger called Dasein – quite generally, like *Sein und Zeit*. And Heidegger's basic characterization of Dasein as Being-in-the-world is taken for granted, as is the distinction between Dasein's inauthentic everyday existence, what Sartre called bad faith, and the possibility of authenticity. Even the defining doctrine of existentialism – that 'existence precedes essence', i.e. that man defines his own essence for himself (see Chapter 3) – had already been anticipated by Heidegger as 'The essence of Dasein lies in its existence' (BT 42). There are many debts to and engagements with others, of which I will mention only two.

One interlocutor is Sigmund Freud. Sartre was clearly taken with the splendid literary qualities of Freud's case histories, and in the *Sketch for a Theory of the Emotions* gave full credit to Freud for recognizing that even the smallest conscious phenomenon had a meaning, that there was something there to be understood. However, he rejected Freud's attempt to see causal mechanisms underlying the production of symptoms: 'the profound contradiction in all psychoanalysis is that it presents *at the same time* a bond of causality and a bond of understanding between the phenomena that it studies' (STE 54). He rejected the idea of the Unconscious (see Chapter 3). And his own 'existential psychoanalysis' rejected the past-orientedness of Freudian analysis, its looking back to a traumatic event as the cause of the present difficulties (Chapter 8).[18]

I also want to highlight the influence of Gestalt psychology, not because it is more important than other influences one might so easily mention, but because it is less obvious and less often highlighted.[19] This school of psychology was developed in the last years of the nineteenth century and the first decades of the twentieth, principally by three German psychologists, Kurt Koffka, Wolfgang Köhler and Max Wertheimer, although the lesser-known Kurt Lewin is also important for Sartre (see Chapter 6). Thus its emergence paralleled that of Husserl's phenomenology, and although it is unclear that there was any direct influence from Husserlian phenomenology, at least in its early stages (see Spiegelberg 1961–9: 54), it was a response to the same 'crisis' (see 'Introduction', above) as Husserl's phenomenology (see Henle 1978); many of its leading lights were, like Husserl, Jewish, and left Germany in 1933. In briefest outline, the Gestaltists set themselves against the atomistic, mechanistic and empiricist scientific psychology of their time; they are best known for their work on perception, although Lewin and others studied emotion, social psychology, child psychology and so on. The German term *Gestalt* literally means 'shape' or 'form' but was used by them specifically to mean a segregated entity, unit, group, or organized whole which stood out against its background. Their argument was that atomistic psychology could not account for the perception of such organized wholes (see Köhler 1970: esp. ch. v). Sartre 'eagerly devoured early popularizations of the Gestalt theory' (Beauvoir PL 39), which he apparently read while he was doing military service (Hayman 1987: 81). Gestaltist concepts were plausibly in the air in conversations with Merleau-Ponty, and many, including 'figure/ground', 'field', and Lewin's notion of 'hodological space', are interwoven into Sartre's discussions of consciousness (see Chapter 3), the lived body (see Chapter 5), space, perception, action, the emotions (see Chapter 6), others (see Chapter 7), and freedom (see Chapter 8).

The Heyday of Existentialism, and its Popular Decline

Cohen-Solal (1987: ch. 3) describes 1945–56 as 'the Sartre years'. Sartre's play *Huis Clos*, generally known in English as *No Exit*, had received its first performance in May 1944. As *La Nausée* is a philosophical novel, *Huis Clos* is a philosophical play. Its three protagonists, Garcin, Inès and Estelle, are in Hell; the play explores the themes of bad faith and being-for-others (Chapters 4 and 7) and it contains the famous line '*L'enfer, c'est les autres*': 'Hell is other people'. It was lauded by serious critics: 'After Anouilli [Anouilh], Jean-Paul Sartre is certainly the most important event in contemporary French theater' (quoted in Cohen-Solal 1987: 213).

Sartre's sudden rise to fame was also given a boost by an attack in the Communist weekly *Action* in June 1945, in which existentialism was denounced as 'idealist' (Hayman 1987: 232): 'idealist' not in the sense that Kant, Brunschvicg or Husserl were idealists but in the sense that was opposed to dialectical materialism, i.e., Marxism. Sartre was regularly derided as a 'bourgeois lackey/hyena/running dog' (Leak 2006: 73). Stung by this misinterpretation, he felt the need to make it clear that existentialism was a philosophy of action, not a philosophy *de luxe* or a philosophy of mere contemplation. Freedom did *not* imply the avoidance of obligations and ties; although his fictional hero Mathieu Delarue held this erroneous view in the first two volumes of Sartre's trilogy of novels *Les Chemins de la liberté* (*The Roads to Freedom*), which appeared in September 1945, Mathieu realizes his error in the third volume; he understands that freedom actually implies commitment (*engagement*).

In October 1945 Sartre gave his famous lecture 'L'Existentialisme est un humanisme'; the organizers had spent a good deal of money on publicity for the event and were worried that no one would show up 'with a title like that'. But, in Cohen-Solal's words, it was an 'unprecedented cultural success. Scrimmages, blows, broken chairs, fainting spells' (1987: 249). Sartre had come by subway and had to fight his way through a dense crowd, which he at first assumed were Communists demonstrating against him. The lecture defended existentialism against the attacks of the Marxists. In that immediate post-war era of reflection, recrimination and reconstruction, it managed to strike just the right note, showing that the existentialist notion of freedom combined a recognition of responsibility for the past and the optimistic possibility of change in the future.

The first issue of the journal *Les Temps modernes*, with Sartre as editor-in-chief and with Aron, Beauvoir and Merleau-Ponty among others on the editorial board, appeared in November. This too was a cultural event: 'The public waited for the first issue of *Les Temps modernes* as much as it had waited for the first two volumes of *The Roads*' (Cohen-Solal 1987: 257).[20] His editorial was a manifesto for 'committed literature' (*littérature engagée*), burdening writers with the responsibility to speak out against oppression and injustice – as the novelist Émile Zola had spoken out in 1898, in the famous pamphlet '*J'accuse*', against the government's anti-Semitism that had led to the unjust charges against the French Jewish soldier Alfred Dreyfus.

Sartre and Beauvoir, that young intellectual couple who were not married and who did not believe in God, were suddenly famous, or notorious.

> Existentialism was fast becoming a fashion accessory . . . young men and women, dressed entirely in black, only coming out at night – and even then wearing dark glasses! – started calling themselves 'Existentialists' and frequenting the jazz cellars of Saint-Germain-des-Prés on the Left Bank. (Leak 2006: 75–6)

The adulation of 'the hairy adolescents of Saint-Germain-des-Prés' (from the weekly *Samedi Soir*, quoted in Cohen-Solal 1987: 261) helped to bring the vitriol of the Catholic Right upon Sartre's head. And what vitriol! While the Communists were calling Sartre a bourgeois lackey, these others were saying that 'we should stop talking about "existentialism" and talk instead of "excrementalism" and how the "Dada movement" had been succeeded by the "Caca [Shit] movement"' (Lévy 2003: 34). Sartre mocked this aspect of the contemporary image of existentialism by telling of 'a lady who, whenever she lets slip a vulgar expression in a moment of nervousness, excuses herself by exclaiming, "I believe I am becoming an existentialist"' (EH 24). The attacks were intensely personal: 'He was accused, in rapid succession, of writing on all fours, of wallowing in filth, of taking delight in toilets, of luring young women along, not to fuck them, but to get them to sniff the odour of Camembert cheese' (Lévy 2003: 35).

Existentialism went out of fashion, as these things do in France. In the early 1960s, Cohen-Solal (1987: 449) tells us, France was excited about Claude Lévi-Strauss, the structuralist anthropologist; Roland Barthes, the literary critic; Jacques Lacan, the psychoanalyst; Louis Althusser, the Marxist philosopher; and Michel Foucault, the postmodernist philosopher and historian of ideas.[21] Sartre paid them little heed, bar a debate with Althusser, where one participant noted the 'treachery of the questions that Althusser's students asked' (quoted in Cohen-Solal 1987: 451). Hence French intellectuals stopped paying heed to Sartre.

Sartre, meanwhile, began to travel all over the world. He went to the United States twice in 1945. The first visit – his first flight and his first time outside Europe (Cohen-Solal 1987: 223) – was in January; he went at the behest of the novelist Albert Camus, who wanted him to accompany a delegation of French journalists and to act as representative for the journal *Combat*. He carried with him a vision of America gleaned from *Buffalo Bill* comic books, novelists such as Dos Passos and Hemingway, and the cinema; but he was stunned by the poverty, oppression and racism he encountered. 'The misery of the farmer is nowhere more profound than in some regions of Texas and New Mexico' (from *Combat*, quoted in Cohen-Solal 1987: 241). Again, '[i]n this country, so justly proud of its democratic institutions, one man out of ten is deprived of his political rights . . . They wait on your table, they polish your shoes, they operate your elevator, they carry your suitcases into your compartment . . . They know they are third-class citizens. They are Negroes' (from *Le Figaro*, quoted in Cohen-Solal 1987: 241).

On Anti-Semitism and Anti-Black Racism

Sartre produced no further major philosophical works during 'the Sartre years', but I want to call attention to two works from this period which might be called 'applied Sartreanism' (see Leak 2006: 79).

In 1946, Sartre published *Réflexions sur la question juive*, best known in English as *Anti-Semite and Jew*. He seems to have been remarkably blind to anti-Semitism during his visit to Berlin in 1933–4, which coincided with Heidegger's appointment to the rectorship of the University of Freiburg when the previous rector resigned in 1933 in protest at the Nazis' moves to rid the German universities of Jews, including Husserl.[22] But he could hardly ignore it during and after the war, especially once the news about Nazi gas chambers and crematoria started filtering out during 1945.

The final passage of *Anti-Semite and Jew* presents a glowing vision of the holistic nature of human liberty: 'What must be done is to point out to each one that the fate of the Jews is his fate. Not one Frenchman will be free so long as the Jews do not enjoy the fullness of their rights. Not one Frenchman will be secure so long as a single Jew – in France or *in the world at large* – can fear for his life' (AS 153). It analyses anti-Semitism as bad faith (see Chapter 4): the anti-Semite believes in a mysterious 'Jewish "principle" ' that magically transforms, for instance, avarice into *Jewish* avarice and thus makes him impervious to the argument that there are Christians who are avaricious and Jews who are not (AS 56). Sartre analyses the situation of the Jew in terms of his notion from BN of the Other who is turned into an object by the Look (see Chapters 7 and 8); he compares this situation to that in *The Trial*, by the Austrian Jewish novelist Franz Kafka: 'the Jew is engaged in a long trial. He does not know his judges, scarcely even his lawyers; he does not know what he is charged with, yet he knows that he is considered guilty' (AS 88).

Perhaps inevitably, 'many criticised the assumptions he made, as a gentile, about Jewishness' (Leak 2006: 79). And perhaps inevitably, in later life Sartre found himself playing a difficult juggling act *vis-à-vis* Israel in its relations to Egypt – he visited both countries in 1967 as a kind of unofficial ambassador and returned to Israel in 1978 – likewise *vis-à-vis* relations between Israel and the Palestinians (see Cohen-Solal 1987: 409ff.; Hayman 1987: 418ff.; Leak 2006: 129f.)

In 1949 he wrote a preface to an anthology of new black and Malagasy poetry entitled *Orphée Noir* ('Black Orpheus'): 'What did you expect when you took away the gag that kept these black mouths shut? That they would sing your praises?' (BO: 115). He ends with this: 'The white man has, for three thousand years, enjoyed the privilege of seeing without being seen. Today, these black men look at us, and our gaze returns and penetrates our own eyes . . .' (BO: 142). This is again a concrete application of his BN doctrine of the Look (see Chapters 7 and 8).[23] 'Black Orpheus' was admired by Frantz Fanon,[24] the Martinique-born psychiatrist who had been sent to Algeria to fight on the side of the French, but who joined the rebels; Fanon also thought highly of *Anti-Semite and Jew* (see Fanon 1986). Sartre met Fanon just before his death in 1961, and wrote the preface to Fanon's *Damnées de la terre* (*The Wretched of the Earth*), an analysis of the Algerian war of independence (1954–62), which has served as an inspiration for many liberation struggles..

'After 1955 his name became virtually synonymous with the cause of Algerian independence' (Leak 2006: 107); he signed the 'Declaration concerning the right of insubordination in the Algerian war' in 1960, which led to war veterans marching the streets crying 'Kill Sartre' (Cohen-Solal 1987: 380); two attempts were made to blow up Sartre's flat, in 1961 and again just before the end of the Algerian war in 1962, apparently for his stance against France (Leak 2006: 116); he was manning the barricades, though beginning to feel his age, during the 1971 demonstrations protesting against the murder of a young Algerian who was apparently a victim of a racist attack (see Thompson 1984: 179). Given France's colonial involvement in Algeria, and given that the war for Algerian independence was constantly in the headlines and divided French society, we should not find it surprising that he was so much more occupied with Algeria than with South Africa; it seems that he did not get involved in the anti-apartheid movement until the 1960s (Leak 2006: 124).

'Les Communistes et la paix' and *Critique de la raison dialectique*

Sartre's relationship with Communism, and with regimes purporting to be Communist, was complex and fraught. We have noted already the attacks by Marxists in the mid-1940s on Sartre's allegedly bourgeois and anti-activist philosophy. In the early 1950s, however, there began to be a rapprochement. Of particular significance was the Duclos affair of 1952. After a massive Communist demonstration against the visit to Paris of the general who commanded the American forces in Korea, a prominent member of the French Communist Party (PCF), Jacques Duclos, was taking pigeons home for his supper; he was arrested and imprisoned on the grounds that these pigeons were carrier pigeons which were going to be used to communicate with anti-state militants. Sartre was on holiday at the time; when he heard about this, '[t]hese sordid, childish tricks turned my stomach . . . An anticommunist is a rat. . . . in the name of liberty, equality, fraternity, I swore to the bourgeoisie a hatred that would die only with me. When I precipitously returned to Paris, I had to write or suffocate' (S 198; cf. Beauvoir FC 262). What he wrote was 'Les Communistes et la paix', published in three instalments in *Les Temps modernes* between 1952 and 1954.

This passionate defence of Communism may seem an extraordinary turnaround. But Sartre, as a defender of freedom, always sided with the oppressed, and at this time not only were Communists being victimized by police in France, they were being witch-hunted in the States by Senator Joseph McCarthy and his House Committee on Un-American Activities. More generally, the whole trajectory of his thinking since his first visit to the States in 1945 showed a dawning awareness of the social and political dimensions of freedom. Beauvoir wrote that when BN was published, 'Sartre thought that any situation could be transcended by subjective effort; in 1951, he knew that circumstances can sometimes steal our transcendence from us; in that case, no individual salvation is possible, only a collective struggle' (FC 242).

The rapprochement with the PCF did not last long, however. Any defender of Communist values must reckon in some way with actual regimes that purport to be Communist. In 1950, the existence of the Soviet 'corrective labour' camps became public knowledge; Sartre and Merleau-Ponty wrote a damning editorial for *Les Temps modernes*, which did nothing to endear them to the PCF. But in 1954 – now on good terms with the PCF – Sartre made his first trip to the USSR, at the invitation of a group of Russian writers. There, he took part in a vodka duel; the Russian challenger 'sank into a heap on the asphalt, a great moment of triumph for Sartre' (FC 320); but Sartre himself, suffering from hypertension and overwork, collapsed and was hospitalized the next day. On his return, he gave an interview of his impressions to *Libération*, which were published under captions such as 'Freedom of criticism is complete in the USSR and the Soviet citizen is continually improving his condition in the bosom of a society making non-stop progress' (quoted in Hayman 1987: 316).[25] When, however, Soviet troops invaded Hungary in 1956, Sartre felt he must 'regretfully but completely' break off relations with his friends in the USSR (quoted in Thompson 1984: 113) and criticized the PCF for its enthusiastic support for this intervention. 'What the Hungarian people is teaching us with its blood is the complete failure of socialism as merchandise imported from the USSR' (quoted in Hayman 1987: 325–6).

The failure of the Soviet brand of socialism did not entail the failure of socialism *tout court*. Sartre had visited Cuba in 1949, before the revolution; he went back in 1960, and met Che Guevara and Fidel Castro. Sartre was impressed by the youth of Cuba's leaders, and by the fact that their revolution was not ideology-led: 'They spoke to me heatedly for a long time about the Revolution, but I tried in vain to get them to tell me whether or not the new regime would be socialist' (SC 150).

> These men, hard at work, without dropping their vigilance for an instant, are fighting under a foreign menace to safeguard their two most precious conquests: freedom . . . and the New Ark of the revolution, the confidence and friendship which unites them . . . The Cubans must win, or we shall lose everything, even hope. (SC 146)

But, as with the Soviet Union, reality struck; and when Sartre spoke out against the torture of the poet Heberto Padilla, Castro dropped him (Hayman 1987: 444).

The year 1960 also saw the publication of Part I of his *Critique de la raison dialectique*, on which he had been working for several years; the unfinished Part II was published posthumously. This difficult book can be described as an attempt at a synthesis between Marxism and existentialism. Much of the subsequent discussion which surrounds it centres on whether Marxism and existentialism are *capable* of any such synthesis, and hence whether the attempt is contradictory in its very conception. A more nuanced question is whether the version of existentialism which permeates the *Critique* is radically different from that developed in BN, i.e., whether the trajectory of Sartre's thinking – about freedom, about responsibility, about interpersonal relations – between 1943 and 1960 contains a discontinuity, or whether there is a more-or-less smooth and natural development (see, e.g., Flynn 1984). Certainly there is a formidable new array of terms: praxis, the practico-inert, seriality, the group-in-fusion. But, it may be argued, these are the heirs, 'with new socialized and extended meanings in the material conditions of history' (Santoni 2003: 35), of an old, if equally formidable, array of terms: being-for-itself, being-in-itself, the Us-object, the We-subject. Arguably, Sartre's increasing attunement to the poverty and injustice in the world, coupled with a deepening conviction that the causes of these evils lie in oppressive structures and institutions and that collective action is necessary to overturn these, induced him to develop, refine, and thicken the earlier conceptions.

Sartre's relationship to Communism cost him dear at a personal level. In one way or another it alienated him both from Merleau-Ponty and from Camus.

Merleau-Ponty and Sartre had met at the École Normale – Merleau-Ponty was just three years younger – when Sartre intervened in a fight between some *normaliens* and Merleau-Ponty, who with a friend 'had sung a few traditional songs that they had found too vulgar' (quoted in Cohen-Solal 1987: 343). They were both passionate about phenomenology, each in his own way. They had worked closely together on *Les Temps modernes* from its inception; but as Sartre began moving toward Communism, Merleau-Ponty was moving away; he resigned as political editor in 1950. He remained joint editor-in-chief, but resigned in 1953 over Sartre's intransigence and editorial heavy-handedness. Sartre, replying to an attack by Claude Lefort, had not only refused to cut out a paragraph which Merleau-Ponty thought went too far, but had omitted, without consultation, a preface written by Merleau-Ponty (Hayman 1987: 309; Stewart 1998a: xxiv–xxv). There was a good deal of bitterness on both sides; Merleau-Ponty's 'Sartre and ultra-Bolshevism' was followed by Beauvoir's 'Merleau-Ponty and pseudo-Sartreanism' (both 1955). Yet Sartre's essay on the occasion of Merleau-Ponty's death in 1961 is soul-searching:

> I still see his last melancholy expression – as we parted, at the rue Claude Bernard – disappointed, suddenly closed. He remains inside me, a painful sore, infected by sorrow, remorse and some bitterness . . . our final misunderstanding – which would have been nothing had I seen him alive again – was made of the same fabric as all the others . . . revealing our mutual affection . . . but it also showed that our lives were out-of-phase . . . (S 225)[26]

Despite the popular association of the names of Camus and Sartre, the two, unlike Sartre and Merleau-Ponty, had never been particularly close. The occasion for the final breach was a review of Camus's analysis of rebellion, revolution and murder, *L'Homme revolté* (*The Rebel*). Sartre did not even write the review; he disliked the book and was inclined simply to ignore it. '[E]ventually the silence of *Les Temps modernes* became more eloquent than a review – no matter how negative – would have been' (Leak 2006: 102). Francis Jeanson, author of a book on Sartre, published a review in May 1952. Camus counter-attacked angrily, directing his fire not at Jeanson but at Sartre; and Sartre – 'displaying an untempered acrimony that excelled the anger demonstrated by Camus' (Santoni 2003: 124) – replied. Sartre and Camus never spoke again; Camus died in a car crash in 1960.

What was at issue between them? Cohen-Solal (1987: 333) sees it as hinging on 'the question of freedom in the USSR': *Les Temps modernes* had denounced the Soviet labour camps but had not gone further to denounce Stalinism at its very roots. But, as Santoni (2003: 8) argues, the core of the disagreement was more fundamental: Camus was arguing that violence, even in the cause of a rebellion against oppression, could never be justified; Sartre appeared to be arguing the opposite. Though neither the *Critique* nor Sartre's preface to Fanon's *The Wretched of the Earth* had yet appeared, his views on violence were beginning to be developed in 'Les Communistes et la paix'. His claim is that in a society based on oppression, violence is inevitable; he consistently denies that violence is *justified* as a means to an end; but some, the pacifist Santoni included, have found his position uneasily close to this.

The *Critique* was the last philosophical work that Sartre published. Not, of course, that he stopped writing; he continued to work on volume II of the *Critique*, his autobiography *Les Mots* came out in 1963, his massive biography of Flaubert, *L'Idiot de la famille*, came out in 1971–2. But after a mild heart attack in 1971 and a more severe one in 1973, and with his eyesight beginning to fail, a lifetime of overwork was beginning to take its toll.

The 1968 Student Unrest, Benny Lévy and *L'Espoir maintenant*

The Vietnam War had been rumbling along for years. In 1966, Sartre was invited to join the International Tribunal against War Crimes in Vietnam, led by one of the few British philosophers to merit the title of 'committed intellectual', Bertrand Russell.

The Vietnam War was one instigating factor in the student unrest of 1967–8. Violent clashes between riot police and students occurred both in the States and in France; in May 1968, 'barricades appeared in the Latin Quarter for the first time since the Commune of 1871' (Leak 2006: 130). Sartre spoke out at the Sorbonne on the side of the students. There was violent street-fighting, and a general strike; the government was threatened with collapse. 'In its aftermath, numerous small, revolutionary groups – *groupuscules* – were formed by young people who saw '68 as only the beginning, not the end, and who distrusted the Communists as much as they detested de Gaulle' (Leak 2006: 132). One of these, the Gauche Prolétarienne, invited Sartre to direct their newspaper *La Cause du Peuple*; through this group, Sartre formed an important friendship with Benny Lévy, a young Maoist who went by the name of Pierre Victor. When Sartre began to lose his sight in 1973, he got Lévy to read to him, and eventually, in 1975, took him on as his secretary.

Shortly before Sartre's death in 1980, Lévy – now turned orthodox Jew – conducted a series of interviews with him; these appeared in *Le Nouvel Observateur* as he lay dying, and were re-published in 1991 under the title *L'Espoir maintenant*: 'a riveting series of discussions between young man and fading star . . . Sartre in conversation with Lévy is challenged to criticize an important part of his life; he moves in unexpected directions, listens to new ideas, and proposes still others' (Aronson 1996: 3).

As with the *Critique*, some of the discussion of these interviews has been about *how* different these unexpected directions of his thinking are from previous directions. For instance, he says that '[t]oday I think everything that takes place for a consciousness at any given moment is necessarily linked to, and often is even engendered by . . . the existence of another . . . In *Being and Nothingness* I left the individual too independent' (HN §4). How fundamental a shift is this? He admits that *Anti-Semite and Jew* focused too exclusively on 'the Jew as the victim of anti-Semitism . . . I now think there is a Jewish reality beyond the ravages that anti-Semitism has inflicted on Jews' (HN §12). Is this anything more than deeper reflection, engendered by his close friendships with a number of Jews, including his adopted daughter Arlette and including Lévy himself?

These interviews have raised questions which the *Critique* just couldn't, however, precisely because they are the words of an old and infirm man in conversation with a young one. Beauvoir was convinced that the arrogant, forceful Lévy had taken advantage of a feeble and accommodating old man; she was 'horrified by the nature of the statements extorted from Sartre' (AFS 119). Others have seen in the interviews as 'containing both his old radicalism in full force and his disposition to contest himself, change, and move in strikingly new directions' (Aronson 1996: 12); yet others, a genuine 'reciprocity' or 'plural thought', to use phrases that entered Sartre's vocabulary in its later phases (Aronson 1996:

12–14). Or was Sartre just 'a great man from whom Lévy expected to get food for his own thoughts' (see quotation from Sartre in Aronson 1996: 14)? Or, as Sartre's own conception of the ambiguity of human reality might attest, are all of these interpretations true in some measure? (See Cohen-Solal 1987: 510–19; Aronson 1996.)

An Italian article (quoted in Cohen-Solal 1987: 521) written on the occasion of Sartre's death said this, and it seems a fitting ending: 'He lived and died running, generously, clearing some obstacles, falling, jumping back up, constantly putting everything into question. A splendid life.'

notes

1 The classic biography is Cohen-Solal's (1987); B-H. Lévy's (2003), massive, idiosyncratic and self-indulgent but often brilliant for all that, made a splash when it appeared, in part because of the flamboyance of Lévy himself; it fed into a renaissance of interest in Sartre, whose star had waned. There are other biographies, e.g. Hayman's (1987) and most recently Leak's (2006). Hayman (1987: 486–511) and Howells (1992: ix–xvi) have useful chronologies, Hayman's lining up events in Sartre's life with world events; Thompson's book (1984) is a year-by-year chronology.

2 Albeit a project in bad faith (see Chapter 4). Charmé 1984 is a valuable study of the relationships between existentialist and Freudian psychoanalysis, between existentialist psychoanalysis and the fundamental project, and between the fundamental project and biography.

3 Beauvoir's letters and autobiographical pieces, even her novels, are considered important sources of information about Sartre's life for biographers.

4 A competitive exam which qualifies one to teach at *lycées* or universities.

5 In 1964, Sartre explained his refusal in a statement entitled 'The writer should refuse to let himself be turned into an institution' (see Thompson 1984: 144–5; Leak 2006: 123).

6 Sartre tried mescaline in 1935; the hallucinations he experienced fed into his discussion of the topic in PsyI IV §3.

7 Manser (1966: 11–12) calls our attention to the images of the body that pervade *Nausea* and indeed are pervaded by nausea; he reads the message as that in place of Descartes's 'I think, therefore I exist', we should say 'I am forced by my body to think and feel, therefore I exist.'

8 See Manser 1966: ch. 1 for a good discussion of the very concept of a philosophical novel.

9 His paper was entitled 'Nietzsche – was he a philosopher?'

10 Lévy reminds us that in his day, Bergson was virtually a Sartrean figure: his lectures at the Collège de France were high society successes, 'the crowds jostling to listen to him, the pretty women and the men of letters mingling with the students of the Latin Quarter' (2003: 102).

11 These lecturers were ridiculed in *Les Chiens de Garde*, by Sartre's friend and contemporary, Paul Nizan. Apparently Brunschwicg was under the

impression that *Sartre* had written this book, and congratulated him on his achievement, ' "although", he said without rancour, "you certainly didn't spare me" ' (S 90).

12 In fact according to Beauvoir he had read Karl Jaspers's monograph *Psychopathology*, itself a landmark in phenomenological psychopathology, in 1927; but apparently the term 'phenomenology' meant nothing to him then and didn't sink in (Beauvoir PL 39).

13 Lévy (2003: 112–13) presents these as two different and partially incompatible versions of his encounter; they surely aren't. He offers a third version (2003: 113), a conversation with Fernando Gerassi, to whom Sartre said that he 'wanted to describe a stone philosophically'; Gerassi replied that that was exactly what Husserl was in the process of doing.

14 Husserl's conception of his own enterprise was constantly changing; I focus here on CM both because the conception expressed there is roughly contemporaneous with Sartre's encounter with phenomenology and because it is a short and relatively accessible work.

15 Husserl was certainly not the first to use the *term*; e.g., Hegel used it in the title of his great work *Phänomenologie des Geistes* (1807), picking up on Kant's distinction between *phenomena* – things as they appear to us, and *noumena* – things as they are in themselves. The term was also used by the roughly contemporary psychologist Carl Stumpf; see Spiegelberg 1961–9, vol. 1: Part I.ii.

16 It is perhaps a reflection of the popularity of existentialism by the time this translation was done that the subtitle *Esquisse d'une description phénoménologique* ended up in the English as: *An Existentialist Theory of Consciousness*!

17 Husserl's transcendental idealism is not identical to Kant's, as he makes clear in the same section.

18 Howells 1979 is a good discussion of the relationships between Sartre and Freud; see also Cannon's superb book (1991); Cannon is herself a practising psychotherapist.

19 This is unmistakable in Merleau-Ponty since he explicitly engages with Gestalt theories in PP; it is less often picked up on in Sartre. Mirvish (e.g., 1984) is a shining exception.

20 Boschetti 1985 argues on sociological grounds for the centrality of *Les Temps modernes* and the institutionalization of existentialism in its pages to the dominance of existentialism during 'the Sartre years'.

21 Again one could give a deeper sociological explanation here of the ascendency of these other intellectuals, one that partly centred on the institutionalization of their thinking in *Critique*, *Les Temps modernes*'s main rival review; see Boschetti 1985.

22 He met Heidegger, just once and very briefly, in 1953.

23 See Gordon 1995, in which this analysis is developed.

24 This did not prevent Fanon from being sharply critical, however; see Fanon 1986.

25 He was similarly taken with China, which he and Beauvoir visited in 1955. Beauvoir expressed their admiration for 'the immensity of the victories won

in only a few years over the scourges that had once held sway in China – dirt, vermin, infant mortality, epidemics, chronic malnutrition, hunger; the people had clothes and clean housing, and something to eat' (FC 345).

26 Stewart 1998a reprints these three items, as well as letters exchanged between Sartre and Merleau-Ponty during the quarrel. Goehr 2005 has an excellent discussion of the different conceptions held by Sartre and Merleau-Ponty of what it was to be an *intellectuel engagé*.

part I

The division of this book into two parts is in a sense arbitrary. The method which Sartre employs – phenonomenology, together with its necessary adjunct which I have called Sartrean therapy – is inextricably interwoven with its results. But because its intertwining with certain of its results – namely its descriptions of consciousness and of bad faith – is more immediately evident than its interweaving with its other results, I have placed the chapters on these two topics together with the methodological chapters in Part I.

phenomenology

artre's monumental work *Being and Nothingness* is subtitled a 'phenomenological essay on ontology'.[1] Phenomenology is the philosophical method which we will be elucidating in this chapter. Ontology is the philosophical study of being, existence or reality, and Sartre, following Heidegger (see 'Sartre's Life', above), sees the starting point of ontology as the exploration of what he calls '*human* reality' – what Heidegger had called *Dasein* or 'there-being'.

My aim in this chapter is to outline what the philosophical method called 'phenomenology' involves, at least for Sartre, not in a historically rigorous but in a practically accessible way.[2] Heidegger (BT 34ff.) takes us back to the etymological roots, in Greek, of the word 'phenomenology': it means the 'logos' – roughly, 'talk' or 'discourse' – of the 'phenomenon', 'that which shows itself'. Since to show oneself is to *appear*, we might say that phenomena are 'appearances', and Sartre does often use the word 'appearance' in place of 'phenomenon'. This, however, is liable to mislead those philosophers who come to this discussion wielding a ready-made 'appearance/reality' distinction; they will suppose that phenomenology studies how things *seem* as opposed to how they really *are*.[3] But no such contrast is intended; how else could there be a 'phenomenological essay on *ontology*'? Back to the Greek! If I say 'A cloud has shown itself on the horizon', or, equivalently, 'A cloud has appeared on the horizon', I am not thereby implying that it merely seems to be a cloud but might not really be one.[4]

At the same time, to appear is to appear *to* someone; and so we could also say that phenomenology is the study of 'experience'. But this term, like 'appearance', is subject to many misunderstandings. Historically, the philosophical orientation known as 'empiricism' – which etymologically suggests a doctrine that takes experience as basic – has transformed the concept of experience unrecognizably. The word 'experience', the philosopher George Santayana suggests, began by referring to 'so much knowledge and readiness as is fetched from contact with events by a teachable and intelligent creature' (1922: 189), the sense in which we speak of 'an experienced train-driver' or 'the wisdom of experience'. It was transformed by the empiricists into a pluralizable term, 'experiences', which designated – not engagement with the world though action, practice and exploration, but – the putative causal upshot in the mind of the perception of putative atomistic qualities of the world: inner, private, atomistic objects also known as 'sensations' or 'impressions' or 'qualia'. By the end of this conceptual mutation, empiricists – those 'practical people' – paradoxically found themselves 'inarticulate sensualists, rapt in omphalic contemplation of their states of mind' (1922: 192). This seems a paradigm case of what Galen Strawson calls 'looking-glassing' a term: i.e., using a term 'in such a way that whatever one means by it, it excludes what the term means' (2005: 43)! The phenomenologists' emphasis on experience can make them sound like empiricists; but their notion of experience is emphatically *not* that of those philosophers known as empiricists. On the contrary, empiricism constitutes one of their principal philosophical targets (see Chapter 2).

Although different phenomenologists will spell this out in different ways, the study of phenomena may be seen as having two stages: the description of phenomena, and the elicitation of their essence from that description. For Sartre and Merleau-Ponty, this second stage is not complete until this essence has been put into relation to some fundamental aspect of human reality. So Sartre, on exploring imagination, observes that when I imagine Pierre, who is in London, he 'appears to me as absent', which 'is enough to distinguish [the imagined object] from the object of perception' (PsyI 261); that in imagination the object is 'given-in-its-absence', whereas in memory it is 'given-now-as-in-the-past' (PsyI 263); and so on. These certainly constitute important features of the essence of imagination; but he refuses to stop there, instead raising the much more fundamental question, 'can we conceive of a consciousness which would never imagine'? (PsyI 260). The answer proves to be 'no', because without the ability to imagine not-yet-existing states of affairs, human beings could never act and hence would not be free (PsyI 269–73). Thus the phenomenological exploration of the essence of imagination as a modality of consciousness requires putting it into relation to an aspect of human reality, freedom, which Sartre sees as absolutely fundamental, and thereby demonstrates that imagination is central to human reality.

The first two sections of this chapter are devoted to looking at these two stages, as they have been explicated and practised by Sartre and Merleau-Ponty. In the third section I work through an example of phenomenology in practice to help to put some flesh on these bones. By this stage, we are in a position to clarify some of the confusion around the term 'existentialism', which for both Sartre and Merleau-Ponty is connected with phenomenology. I end by considering a very general objection that may be made to the whole phenomenological enterprise, an objection that might be put by asking: 'Isn't phenomenology just *assuming* that phenomena are *real*? And might that assumption not be false?'

The Phenomenological Reduction: Description of Phenomena

Husserl introduced the 'phenomenological reduction' – what he also called the 'phenomenological *epoche*', the '"parenthesizing" of the Objective world', and 'putting [things] out of play' (CM 20) – as in a certain sense parallel to Descartes's doubt, i.e., suspension of judgement. We have already noted that part of what Husserl required us to 'put into parentheses' or 'bracket off' was the truth of the claim to existence made by perceived objects such as Husserl's famous die. As we also observed, Sartre held this aspect of the phenomenological reduction to be impossible: Roquentin's encounter with the chestnut tree root in Sartre's novel *Nausea* showed that; and *Merleau-Ponty*'s use of the term 'existentialism' – or anyway 'existential philosophy' – refers to 'the impossibility of a complete reduction' (PP xiv), that is, the impossibility of suspending judgement on such existence-claims.

Yet there is still in Sartre's and Merleau-Ponty's view an important role for something *like* the phenomenological reduction. The phenomena which phenomenology aims to describe are absolutely familiar, and paradoxical though it may seem, this very familiarity is one of the principal obstacles to describing them. As Wittgenstein put it, '[t]he aspects of things that are most important for us are hidden because of their simplicity and familiarity. (One is unable to notice something – because it is always before one's eyes.)' (PI §129). It is this fact that gives point to the so-called 'phenomenological reduction' *à la française*: in the hands of the French phenomenologists, this becomes suspension, not of judgement, but of what might be called *unastonishment*, a recovery of what Merleau-Ponty calls ' "wonder" in the face of the world' (PP xiii); we must 'allow ourselves to be struck' by or 'find surprising' things which we take for granted. (For example, 'Don't take it as a matter of course, but as a remarkable fact, that pictures and fictitious narratives give us pleasure', Wittgenstein PI §524.) The aim is not to find a new epistemological foundation for our former opinions, but to put ourselves in a position to describe the familiar. This suspension of unastonishment is vital for the phenomenological aim of describing the experienced world and our relationships with it, '[n]ot because we reject the certainties of common sense and a natural attitude to things . . . but because, being the presupposed basis of any thought, they are taken for granted, and go unnoticed' (PP xiii).

Anyone who has ever been, as we say, 'taken for granted' can testify that the familiar can become in a certain sense invisible! There are various techniques we might adopt for suspending unastonishment and thus rendering the invisible visible:

One, very straightforwardly, is the technique which Wittgenstein labelled 'assembling reminders' (PI §127): rendering into words what is normally unreflected-on. Sartre's literary talents are exhibited to fine effect in his descriptions of such familiar experiences as this:

> I have an appointment with Pierre at four o'clock. I arrive at the café a quarter of an hour late . . . Will he have waited for me? . . . When I enter the café to search for Pierre, there is formed a synthetic organization of all the objects in the café, on the ground of which Pierre is given as about to appear . . . But now Pierre is not here . . . I expected to see Pierre, and my expectation has caused the absence of Pierre *to happen* as a real event concerning this café. (BN 9–10)

'Do we not say, for example, "I suddenly saw that he was not there"?' (BN 9). Such experiences are familiar; this is also, it happens, a crucial example for Sartre: absences are instances of what he terms *négatités*, concrete 'nothingnesses', which play a starring role in, *inter alia*, his discussion of freedom. Yet we in all probability had never made the experience of absence explicit to ourselves. We recognize descriptions of these experiences because they are familiar, yet we find such descriptions illuminating or even revelatory precisely *because* we have not previously made them explicit to ourselves.

Another technique takes off from the observation that familiar things can be invisible simply through lack of contrast. At a basic level, we can even grasp this as a *sensory* phenomenon: we cease to hear the ticking of the clock because it is a constant sensory accompaniment. We can also fail to notice or be struck by familiar aspects of our own country or culture because we have nothing with which to contrast them; one of the potential benefits of foreign travel is precisely that, by providing such a contrast, it may get us to notice these features in our own land or culture: accents, styles of dress or architecture, landscapes, customs. Though this technique seems to be less prominent in Sartre, one purpose of Merleau-Ponty's descriptions of unfamiliar experiences, for example, his discussion of phantom limbs and anosognosia, or of the brain-injured war veteran Schneider, or of experiments with inverting spectacles, is to illuminate the familiar by way of contrast.[5]

A final point: there is a widespread but misguided impression among some philosophers and psychologists that phenomenological reflection is what is sometimes called 'introspection': philosophers, particularly those sceptical of the notion, tend to characterize introspection as a kind of metaphorical peering into the private contents of one's own mind, therein catching fleeting glimpses of those 'experiences' and 'qualia' invented by the empiricists. If we have conflated phenomenological reflection with introspection, we may demand to know what licenses the phenomenologists' easy glide from the first-person singular ('*I* expected to see Pierre'), to the first-person plural ('Do *we* not say, for example, "I suddenly saw that he was not there"?'). We may, like the philosopher D. C. Dennett, charge the phenomenologists with making what he terms 'the first-person plural presumption' (1991: 67): if all Sartre is really talking about is the private contents of his own mind, is not such a presumption not only presumptuous but untestable?

Phenomenological reflection is not introspection, however; the phenomenologists' examples are clearly *not* meant as reports of what is going on inside their own minds. When Sartre describes the experience of absence, he is describing not the contents of his own mind but the *world*; and we, Sartre's readers, are meant to *recognize* something in this description, a recognition which may be manifested in our spontaneously relating Sartre's description to occasions when *we* have experienced an absence. His shift to the first-person plural is hardly presumptuous; and far from his descriptions being untestable, we might say that our recognition is a *criterion of correctness* for a phenomenological description: 'When we focus on some feature of our dealing with the world and bring it to speech, it doesn't come across as a discovery of some unsuspected fact, like for example the change in landscape at a turn in the road' (Taylor 2005: 35).

There is, however, a complication, namely that the failure to recognize the description may be due to intellectual prejudices. Dennett is fond of citing cases where people are surprised by their own perceptual experience; this surprise is engendered by the fact that people are inclined to describe what they *think* the perceived world must be like, without actually looking.[6] For example, we may be surprised to discover that we cannot identify a playing card until it is virtually directly in front of our eyes, *because*, Dennett suggests, we tend to think of our visual field as a kind of inner picture composed of coloured shapes, so that it 'stands to reason that each portion of the canvas must be colored *some* color' (1991: 68). But that the phenomenological enterprise of describing experience is endangered by intellectual prejudice is hardly news to the phenomenologists, who devote a good deal of effort to identifying and attempting to undermine such prejudices. Indeed Dennett's diagnosis sounds just the sort of diagnosis that a phenomenologist might well give (though contrast Merleau-Ponty's actual diagnosis, PP 6). Some of the more pernicious patterns of thinking identified by the phenomenologists will be explored in Chapter 2.

'True philosophy consists in re-learning to look at the world', says Merleau-Ponty (PP xx); there is a great deal that needs to be re-learned – and unlearned.

The Eidetic Reduction: Essences and Meanings

Husserl spoke also of the 'eidetic reduction' or 'the intuition of essences'. The notion of essence has a long history within philosophy, and the phenomenologists are eager to distinguish their conception of essences from others'. Two conceptions of essence in particular are in the background of their discussions: the scholastic conception and the logical-positivist conception, itself formulated largely as a reaction against the scholastic conception.

The scholastic conception of essence. The term 'scholastics' is applied to a loosely defined set of medieval philosophers and theologians whose fundamental project was to integrate the teachings of the Bible with those of the great Greek philosophers, particularly Aristotle. Their writings form the backdrop for Descartes, whose own writings are such an important part of the backdrop to the phenomenologists. A basic distinction which Descartes and the scholastics made is that between two kinds of properties: *essential* and *accidental*. Essential properties belong to *kinds* of things, and do so eternally; every instance of a particular kind necessarily exemplifies that kind's essential property or properties: it is that in virtue of which the instance *is* an instance. Essences are expressed in what the scholastics called 'real definitions' or definitions of *things* as opposed to the more superficial nominal definitions or definitions of *words*. Accidental properties belong to individuals, i.e., instances of kinds, and need not be exemplified by other individuals of the same kind. Thus the essence of a triangle is: *a three-sided plane figure*. A particular triangle *must* exemplify that property since otherwise it would not be a triangle, but it might be right-angled, or isosceles, or scalene; these are accidental properties, which other triangles may or may not have. Again, the essence of a human being is (at least according to many scholastics) *a rational animal*; an individual human being *must* exemplify this property since it is this in virtue of which he is a human being, but might possess the accidental properties of being French, or male, or aged 49, which not all human beings need possess.

One type of property was of especial consequence for the scholastics: existence, which was always an accidental property – except in the case of God, who exists necessarily: his existence, uniquely, is part of his essence. The real definition of a triangle or a human being does not mention existence; we can know what a triangle *is*, what it is to *be* a triangle, without knowing whether any triangles actually exist. This point might be articulated by saying that essences were a kind of blueprint in the mind of God prior to his creating things which fulfilled the blueprint. The scholastics expressed this basic principle as: 'Essence precedes existence'.[7] Sartre's principle 'Existence precedes essence', the defining axiom of *his* existentialism, is a deliberate reversal of the scholastic axiom (see below).

The logical-positivist conception of essence. Merleau-Ponty's target is less the scholastics than the logical positivists, those twentieth-century empiricists of the so-called Vienna Circle whose basic premise was that every meaningful sentence is either 'analytic' – true in virtue of the meanings of the words, as for example 'All bachelors are unmarried' – or verifiable through 'experience', i.e., empirically. The logical positivists were in part self-consciously setting themselves against certain aspects of the scholastic notion of essence; their main complaint was that the scholastics had elevated the notion of essence into something metaphysical, as their emphasis on the word 'must' and their grandiose language of 'eternal' or 'unchanging' indicated. The positivists wanted to replace that notion with the much more down-to-earth notion of an analytic proposition whose truth was grounded in the meanings of words, themselves the product of conventions. Thus instead of saying 'Man is a rational animal', which is apt to be understood as expressing a metaphysical insight deep into the nature of human beings, it is less misleading to say 'The sentence "Man is a rational animal" is analytic' or 'The word "man" means "rational animal".'[8] They rejected the very intelligibility of a 'real definition', a definition of the thing as opposed to the word; only words, not things, have meanings. We can't talk about the meaning of life, only about the meaning of (the word) 'life'!

The logical positivists, however, shared with the scholastics the principle that essence, re-interpreted as word-meaning, precedes existence, for one can, on the positivist view, know what a word means independently of knowing whether that word refers to anything which actually exists.[9] (Nor would they see God as an exception to this principle.) And Merleau-Ponty is as critical of this axiom as Sartre was, though on different grounds; his conclusion will be not that 'existence precedes essence': rather, phenomenology 'puts essences back into existence' (PP vii), essence and existence are intertwined.

The core of Merleau-Ponty's critique of the positivists is a critique of their conception of language: they see its 'office' as 'caus[ing] essences to exist in a state of separation [from existence]'. Their essences are word-meanings, and they understand word-meanings as the product of arbitrary convention, ungrounded in what Merleau-Ponty refers to as 'the ante-predicative life of consciousness' (PP xv). It is as if positivists have forgotten that they are human beings and that language is a human, expressive phenomenon. If we wish to say that the meanings of words are the result of conventions, we must not exaggerate their arbitrariness. Let us not forget that conventions are the product of *human* activities, activities of beings-in-the-world, which take place in a *situation*. The claim that the conventions which produce word-meanings are arbitrary is commonly justified by the apparent arbitrariness of the connection between – to take a typical if apparently trivial example – a particular type of animal and the word 'dog', as evidenced by the fact that the same type of animal is called *Hund* or *chien* in other languages. Yet to call the conventions governing the use of these words arbitrary is to suggest, on the one hand, that it was simply decided by *fiat* that *these* animals would henceforth be called 'dogs' (or *Hunds* or *chiens*); this is to ignore the fact that the name of this type of animal in a given language itself has a history and presupposes a whole culture. And it seems to suggest, on the other hand, that it was an arbitrary matter to pick out this type of item from the world and to give it a name in the first place, as if perceptual saliences are unrelated to human needs, be they for companionship, food or safety. Thus Merleau-Ponty says that '[i]n the silence of primary consciousness can be seen appearing not only what words mean, but also what things mean' (PP xv); his language echoes the scholastics' distinction between real and nominal definitions, and also helps to clarify the shift between talk about essence and talk about meaning that we sometimes see in phenomenological writers. Word-meanings and thing-meanings (essences) are inseparable; both have their roots in existence, i.e., in the experienced world; and ultimately both refer to fundamental features of human reality.

The question of how we actually arrive at characterizations of the essence or meaning of a phenomenon from a description is best considered by way of example.

The Practice of Phenomenology: an Example

What then does a phenomenologist do in order to exhibit the essence or meaning of a phenomenon? We should expect already that this will fall roughly into two phases: the execution of the phenomenological reduction and the execution of the eidetic reduction.

Take again the example from earlier: Sartre's description of the experience of the absence of Pierre. We exhibit our recognition of this description and thereby confirm its correctness by spontaneously relating it to our own experiences of absence – say, the time I was meant to be meeting Sue off the plane, but she had missed her flight. We may not understand or grasp the full implications of some of his language (e.g., 'synthetic organization'), but whatever it is that we recognize in the description helps us in grasping that language; we reflect on our own experience, perhaps we note that the passengers who are *not* Sue, the terminal itself, the announcements, all *merge into* one another as background with a Sue-shaped hole, as it were, waiting to be filled, although that hole is not in any precise location. Thus we, upon reading Sartre's descriptions with understanding, begin to notice things in our own experience which are perfectly familiar but to which we had, chances are, never been attuned before. We have suspended our unastonishment, and thus, at least incipiently and in a small way, performed the phenomenological reduction; and we can begin to describe our experience, perhaps to supplement or even to correct Sartre's description.

Sartre's description and our confirmation of it enable us to say that 'an absence can *happen* as a real event'. In so doing, we have *already* moved beyond the particular experience, either that described by Sartre or that which we brought to mind in order to understand his description. We are now talking about a *kind* of experience: experiences of absence. We are then in a position to perform the eidetic reduction; and the first step here consists in a technique which Husserl labelled 'free imaginative variation'. We might, for example, think of other people who did not get off the plane – the Queen, Martin Heidegger – and confirm that *their* non-appearances did not 'happen as real events'; there was no Queen-shaped hole in the airport terminal. So we can now say that there is a difference between absence and mere non-presence; I am just amusing myself if I say 'The Queen was not on the plane', whereas 'Sue was not on the plane' bears a real significance (cf. BN 10); it means phone calls, worrying, changes of plan. The difference, as we can confirm by imagining that we had gone to the airport in order to meet the Queen off the plane, is that experiences of absence only occur in the context of an *expectation*: 'I expected to see Pierre, and my expectation has caused the absence of Pierre *to happen* as a real event concerning this café' (BN 9–10). It was my *expectation* that caused Sue's absence to happen, my expectation that brought it about that her non-presence, unlike the Queen's, was an *absence*.

For the French phenomenologists, however, we do not yet fully grasp the meaning of the phenomenon of absence until we have succeeded in relating our description of this type of experience to some fundamental aspect of human reality. Although it takes Sartre many pages to get there, what we learn, through a series of increasingly penetrating questions, is that '[m]an is the being through whom nothingness comes to the world' (BN 24). And man's ability to 'secrete his own nothingness' (see BN 24, 28) is nothing other than *freedom*. A positivist would have said that the meaning of absence is the meaning of the *word* 'absence', and this is roughly what you might find in a dictionary, perhaps 'the state of being away or not present'. How very distant this is from the phenomenologists' answer: that the meaning of absence is that human beings are free!

We will see a number of phenomenological descriptions in what follows; although I won't always distinguish as explicitly as I have here between the two principal phases, this discussion should set the scene for these. Before considering a general objection to the whole enterprise, I want first to say something about the connections between existentialism and phenomenology; many people find this puzzling, and we now have the necessary materials to explain it.

Existentialism and Phenomenology

The term 'existentialist' has been applied to a wide range of thinkers, invariably including Sartre, but also including, just for example, Kierkegaard, Nietzsche, Dostoevsky, Heidegger, Jaspers, Marcel and Camus. Most of those who had the opportunity to – including Sartre at times – have repudiated the title; and curiously, Merleau-Ponty seldom figures on this roll-call. Many books and articles with titles like *Existentialism* and *Introduction to Existentialism* have tried to identify something in common between all these thinkers; others have given up on the task, or rejected the applicability of the label to one or more of the thinkers commonly listed. I will confine myself to indicating what Sartre and Merleau-Ponty understood by the term 'existentialism'.

In Merleau-Ponty's usage, 'existentialism' or 'existential philosophy' is simply part of phenomenology as he understands it; phenomenology must be an *existential* philosophy because the phenomenological reduction cannot be taken to the point of suspending judgement on the truth of the existence-claims made by perceived objects. Sartre shares this understanding of phenomenology and of the reduction; the primary intuition to which *Nausea* gave expression – the intuition that at first drew him to Husserlian phenomenology and afterwards repelled him from it once he had understood the idealist tendencies of Husserl's version of phenomenology – was the intuition of the contingency and at the same time the indubitability of the existence of things. Thus we can say that Sartre is an existentialist in Merleau-Ponty's sense of the term, even though this is not the sense in which Sartre uses that term.

When Sartre uses the term 'existentialism', it refers not to an aspect of the method of phenomenology but to one of its foremost *results*: the idea that human beings do not possess a pre-given essence. He expresses this claim by saying that existence precedes essence, a deliberate reversal of the scholastic claim that essence precedes existence. Just as the artisan who produces a paper-knife has a conception of a paper-knife and at the same time is aware of 'the pre-existent technique of production which is a part of that conception', so too, according to the scholastics, for the 'supernal artisan', God. On this picture 'God makes man according to a procedure and a conception, exactly as the artisan manufactures a paper-knife' (EH 27). Sartre himself rejects the notion of God. But even if 'the notion of God is suppressed', there is still a tendency to invoke 'human nature' to fulfil a parallel role; it means that 'each man is a particular example of a universal conception'. So even on this picture, 'the essence of man precedes that historic existence which we confront in experience' (EH 27). Existentialists, by contrast, say that 'man first of all exists . . . and defines himself afterwards' (EH 28). This conception of human beings is integral to Sartre's conception of freedom and will be explored later (Chapter 8).

Note several things: first, when Sartre develops this principle in EH, it applies solely to human beings. Rather as God was the exception to the scholastic principle that essence precedes existence, human beings are, it seems, exceptions to that same principle for Sartre. Nor by the way is this comparison inapt; as we will see, man is rather closer to the scholastics' God than we might expect! Thus despite its seemingly general formulation, he is not proclaiming 'Existence precedes essence' as a general principle applicable to all kinds of things. Second, 'essence' for Sartre belongs to *individual* human beings, not the kind 'human being', and this is a feature which is radically at odds with the scholastics' understanding of essence. When he says 'man first of all exists . . . and defines himself afterwards', he means that *each individual* human being defines himself, through his actions; that is, as Sartre sometimes puts it, each human being *creates his own* essence, which is utterly unique to him. (Sartre does, of course, make general claims about fundamental aspects of human reality; that is after all the subject-matter of BN, but this is not what *he* has in mind when he uses the term 'essence'.) Third, unlike scholastic essences, these self-defined individual essences are not eternal; indeed, through a radical conversion of one's 'fundamental project' (see Chapter 8), one can *change* one's own essence. One might be forgiven for concluding that Sartre's famous principle is simply if memorably playing with words: he has 'looking-glassed' the term 'essence'. This obviously diminishes the value of his existentialism as a critique of the scholastic conception of essence, but does not, of course, diminish the value of his existentialism per se.

Appearance and Reality Revisited

I want to end by considering what might seem to be a fundamental objection to the entire phenomenological endeavour. We noted earlier that although phenomena may be characterized as 'appearances', this term was not to be understood against the background of a distinction between appearance and reality; we are not to understand the phenomenological enterprise as one of describing how things seem as opposed to how they really are. But are the phenomenologists not then assuming that to describe phenomena is to describe *how things really are*? And, worse yet, might that assumption not be false? These questions themselves, I suggest, manifest intellectual prejudices.

This objection has been put forcefully for many years by Dennett. He develops what he takes to be an analogy: he imagines a tribe which believes in a god called Feenoman and considers the various positions which anthropologists might take toward the tribe's beliefs about this deity. Some, the Feenomanists, go native and start to 'believe in the real existence and good works of Feenoman'. Others, the Feenomanologists, gather descriptions of Feenoman from their native informants, questioning them closely to eliminate disagreements wherever possible; they catalogue and inventory the relevant 'belief-manifolds' of the natives and arrive at as definitive a description as possible of Feenoman considered as an 'intentional object' whose actual *existence* they have bracketed. Yet others take the Feenomanologists' descriptions of the natives' belief-manifolds and set out to plot their normal *causes*, which may or may not turn out to be the words and deeds of Feenoman. If they do not – if in fact their beliefs are caused by the trickery of Sam the Shaman – then we might either conclude that Sam the Shaman *is* Feenoman or that Feenoman does not exist, depending on how many of Feenoman's central properties Sam possesses (Dennett 1978: 182–3; cf. 1991: 82–3).

This *looks* like an elegant way to raise the general question about the phenomenological enterprise. What the phenomenologists, by analogy with the Feenomanologists, are doing is cataloguing our beliefs about ourselves and the 'life-world'; and that is in and of itself an irreproachable activity. To the extent that they assume that these beliefs are true, however – i.e., to the extent that they assume that the normal causes of our belief-manifolds are sufficiently like what we take their causes to be – they are open to refutation by philosophers who take the third approach. Since Sartre and Merleau-Ponty, unlike Husserl, do *not* 'bracket off' existence, they apparently make the very assumption that is open to refutation.

We might begin by observing that Dennett's anthropology would ring an old-fashioned note to many modern anthropologists: Dennett's Feenomanologists sound rather like J. G. Frazer, writing in 1922: 'In various parts of Mecklenburg, where the belief in the Corn-wolf is particularly prevalent, every one fears to cut the last corn, because they say that the Wolf is sitting in it' (quoted in Wittgenstein RF n.11), or W. H. R Rivers, writing in 1924:

in Torres Straits, disease is believed to occur by the action of certain men who, through their possession of objects called *zogo* . . . have the power of inflicting disease. Thus, one *zogo* is believed to make people lean and hungry and at the same time to produce dysentery, another will produce constipation, and a third insanity. (quoted in Good 1994: 18)

The anthropologist B. J. Good focuses on the word 'belief' in such passages; etymologically it is related to 'beloved' and the archaic 'lief'. In its older use, still retained in some contexts today,

The affirmation 'I believe in God' used to mean: 'Given the reality of God as a fact of the universe, I hereby pledge to him my heart and soul . . .' Today, the statement may be taken by some as meaning: 'Given the uncertainty as to whether there be a God or not . . . I announce that my opinion is "yes".' (W. C. Smith, quoted in Good 1994: 16)[10]

Within the old-style anthropology, as well as in philosophy, it clearly bears the latter meaning. For Dennett and his imaginary anthropologists, beliefs are opinions, not commitments to ways of life.

More recent anthropologists such as Good have come to question both the epistemology and the politics underlying such belief-discourse. Their concerns are directly relevant to ours, because their grounds echo those of the phenomenologists, as well as Wittgenstein's 'Remarks on Frazer's *Golden Bough*'; it is no coincidence that many modern anthropologists, Good included, actually draw on phenomenology for their theoretical framework.

First, anthropology since Pierre Bourdieu (esp. 1977) has tended to focus on practices rather than beliefs. Bourdieu, himself influenced by both Wittgenstein and Merleau-Ponty, argued, against the prevailing intellectualist or 'mentalistic' (Good 1994: 23) trend, that the learning of a cultural practice was – not the acquisition of a set of beliefs but – the acquisition of a set of embodied *habits* through imitation and training. Moreover, as Wittgenstein himself argued, cultural practices were not to be explained by *reference* to beliefs. When Frazer states that the king in a particular culture 'must be killed in his prime, because the savages believe that otherwise his soul would not be kept fresh', Wittgenstein comments that 'the practice does not spring from the view' (RF 62), any more than kissing the picture of one's beloved springs from the opinion 'that it will have some specific effect on the object which the picture represents' (RF 64). And the phenomenologists – admittedly Merleau-Ponty more assiduously than Sartre – have made parallel anti-intellectualist arguments in other arenas. Dennett's discussion simply bypasses these arguments via his assumption that the subject-matter of phenomenology is *beliefs about* experience rather than experience.[11] It exhibits a version of what we in Chapter 2 label 'the prejudice in favour of knowing over living'.

Secondly, belief as Dennett understands it is closely akin to 'opinion', as in the Smith quotation, or to 'assumption', as in our original question. An opinion is at the least something which it makes sense to doubt, and such that it makes sense to ask for grounds; the word 'assumption' might be characterized as something such that it makes sense to ask for grounds but for which one is not presently giving grounds. But what Dennett in his critique of phenomenology calls 'beliefs' are in fact *lived certainties*. That is, they are such that the notion of doubt makes no sense, and such that it makes no sense to ask for grounds; hence they are precisely *not* opinions or assumptions. We will see many examples of lived certainties in what follows; a paradigm case is the existence of other conscious subjects (see Chapter 7). Unlike Dennett (see 1991: 95), we don't *assume* that our friends aren't zombies, i.e., human beings who exhibit 'perfectly natural, alert, loquacious, vivacious behavior' but are 'in fact not conscious at all' (1991: 73). In Wittgenstein's words, ' "I believe that he is not an automaton" [or a zombie], just like that, so far makes no sense . . . I am not of the *opinion*' that he is a conscious subject (PI p. 178). The suggestion that phenomenologists *assume* or *believe* that other conscious subjects exist embodies a widespread intellectual prejudice; it is what we will label (Chapter 2) 'the prejudice in favour of knowledge over certainty'.

Thirdly, Dennett, like the earlier anthropologists, is clearly treating the tribe's beliefs about Feenoman as proto-scientific: Feenoman's powers are seen as a 'primitive' causal explanation of various events the tribesmen observe in the world around them. Wittgenstein's comment on Frazer seems equally applicable to Dennett. Both present 'primitive' practices 'as, so to speak, pieces of stupidity' (RF 61); so to represent these practices is not just, as we today might say, 'politically incorrect', but obviously wrong.[12] Wittgenstein refers to 'a Rain-King in Africa to whom the people pray for rain *when the rainy period comes*. But surely that means that they do not really believe that he can make it rain, otherwise they would make it rain in the dry periods of the year' (RF 71–2).[13] 'What a narrow spiritual life on Frazer's part!', he exclaims (RF 65); 'Frazer is much more savage than most of his savages' (RF 68). In anthropology, analyses of such practices as proto-scientific are 'now largely discounted' (Good 1994: 22). The old-style anthropologists who employed the term 'belief' in connection with 'primitive' tribes tended to use the word 'knowledge' in reference to their *own* assented-to propositions, thereby suggesting that their own beliefs are true whereas those of the culture they are studying are false; 'the representation of others' culture as "belief" authorizes the position and knowledge of the anthropological observer' (Good 1994; 20). Although Dennett is somewhat disingenuously purporting to remain neutral with regard to the truth of the tribe's beliefs about Feenoman, he does have a clear view of what would count as showing these 'beliefs' to be false. For him, as for the old-fashioned anthropologists, *science* has the role of 'arbiter between knowledge and belief' (Good 1994: 22). This attitude exhibits scientism, which embodies a veritable bouquet of intellectual prejudices (see below and Chapter 2).

The objection we are considering assumes that there *is* a contrast to be drawn between how things seem and how they really are (cf. Austin 1962). No doubt in particular cases we can make such a distinction for particular purposes, but it will not carry the weight philosophers tend to want it to bear. Consider a so-called visual illusion (see BN 312): a paradigm occasion for making the appearance/reality distinction. It is commonly said of the lines in the Müller–Lyer illusion (see figure) that they *look* different lengths but are *really* the same length.

The Müller–Lyer illusion

In the first place, however, this is a careless description of how they *look*; the fact is that they look the same length if you ignore or cover up the arrowheads, and different lengths if you do not – so that they do not unambiguously look either the same length or different lengths.[14] In the second place, the temptation to say that they *really are* the same length rests on the preconception that the measurable is more real than the non-measurable; the criterion for saying that they are 'really' the same length is simply that they reach the same point on a ruler (cf. PP 6ff.).[15]

To apply the word 'real', however, is to make a value-judgement: reality is contrasted with '*mere* appearance'; to call something real is to give it our philosophical seal of approval. But once we recognize that 'real' simply means 'measurable' in this context, we might be in a position to raise the question of why the measurable is supposed to be more valuable than the non-measurable. We can even grant that for certain purposes, e.g., building a bridge that will not fall down, it is; for others, e.g., judging the aesthetic quality of the bridge, it is not. As Carman nicely puts it, scientific purposes 'are not our only, and certainly not our most cherished, purposes'. If, as Carman goes on to suggest, we define scientism as the 'insistence on equating reality with scientific utility' (2005a: 70 n. 5), this critique of phenomenology – like Dennett's – is a paradigm instance of scientism.[16] It is a cousin of what we will label

(Chapter 2) 'the prejudice in favour of the existent'. This is not, of course, to devalue science: science 'has its own magnificent work to do'; it is, however, to wish to restrain its hegemonic pretensions; science 'does not need to rush in and take over extraneous kinds of questions (historical, logical, ethical, linguistic or the like) as well' (Midgley 2004: 6).

Finally, there is a crucial disanalogy between Dennett's anthropologists and the phenomenologists. Dennett's Feenomanologist anthropologists are what he calls 'heterophenomenologists' (see 1991: 72ff.), i.e., *inter alia*, they are studying subjects other than themselves, from the 'third-person point of view'.[17] But the 'tribe' which the phenomenologists are studying is *us* – us human beings, us conscious beings-in-the-world. There is no taking an external point of view on these subjects; even Dennett cannot conduct heterophenomenology *vis-à-vis* human reality.

I have attempted to present the phenomenological method in a practically accessible way, as well as to clarify its relations to existentialism. We have seen that the familiarity of the phenomena which phenomenologists seek to describe tends, for a variety of reasons, to render those phenomena 'invisible', and to make the invisible visible calls for a variety of techniques. We have also, in considering an objection to the whole phenomenological enterprise, seen glimpses of another formidable obstacle: widespread intellectual prejudices. These, and some of the techniques for overcoming them, are the focus of the next chapter.

notes

1 The subtitle of BN is, in French, *'essai d'ontologie phénoménologique'*, which, as others have noted, might be translated either as 'essay on phenomenological ontology' or as 'phenomenological essay on ontology'. Barnes chooses the former; I have chosen the latter since I think it makes it a little clearer that phenomenology is the method whereby being is to be explored philosophically.

2 See, e.g., Spiegelberg's classic study of phenomenology (1961–9) or Moran's excellent introduction (2000), for more historically rigorous outlines of phenomenology.

3 McCulloch (1994) reads phenomenology in this way, thus misleading a whole generation of Sartre students.

4 See Austin's (1962) discussion of the terms 'appear' and 'appearance'.

5 Wittgenstein does something similar sometimes, although often with imaginary examples, e.g., his human beings who speak only in monologue (PI §243); in RF he considers anthropological descriptions of the practices of other cultures, but he also comments 'that we ourselves could think up all the possibilities' (RF 66).

6 Cf. Wittgenstein PI §66; cf. Sartre's charge against Bergson that instead of 'looking' at his images he 'appeals' to 'a priori deduction' (I 56).

7 Different scholastic and post-scholastic thinkers will express these points differently and some may disagree about the details; this is accurate enough for present purposes.

8 Cf. Carnap (1937, Part V.A) on the 'material mode' vs. the 'formal mode' of speech.

9 Unlike the scholastics, this is not because they think of existence as an accidental property; indeed they reject the view that existence is a property at all.

10 Cf. Sartre's use in BN Part I.2, where he tries to make it clear that in this context 'belief' means 'faith'; see Chapter 4.

11 Carman 2005a and 2005b have excellent discussions of Merleau-Ponty's anti-intellectualist arguments which explicitly engage with Dennett.

12 On this point, words such as 'primitive', 'savage' and even 'tribe' have disappeared from the anthropological vocabulary; I trust that I won't be seen as endorsing the use of these words.

13 There is a whole literature in Christian theology on the efficacy of prayer, much of which makes a parallel point.

14 Merleau-Ponty will add that 'same length' and 'different length' don't figure in our experience anyway, at least insofar as the word 'length' refers to measurable length (PP 6). For example, we can't ask 'How much longer does the one line look than the other?'

15 Again, Dennett asserts that '[p]eople do undoubtedly believe that they have mental images'; but it is 'an empirical matter to investigate' 'whether items thus portrayed exist as real objects, events, and states in the brain' (1991: 98). The word 'belief' again shows his commitment to intellectualism; his phenomenology of mental images is seriously inaccurate (see Sartre, I); and his presupposition about what it would be for this belief to be true is scientistic (see below, in this chapter).

16 Debates about scientific realism in philosophy of science – e.g., whether subatomic particles are 'real' or merely 'theoretical constructs' – would be interesting to consider here. 'Real' means 'existent' in either case; those who think of, say, subatomic particles as theoretical constructs often characterize them as 'useful fictions', hence accord them a certain 'heuristic' value, from which it follows that they recognize values other than reality – though still, of course, a value only for *scientific* purposes. Some of those who insist that subatomic particles are real may be assuming that the criterion for existence and hence for reality is, precisely, scientific usefulness.

17 In fact there is a whole literature on what is sometimes called 'anthropology at home' (e.g., Peirano 1998 and her bibliography), which shows a sensitive awareness of both the advantages and the difficulties of studying one's own 'tribe'.

intellectual prejudices and sartrean therapy

henomenology's starting point, as we saw in the previous chapter, is the unprejudiced description of familiar phenomena. The phenomenologists identify a number of wide-ranging and pernicious 'intellectual prejudices' (BN 241–2) that commonly distort such descriptions, and I want to spotlight these as early as possible. This is imperative for two reasons: first, many *non*-phenomenological philosophers and other thinkers are – we have seen an example of this already – in the grip of the very prejudices which the phenomenologists are at such pains to diagnose and to attempt to remedy. This in itself constitutes one of the most serious barriers to mutual understanding. Second, many of the peculiarities of style and expression which characterize phenomenological writings and which may serve to alienate non-phenomenological thinkers are, I want to suggest, to be seen as subserving their attempts at therapy to treat these prejudices.

The term 'prejudice' and similar terms, referring to intellectual prejudices, echo through the historical tradition in which Sartre is working. Think of Husserl's ringing call to arms, which expressly places itself in the tradition of Descartes's stated aim of 'freeing us from our preconceived opinions': 'Must not the demand for a philosophy aiming at the ultimate conceivable freedom from prejudice . . . and therefore absolutely self-responsible . . . be part of the fundamental sense of genuine philosophy?' (CM §2); Heidegger refers to 'the presuppositions and prejudices which are constantly reimplanting and fostering the belief that an inquiry into Being is unnecessary' (BT 2); Merleau-Ponty's introduction to PP is entitled 'Traditional prejudices and the return to phenomena', and what he calls the prejudice of objective thought is the *Leitmotiv* of the entire book. I don't want to insist on the *word* 'prejudice'; in fact it is not all that prominent in Sartre's own philosophical works.[1] He is more prone to use the term 'illusion', as in 'the illusion of the primacy of knowledge' (BN xxviii, cf. xxx, 175–6), the 'substantialist illusion' (BN 84, cf. 557), or the 'illusion of immanence' the combating of which dominates PsyI (cf. BN 27, 450). One might equally, as Taylor (2005) does, speak of thraldom to a *picture*; other Wittgensteinian terms like 'dogma' and 'superstition' could serve something of the same purpose; and so too could Sartre's own term 'bad faith' (see Chapter 4), which he uses from time to time in application to intellectual positions.[2] The point is not the word but the concept, and neither, I think, is given sufficient weight by most commentators on these authors. I submit that by 'prejudice' these authors intend something more than a mere preconception or prior judgement that is readily overturned by evidence and argument; they mean to call to mind everyday prejudices such as racism and anti-Semitism, which are precisely – though to a greater or lesser degree in individual cases – *resistant* to such measures.[3] These other terms – 'dogma', 'illusion', etc. – similarly connote what I will call 'perverse' thinking.

The phenomenologists identify a number of intellectual prejudices which appear to be widespread not only among philosophers, but also among psychologists, sociologists and anthropologists who, so the phenomenologists will urge, ought to *begin* with unprejudiced descriptions of the aspects of human reality which they wish to go on to explain or analyse; but they frequently fail to do so and hence undermine the foundations of their own theories. I begin by sketching the most significant of these patterns, before considering in general terms what therapy for such intellectual prejudices might involve.

Patterns of Intellectual Prejudice

The prejudice in favour of external relations

The notion of an internal relation is arguably the single most important one for understanding the writings of the phenomenologists.[4] Very roughly, to say of 'two' things that they are internally related is to say that neither would be what it is were it not for the other; an internal relation is a duality in a unity. We might explicate this duality-in-a-unity via the term 'ambiguity', which figures heavily in phenomenological descriptions of human reality; but, though helpful up to a point, it will be misleading if the model of ambiguity one has in mind is that of an ambiguous *word*, like 'bank', where the two meanings of 'financial institution' and 'side of a river' appear to be totally unconnected with one another. A better model might be an ambiguous *picture* – and especially, perhaps, one where the ambiguity is a figure/ground ambiguity (see figure).

The word 'bank' could lose its meaning of 'side of a river' with no effect whatsoever on its meaning of 'financial institution': these two meanings are externally related. The vase, by contrast, would disappear

Figure/ground ambiguity

if the black background disappeared, the profiles would disappear if the white background disappeared, and one might say that the vase *is* the possibility of being seen as two profiles on a white background: figure and ground are internally related.

This is an instance of an internal relation as well as an analogy for more central examples; but any example is necessarily controversial, precisely because many thinkers reject the very idea of an internal relation. The phenomenologists will often signal internal relations with such language as 'synthetic unity', 'totality', 'field', and 'organization', and they see many things as internally related which other thinkers see as externally related: the bodily reactions, the behaviour and the consciousness of the object (say, a frightening tiger) of an emotion (say, fear); 'different' qualities of perceived objects (e.g., we do not perceive the texture and the colour of a carpet as two separate qualities but as a 'fleecy red' or 'woolly red'; PsyI 276; cf. PP 5); past, present and future; perception and action; action, motive and end; consciousness and body; I and the Other; freedom and situation, and so on. To say of two things that they are *externally* related is to say that each is what it is independently of the other thing. The phenomenologists often mark external relations by such terms as 'association' or 'series'. Sartre often uses the image of a witness: if two things are not related internally – say, the lamp and the book – we need an observer to bring them into relation with one another, to say 'The lamp is to the left of the book' or 'The lamp and the book are both on the table' (see, e.g., BN 231).

Crucially, verbal expressions of internal relations can often sound contradictory, because if 'two' things a and b – say, past and present – are internally related, one cannot say that $a = b$: the claim is not that the past is the *same* as the present. But nor can one say that $a \neq b$; this would seem to suggest that past and present are wholly independent, i.e., externally related. Sartre often in fact ends up saying that a both *is* and *is not*

intellectual prejudices and sartrean therapy

identical to b, i.e. ($a = b$ and $a \neq b$) – which is, in logical terms, contradictory, but he is trying to express an internal relation. For example, one finds Sartre saying, within the space of a few pages, both 'I am my past' and 'I am not my past' (BN 110–18). I *am* my past rather than *having* my past: 'one cannot "have" a past as one "has" an automobile or a racing-stable . . . [because] possession ordinarily expresses an external relation of the possessor to the possessed'; this would render past and present 'two factual givens without real communication' (BN 112–13). At the same time, 'I am not my past. I *am* not it because I *was* it' (BN 116). The internal relation between past and present can be brought out by saying that my past 'is originally the past of *this* present' (BN 110); *this* past is what it is only in virtue of being the past of *this* present; moreover *this* present is what it is only in virtue of having *this* past. A similar analysis will apply to such statements as 'I *am* my body to the extent that I *am*; *I am not* my body to the extent that I am not what I am' (BN 326). Such seemingly paradoxical claims are a perpetual hazard for anyone who wants to express internal relations; we find them, for example, in Wittgenstein as well. In trying to articulate the internal relation between pain and pain-behaviour, he ends up saying 'It [the sensation] is not a *something*, but not a *nothing* either!' (PI §304).

The *locus classicus* for a description of external relations might be the arch-empiricist Hume's discussion of causation. For Hume, the cause and the effect are 'objects' such that 'the effect is totally different from the cause, and consequently can never be discovered in it' (*Enquiry* IV.i.25). Cause and effect are what they are quite independently of the other, i.e., they are externally related.[5] According to a widespread intellectual prejudice, all relations between things – things as opposed to words or ideas – are external: everything there is is a *Humean* object. What Merleau-Ponty labels 'scientific points of view' (PP ix) rely on this prejudice. As Sartre argues in his critique of scientific psychology, the very aim of formulating laws and devising explanations tends to force the scientific psychologist to isolate various factors. For example, a scientific psychologist studying emotion will be encouraged to identify as separate factors the bodily reactions such as increased adrenalin, behaviour such as 'fight or flight', and 'the state of consciousness properly so-called', say the awareness of the crouching tiger (STE 20), in order to come up with causal laws relating them and causal explanations for the behaviour.[6] To do so is to treat these as externally related when phenomenology reveals them as internally related. We will encounter numerous other examples.

There is a strand in analytic philosophy which inclines toward the prejudice in favour of external relations for somewhat different reasons. First, to talk of internal relations is to talk of some sort of 'necessary connection', and some analytic philosophers seem inclined to accept the logical-positivist axiom that all necessity is *logical* necessity. Just as we cannot in their view talk about the meanings of things, only about the meanings of words (Chapter 1), so we cannot talk about internal relations between things, only between words or expressions. They will endorse Hume's claim that *the cause A* and *the effect B*, i.e., the objects, cannot be said to be internally related, though if you redescribe A as 'the cause of B', you can say that the *descriptions* 'the cause of B' and 'B' are internally related: 'The cause of B caused B', trivially, expresses a necessary connection (Davidson 1980: 14). Anything less trivial than that will be deemed inadmissible. Second, some analytic philosophers make expressibility in logical notation a criterion for coherence, and the names which logical notation uses are *meant* to refer to Humean objects, objects which are externally related.[7] This is why there are inherent difficulties in expressing internal relations within standard logical notation.[8]

Thus certain strands of analytic philosophy unite with scientific points of view in condemning the very idea of internal relations. Yet our experience, the phenomenologists claim, reveals many relations as internal. The rejection of internal relations on the part of these philosophical outlooks is grounded in prejudice.

Prejudices in favour of the existent

The very title of Sartre's great work *Being and Nothingness* indicates that the non-existent, the non-factual, the absent, and the possible play a central role in phenomenological accounts of human reality. Lest it seem puzzling that a philosophy of existence – existentialism – should simultaneously be a philosophy of *non*-existence, we must note that the existent and the non-existent are internally related. For example, although neither the past nor the future exist – else they would not be the past or the future – past, present and future are internally related.

Let us be clear: the claim is not, of course, that the non-existent *exists*! A. J. Ayer, the British empiricist who came back from his visits to Vienna bearing the message of the logical positivists, misunderstood this point; he accused Sartre of using the word 'nothing' to name 'something insubstantial and mysterious', like the 'nobody' whom the Red King's eyes lacked the acuity to spot (1945: 19). Nor are absences present, or possibilities actualities, or values facts – that is the whole point! Granted that Merleau-Ponty will say that the unseen sides of the lamp are 'present in their own way' (see Chapter 3), and that '[t]he normal person reckons with the possible, which thus, without shifting from its position as a possibility, acquires a sort of actuality' (PP 109); Sartre will say that 'For Pierre to be absent in relation to Thérèse is a particular way of his being present' (BN 278). The point is to contrast those unseen profiles which form a horizon of the perceptual experience with those unseen things which have nothing to do with it (Chapter 3), to contrast *lived* possibilities with abstract conjectures (Chapter 4), and to contrast absence with mere non-presence (Chapter 1).

There is, however, a widespread intellectual prejudice against the non-existent, the non-factual, the non-actual, and the absent, as well as the non-quantifiable and the non-measurable (cf. Chapter 1).[9] I sum these up with the phrase 'prejudice in favour of the existent'.[10] The prejudice might be expressed as: only the existent is *real*.

We have observed already that to apply the word 'real' is to make a value-judgement; and often on close inspection, philosophical critiques of the non-existent in its various guises amount to no more than the claim that the non-existent does not exist – which of course is already not only granted but insisted upon – together with a negative evaluation of that fact! For example, the influential analytic philosopher W. V. O. Quine famously ridicules the idea of 'unactualized possibles':

> Take, for instance, the possible fat man in that doorway; and, again, the possible bald man in that doorway. Are they the same possible man, or two possible men? How do we decide? How many possible men are there in that doorway? Are there more possible thin ones than fat ones? (1963: 4)

One could be forgiven for thinking that this simply amounts to the observation that unactualized possibles are not *actual* – they don't share the logic of the actual – and that they are the worse because of that.

Humean empiricism and scientific points of view are blind to the non-existent; this blindness is partly fed by that strand of the prejudice in favour of external relations which sees causal relations in many places where phenomenologists would discern internal relations, since causes as empiricists understand them must *exist*. Their analyses of perception, for example, are causal, and this is part of what makes it difficult for them to make sense of the phenomenologists' notion of a horizon, e.g., of the idea that the unseen sides of the lamp form the horizon of our perceptual experience of the lamp (see Chapter 3): if the unseen sides are not actually seen – which they cannot be since they are not in the 'line of sight' – they cannot play any causal role and so, they reason, cannot be any part of perceptual experience. Again, empiricists cannot make sense of Aristotle's 'final' causes, where the cause is in the future as a not-yet-existent end. To say that the cause of my going to the shops to buy milk is a not-yet-existent end, namely a milky mug of tea, can only be an elliptical way of saying that a *present, existent* desire for a milky mug of tea combined with a present belief that milk can be obtained from the shops was the *efficient* cause of my action. Again, they can make little sense of the idea that memory puts us in direct contact with the past; memory can only operate via *present* traces, say, in the brain: 'Since the past is no more . . . if the memory continues to exist, it must be by virtue of a present modification of our being' (BN 108).

The phenomenologists will say that the non-existent is real, i.e., part of human reality, the life-world (Husserl: *Lebenswelt*) which is 'the seat and as it were the *homeland* of our thoughts' (Merleau-Ponty PP 24). There is in fact a long tradition within philosophy of distinguishing, in a variety of ways, between existence and reality. What is unique about phenomenology is that it exhibits the real but non-existent as a constitutive aspect of the life-world. We can see in this a Nietzschean revaluation of values: the phenomenologists are re-appropriating the word 'real', already indicative of a positive value-judgement, to remind us that the non-existent, the absent, possibilities, and values – and let us add for good measure the ambiguous, the indeterminate and the non-measurable – are central aspects of human experience, so that to devalue them is to devalue human reality, that is, as Nietzsche would put it, *life.* And they will add that the positive value placed by prejudiced thinkers upon the existent, the present, the factual and the actual is, like all values, a *human* value – one that, paradoxically enough, devalues the value of the human.

Prejudices in favour of knowledge

I will here highlight two closely connected prejudices: *the prejudice in favour of knowledge over certainty;* and *the prejudice in favour of knowing over living.* I could also include under this heading *the prejudice in favour of knowledge over the emotions.* Sartre accuses the philosophy of his day of 'understand[ing] little besides epistemology'. But 'our consciousness of things is by no means limited to knowledge of them. Knowledge . . . is only one of the possible forms of my consciousness "of" this tree; I can also love it, fear it, hate it' (IFI 5; cf. BN xxviii); emotions give us a different kind of access *to the world.*[11]

Prejudice in favour of knowledge over certainty. Sartre's distinction between knowledge and certainty requires some explanation; but first, it may be important to distinguish his use of the word 'certainty' from a usage according to which it means something like 'strong subjective conviction', as in 'I'm certain it's going to rain this afternoon', a conviction that can of course prove wrong;[12] this is not at all what Sartre means. His use is more like the impersonal 'It is certain that . . .'

Sartre connects the concept of knowledge with two other concepts (see BN 250–1, 276, 302): that of *probability* and that of *evidence* or *validation/invalidation.*[12] These concepts are all part of the 'language-game' of knowledge, to borrow Wittgenstein's phrase, and have no part in the language-game of certainty.

The connection between knowledge and probability might be cashed out in terms of the idea that where it makes sense to speak of knowledge it also makes sense to speak of doubt; from this point of view I can be said to know that another is in pain but not to *know* that I am in pain, since in the latter case it makes no sense to speak of doubt (cf. Wittgenstein, PI §246). However, just because it makes sense to speak of doubt does not entail that doubt is always possible: cf. 'Just try – in a real case – to doubt someone else's fear or pain' (PI §303). Sartre uses the somewhat curious phrase 'infinite probability' for such cases. The connection Sartre draws between knowledge and evidence or validation and invalidation might be cashed out in terms of the applicability of the question '*How* do you know?' Wherever it makes sense to say that you know, it also makes sense to ask 'How do you know?'

By parity of reasoning, we can then see that the language-game played with *certainty* in Sartre's usage is one in which it makes no sense to talk of doubt and one in which the question 'How, i.e., on what basis, are you certain?' cannot arise.

The philosophical inclination to insist that the question 'How do you know?' is always appropriate exhibits the prejudice in favour of knowledge over certainty. If the inapplicability of the question is mistaken for the inadequacy of the answer, the question will fuel scepticism about the existence of the external world, other minds and so on. As Heidegger famously said, 'The "scandal of philosophy" [*pace* Kant] is not that this proof [of the existence of external things] has yet to be given, but that *such proofs are expected and attempted again and again.*' As he goes on to note, the idea that the existence of things must ' "be taken merely on faith" . . . would still fail to surmount this perversion of the problem. The assumption would remain that at bottom and ideally it must still be possible to carry out such a proof.' Likewise with the suggestion that 'the subject must presuppose and indeed always does unconsciously presuppose' the existence of the external world (BT 205–6).[13]

Sartre does give what he calls an 'ontological proof' of the existence of things outside of consciousness; the intentionality of consciousness implies (see Chapter 3) that 'consciousness is born *supported by* a being which is not itself' (BN xxxvii). But he himself distances this 'proof' from more traditional attempts at such a proof: 'It is not a question of showing that the phenomena of inner sense imply the existence of objective spatial phenomena [as Kant purported to do], but that consciousness implies in its being a non-conscious and transphenomenal being' (BN xxxviii). He also addresses solipsism, or scepticism regarding the existence of conscious subjects other than oneself. Here he deliberately resists the word 'proof': a theory of the Other's existence 'can not offer a new proof of the existence of others, or an argument better than any other against solipsism . . . far from inventing a proof, it must make explicit the very foundation of that certainty' which the Other's existence possesses (BN 250–1). Commentators exhibit the prejudice in favour of knowledge over certainty when they attempt to reconstruct Sartre's enterprise in terms of a proof, and equally when they conclude that in fact he is not attempting to prove the existence of others, he is simply assuming it.[14]

Prejudice in favour of knowing over living. The phenomenologists draw a related contrast between knowing and living. The language-game which encompasses knowledge, probability and evidence also encompasses objects, that is, objects which one perceives or uses. The distinction is particularly important in relation to the body, which may be either known, as the body of another person is, or lived, as one's own body is in one's normal dealings with the world (see Chapter 5).[15] One does not normally perceive or use one's body; the 'body-for-itself' is rather the unperceived centre of the fields of perception and of instrumentality. Thus the relation between consciousness and the body-for-itself is not epistemological, not one of knowledge, but *existential*: Sartre will sometimes use 'exist', as well as 'live', as a transitive verb, e.g., 'consciousness exists its body' (BN 329), in order to make this point.

Philosophers in the grip of this prejudice – what Sartre calls 'the illusion of the primacy of knowledge' (e.g., BN xxviii) – seem driven to convert this existential relationship into an epistemological one. We will, for example, see that on those rare occasions when philosophers focus on one's awareness of one's own body, they tend to posit special sense-modalities, e.g., proprioception, to provide the answer to the question 'How do you know the position of your limbs?' This exhibits not only the prejudice in favour of knowledge over certainty, in the sense that normally the question 'How do you know?' is inapplicable here, but also the prejudice in favour of knowing over living. In truth, I don't normally *know* the position of my limbs, because I normally *live* my body, I *exist* it: it is not an *object* for me.

A consequence: the impoverishment of perceptual experience

One pervasive consequence of the confluence of the prejudices already described is the impoverishment of perceptual experience (Merleau-Ponty PP 24; cf. Taylor 2005: 45); it is so striking and so characteristic of much non-phenomenological philosophy that it merits special mention. Although rationalists or intellectualists as well as empiricists impoverish perceptual experience, it is perhaps most startling that empiricists do so, since, as their name indicates, they purport to be starting from *experience*. Yet they bring these prejudices to bear on their descriptions of perceptual experience – deciding in advance what we can, 'strictly speaking', perceive – and thereby jettisoning much of the richness of the perceived world from their descriptions.

The perceived world contains *absences*: think of Pierre's absence from the café. It contains *internally related qualities* – recall the fleecy red of the carpet – which themselves reveal internal relations between the sensory modalities: 'if I poke my finger into a jar of jam, the sticky coldness of that jam is the revelation to my fingers of its sugary taste' (BN 186). It contains *the future*: 'I could see that coming', we say, as the cat, intent on catching a fly, knocks down the vase. It contains *concrete possibilities*: the possibility of rain 'belongs to the sky as a threat' (BN 97). We perceive *values*, which are 'sown on my path as thousands of little real demands, like the signs which order us to keep off the grass' (BN 38). We perceive the joy in another person's face; we perceive melancholy in a landscape; things 'unveil themselves to us as hateful, sympathetic, horrible, lovable' (IFI 5). We perceive meaning in a text; objects have a 'sensible significance' (PP 230), a *physiognomy* (PP 131–2), they make *demands* on us and *promises* to us: the hammer calls out to us to be picked up by its handle (cf. BN 322). In short, '[t]he world is human' (BN 218).

This rich, lush, overflowing world of perception appears pallid and drab in the writings of many philosophers and psychologists. Since, according to their view, there are no internal relations between things, since things do not possess potentialities, values, emotions, absences or meanings, and since emotions cannot be said to reveal qualities in things, philosophers and psychologists have denied that what we perceive has any of these features. Often they will say that our supposition that these are qualities of the perceived world rests on the fact that we 'project' our own inner states on to the world, although the mechanism of such projection remains wholly mysterious.

> Joy and sadness, vivacity and obtuseness are [they say] data of introspection, and when we invest landscapes or other people with these states, it is because we have observed in ourselves the coincidence between these internal perceptions and the external signs associated with them. (PP 24)

Thus the world described by poets and depicted by painters, the world, that human world, in which we live and move and have our being, is obscured from us through the intellectual prejudices of philosophers.

Therapy for Intellectual Prejudices

Intellectual prejudices lead philosophers and psychologists to doubt lived certainties, to deny things that we as human beings recognize to be true from our own experience, and to misdescribe our lived experience. So how can one help another, or indeed oneself, to overcome them?

If intellectual prejudices were mere mistakes or logical fallacies, our task would in principle be easy, or at least straightforward: we could point to the logical flaw, or provide counterexamples, or attempt to construct an argument that logically demonstrated the opposite. But if we take the analogy between intellectual and everyday prejudices seriously in the respects intended, such procedures are unlikely to be any more effective in dissuading a philosopher from saying such things than they would be in persuading a racist or anti-Semite to change his view or a smoker to quit (see Chapter 4). Prejudices are 'cognitive and emotional habits' (as Midgley (2004: 5) says of 'myths'), and like any long-standing habit, they are difficult to break; as 'structures that shape our thinking' (ibid.; cf. Taylor 2005: 28), they are characterized by what might be called a 'perverse' attitude toward evidence and logical argument. This is why we need something like therapy.

Sartre brings out the perversity of the thinking of someone in the grip of an everyday prejudice in his description of the anti-Semite: 'A classmate of mine at the *lycée* told me that Jews "annoy" him because of the thousands of injustices . . . [such as this]: "A Jew passed his *agrégation* the year I failed, and you can't make me believe that that fellow . . . understood . . . Virgil better than I" ' (AS 11–12). This classmate

> ranked twenty-seventh on the official list. There were twenty-six ahead of him, twelve who passed and fourteen who failed . . . even if he had been at the top of the list of unsuccessful candidates, even if by eliminating one of the successful candidates he would have a chance to pass, why should the Jew Weil have been eliminated rather than the Norman Mathieu or the Breton Arzell? . . . [But] it was the Jew who robbed him of his place. (AS 12–13)

Do we expect the anti-Semite to be persuaded by this argument to give up his resentment against Weil? Again, the anti-Semite *may* be persuaded by the evidence that Jews are intelligent – but, it will turn out, he admits this because that makes them more dangerous. Indeed it allows him to disdain intelligence because it is Jewish: 'The true Frenchman . . . does not *need* intelligence' (AS 25). We are up against perversity.

In regard to intellectual prejudices, what he sometimes calls dogmas, Wittgenstein brings out the perversity thus: 'dogma is expressed in the form of an assertion, and is unshakable, but at the same time any practical opinion *can* be made to harmonize with it; admittedly more easily in some cases than in others . . . This is how dogma becomes irrefutable and beyond the reach of attack' (CV 28). We can see this description at work in this methodologically interesting passage from Merleau-Ponty. Referring to the perceptual relationships, highlighted by Husserl and Gestalt psychology, of 'figure' and 'background', 'thing' and 'non-thing', and temporal horizons (see Chapter 3), which appear 'to be structures of consciousness irreducible to the qualities which appear in them', Merleau-Ponty comments that

> Empiricism will always retain the expedient of treating [these as] . . . the product of some mental chemistry. The empiricist will concede that every object is presented against a background which is not an object, the present lying between two horizons of absence, past and future. But, he will go on, these significations are derivative . . . [He] must reconstruct theoretically these structures with the aid of the impressions whose actual relationships they express. (PP 22–3)

The movement of thought which Merleau-Ponty here ascribes to the empiricist is characteristic of someone gripped by a prejudice. The empiricist attempts to explain the apparently contrary phenomena away, for example, reconstructing them as derivative of items whose existence he recognizes – impressions and their 'chemical combinations' – although this reconstruction is surely done 'more easily in some cases than in others'. As Merleau-Ponty observes, 'On this footing empiricism cannot be refuted. Since it rejects the evidence of reflection . . . there is no phenomenon which can be adduced as a crucial proof against it' (PP 23).

So how is one to rid someone of a fixed habit of thinking that so structures his very responses to evidence and argument that it has 'become irrefutable and beyond the reach of attack'? There can be no set formula for performing therapy on intellectual prejudices, and no guarantee of success; moreover, not everyone will be a good candidate for therapy. A prerequisite for a thinker's accessibility to therapy will be a susceptibility to *unease* in the face of his doubt or denial of what his own experience reveals as certain; and those who we might call fanatics[16] – philosophers who in Wittgenstein's words suffer from 'loss of problems' (Z §456)[17] – are not so susceptible. We might compare them to those smokers who do not *want* to quit (see Chapter 4), who go along cheerfully untroubled by the negative consequences of their habit on their own and others' health. Such thinkers may even see as a virtue the fact that their thinking is contrary to everyday experience, as Russell does here: 'the point of philosophy is to start with something so simple as not to seem worth stating, and to end with something so paradoxical that no-one will believe it' (1956: 193). They may see phenomenology as 'debasing itself before common sense as Tolstoy debased himself before the peasants', as Russell said of the later Wittgenstein (1959: 214), and dismiss existentialism, as Lévi-Strauss did, as *métaphysique pour midinette* ('shopgirl metaphysics').[18]

It may be that we can manage to *create* concern and unrest in such a thinker; unless we can do so, there is nowhere for therapy to gain a foothold. Unless the fly wants to get out of the flybottle, it is no good showing him the exit (cf. PI §309)! Precisely because of the perversity of thinking which characterizes intellectual prejudices, the possibility of purely rationally unhooking a thinker from his dogmatic philosophical position through refutation – providing counterexamples, pointing out fallacies, etc. – is doomed to fail. It does not follow that providing arguments is necessarily useless, and there are plenty of these in the phenomenologists' writings; likewise, descriptions of experience, be they in Sartre's philosophical texts or in his or others' novels. These arguments and counterexamples *can* have a cumulative persuasive force, not because they function as refutations – after all, the philosopher retains the expedient of explaining them away – but because they help to create the unease that is a prerequisite to successful therapy.

However, the Sartrean therapist meets up with perverse thinking even in the fly who is desperately trying to escape from the flybottle. Like the psychoanalyst, the phenomenological therapist is working against resistance, even in the patient who genuinely wishes to be healed. And this is because at the root of the intellectual prejudice is a picture: of the eye as a camera, of the body as a machine, of memory as a storehouse (or, these days, a CD-ROM), of motives as miniature cattle-prods, etc. A person's thinking, in Sartre's term, 'crystallizes' around such a picture, which thereafter exerts a kind of irresistible fascination. As long as the philosopher supposes that it encapsulates how things *must be*, it operates like a hidden magnet which distorts the straight lines of his thinking. Getting the person to acknowledge the picture at the heart of his thinking is one important stage in uprooting a prejudice; another is offering an alternative picture around which a fresh way of looking at things can crystallize. The value of this does not lie in the alternative picture's being true but in its being *alternative*; to acknowledge that there is a different way of looking at things is already no longer to be in thrall to the original picture.

We noted in the Introduction a number of stylistic features of Sartre's writing that could lead to the charge of obscurantism: he expresses himself paradoxically, he plays with words, he has a rather unhealthy penchant for negative-sounding language, his statements are at times hysterical and hyperbolic. I have already suggested that the paradoxicality is all but inevitable given the difficulties of expressing internal relations. Other features – and possibly even the paradoxicality – are often, I submit, to be seen in the light of his efforts at performing these therapeutic tasks.

Thus, the greatest benefit of Wittgenstein's picture of thinking as 'operating with signs' lay in its re-orienting our thinking about thinking away from the dominant picture according to which thinking is a hidden inner accompaniment to our words.[19] And in like manner, much of Sartre's hyperbole – which encompasses some of his more negative-sounding statements – is aimed at effecting a similar decrystallization and a subsequent recrystallization of meaning. For example, his arresting assertion that 'the world is human' is meant to orient us away from the picture according to which what is real is what there would be independently of human beings. His announcement that '[m]y body is co-extensive with the world' (BN 318) provides a counterweight to the picture according to which the body is simply one more physical object in the midst of the world. And when he makes the – both hyperbolic and negative-sounding – claim that when another person comes along, 'suddenly an object has appeared which has stolen the world from me' (BN 255), this is meant to shift our thinking off the idea that what we see when we see another human being is simply a physical object that moves.

As for Sartre's 'playing with words': although Sartre's humour is seldom appreciated, it seems to me that often he is literally playing, being playful, having fun. Certainly many of his hyperbolic and negative-sounding images are amusing; likewise, with his paradoxical assertions – 'man is the being who is what he is not and is not what he is' (see Chapter 4) – one's first response might well be to laugh. It is often observed that humour can be a very powerful weapon in the therapeutic armoury;[20] and we might see Sartre's humour in the light of his own proposal that play and irony are activities which stand in opposition to what he calls 'the spirit of seriousness', a 'dismissal of human reality in favour of the world' (BN 580). The spirit of seriousness, in which man 'takes himself for an object' and in which, in particular, he sees values as written into the world independently of his own free choices, is a manifestation of bad faith;[21] and play opposes this spirit because it 'releases subjectivity', opens up possibilities, and devises its own rules (BN 580–1). One might see many of the widespread intellectual prejudices under investigation here as exemplifying that same spirit of seriousness. Sartre uses irony and caricature both to cajole the 'serious' thinker into laughing at himself – as when he characterizes Bergson's conception of the being of the past as 'preserving for it the existence of a household god' (BN 109–10) – and to begin to rejoice in new vistas of possibility, as with his hyperbole and paradox.

When we as philosophers read Sartre, therefore, we ought not always to be asking ourselves 'What are his arguments for this view? What are his arguments against those he is criticizing?' Much of what he is doing does not fit this pattern. To the extent that he has got the phenomenological description right, it doesn't *need* argument; and as for those he is criticizing, the question for Sartre will always be 'What – which *prejudice* – is getting in the way of this thinker acknowledging what he as a human being recognizes as true, and how can we help him to overcome that prejudice?' I am well aware that this is apt to suggest to some that Sartrean therapy is non-rational, and that they may see in this support for the conviction that phenomenology is not proper philosophy. There is a kind of meta-prejudice which insists that anything that isn't argument is mere assertion, that 'appeals to the head' and 'appeals to the heart' – or appeals to the intellect and appeals to the will (cf. Wittgenstein, CV 17) – are mutually exclusive and exhaustive of the field of methods of convincing (unless we include coercion, as in Warnock's (1965: 10) portrayal of Sartre as 'bludgeoning his readers into accepting a certain view of the world'), and that only 'appeals to the head' are rational or reasonable.[22] Perhaps this book as a whole may help to exorcise this particular philosophical demon.

A final point: it might be supposed that to speak of therapy is to presuppose that intellectual prejudices are wholly problems belonging to *individuals*. Yet just as there are whole societies which are racist or anti-Semitic, the intellectual prejudices identified by the phenomenologists – and perhaps too the meta-prejudice just sketched above – are inherent in western technology-oriented, science-worshipping society. Indeed these patterns of thinking may be said to be symptomatic of the very 'crisis' in European culture that sparked off Husserl's development of the phenomenological method. Certainly Sartre in his later thinking became sensitized to the ways in which social structures made authenticity – freedom from bad faith – more difficult. As Beauvoir's Sartrean character Dubreuilh put it, 'In a curved space, it is impossible to draw a straight line' (*Les Mandarins*, quoted in Manser 1966: 139). Yet unless one thinks of society and individuals as externally related, the tasks of combating prejudices in individuals and in the social structures of their society are not independent.

Sartre highlights a number of widespread patterns of thinking – what I have labelled the 'prejudices in favour of external relations/the existent/knowledge' – which constitute important obstacles to the descriptions and the elicitations of essences and meanings which are the central tasks of phenomenology. We will see the influence of these prejudices under various guises and in a variety of environments throughout the remainder of the book. In the next chapter we look at consciousness, which is both phenomenology's principal tool and one of its primary topics for investigation. As we will see, the intellectual prejudices we focused on in this chapter are a threat to the correct description of consciousness, and Sartre must employ all the therapeutic techniques at his disposal to combat those prejudices.

notes

1 Apart from BN 242, it occurs in BN just twice: xl and 77; at I 3 he uses 'unprejudiced'.
2 E.g., BN 113, 249, 534; cf. also I 46, EH 51.
3 This is a resistance which we may see as stemming from the attitude toward evidence lying at the heart of bad faith (Chapter 4). The connection between bad faith and prejudice is one which Sartre himself makes, at least when speaking of everyday prejudices; see his celebrated analysis of anti-Semitism (AS), likewise Gordon's (1995) analysis of anti-black racism, and Beauvoir's analysis (SS) of what we today call sexism.
4 It also figures in Wittgenstein; or to be precise, the expression figures rather little (e.g., PI p. 212 is the sole instance in that book), but the concept figures very heavily.
5 This is at any rate how Hume is commonly read.
6 This is not to say that a phenomenologically grounded, an 'honest' (cf. PP viii) scientific psychology is impossible; science need not hold a 'scientific point of view' in this sense. The neuropsychologist A. R. Luria, author of such books as *The Man with a Shattered World*, and more recently Oliver Sacks, author of such books as *The Man Who Mistook His Wife for a Hat*, personify to an extent a possible vision of such a science. Thus phenomenology is not anti-science; it is opposed to the hegemonic encroachment of science on alien territory and it is opposed to a science which falsifies in its descriptions what it purports to explain.
7 This is the upshot of Quine's celebrated slogan 'To be is to be the value of a bound variable' (1963).
8 Again, this perhaps does not rule out the possibility of a phenomenologically grounded logical notation.
9 Admirers of Derrida may recognize some resemblances between what he calls 'the metaphysics of presence' and this prejudice, and perhaps also between the prejudice in favour of external relations and Derrida's remarks on binary opposites.
10 Since beings-in-themselves (see Chapter 3) possess only external relations, and contain nothing that is non-existent – no possibilities or potentialities, no gaps, lacks or absences, and no values or any reference beyond the present – we could have summed up both the prejudice in favour of external relations and the prejudice in favour of the existent as a prejudice in favour of the in-itself.
11 Merleau-Ponty might wish to add: *the prejudice in favour of the conceptualized over the pre-conceptual*; see Chapter 3.
12 Readers should be warned that the term 'evidence' in the phenomenologists is sometimes used, not in the sense here of 'having evidence for something' or 'validation and invalidation' but in the sense of 'something's *being* evident', i.e., certain. There is a real danger of confusion here; see especially the final paragraph of BN III.1.
13 Cf. the remarks in Chapter 1 about the word 'assumption'.
14 See K. J. Morris 1998.
15 Other terms used by phenomenologists are often rendered into English in terms of 'lived'; Husserl's *Lebenswelt* is often rendered as *the lived world*,

and one also comes across expressions like *lived space* and *lived time*. It seems to me that these involve a different sense of the word 'lived': the point isn't that these are lived as opposed to known, but rather that to speak of the lived world or lived space or lived time is to speak of the world, space and time as they are experienced rather than as they are conceived by scientific points of view. I tend to used 'life-' in place of 'lived' for this reason, e.g., in 'life-world'. But the body-for-itself is *lived* as opposed to known; so I retain the expression 'lived body'.

16 In something like Hare's sense (1963: esp. ch. 9).

17 Cf.: empiricism 'can always retort that it *does not understand*' (PP 23).

18 Quoted in Moi 1990: 28.

19 Cf. Baker 2004: ch. 8.

20 This is a point clearly recognized by philosophers such as Nietzsche and Wittgenstein, though seldom thematized. Kathleen Higgins's book on Nietzsche's *The Gay Science, Comic Relief*, is premised on something like this point. Wittgenstein famously once said that one could write a whole philosophical book that consisted of nothing but jokes, and in fact there are many jokes in PI that are seldom recognized as such.

21 A number of commentators (most notably, perhaps, Bell (1989: ch. 5)) have made use of the contrast between play and seriousness in considering his remarks on ethics; my proposal here is that we also see it as playing a central role in the therapeutic strand of his philosophical methodology.

22 Cora Diamond (1991: esp. ch. 11) has done much to combat this particular meta-prejudice.

consciousness

'What is consciousness?' We may feel that we knew what it was before we asked ourselves the question, but now, asked to give an account of it, no longer do;[1] it may seem to us something mysterious and ineffable. It may be helpful here to remind ourselves, mundane as this may seem, of how we talk about consciousness, of our ordinary uses of the words 'consciousness' and 'conscious'.

Our preliminary investigation will focus on the verb 'to be conscious' rather than the noun 'consciousness'; there is a therapeutic benefit to this. There are many intellectual prejudices which are apt to interfere with our grasping consciousness aright. Part of the reason that we are inclined to think of consciousness as something mysterious and ineffable is surely that we are inclined to think of it as *something* in the first place. Focusing on the verb rather than the noun, asking 'What is it *to be conscious*?' or 'What is it *to be conscious* of something?' rather than 'What is consciousness?', may remove the temptation to think of consciousness as a thing, to 'reify' it, as the philosophical jargon has it;[2] and when Sartre says, as he sometimes does, that consciousness is 'nothing', part of what he means is just that: consciousness is *no thing*, not a *something*.

The most prominent landmark in this field is the fact that the verb 'to be conscious' may be either intransitive or transitive, i.e., we can speak either of *being conscious* (as opposed to unconscious or non-conscious), or of *being conscious of* . . . or *that* . . . When it is intransitive and opposed to 'unconscious', it generally means something like 'to be awake' or 'no longer in a coma', etc. ('Is the patient conscious yet?') When it is opposed to 'non-conscious', it often refers to something like 'the capability of being conscious (in its transitive use)', as when we say 'Human beings are conscious', meaning that they are capable of being conscious *of* . . . or *that* . . . , or when we ask 'Are fish conscious?', wondering whether they are capable of being conscious *of* . . . or *that* . . . This is one usage which is relevant for understanding Sartre; for him, the most fundamental question to ask about anything is, precisely, whether it is conscious in this sense or not, although curiously enough he does *not* ask it of fish or indeed any other non-human animal. The primary ontological division for him is between conscious beings, paradigmatically human beings, which he terms 'beings-for-themselves', and non-conscious beings, which he terms 'beings-in-themselves'. His examples of the latter are generally tables, inkwells, books and the other paraphernalia of a Parisian mid-twentieth-century intellectual; it is unclear where animals might fit in.

In the transitive use in *English* of 'to be conscious', one may be either conscious *of . . .* or conscious *that . . .* French does not allow the expression *'conscient que'* as opposed to *'conscient de'* or *'(avoir) conscience de'*; many instances of what we in English would express as 'conscious that . . .' can be expressed as having *'conscience du fait que . . .'*, i.e., 'consciousness of the fact that . . .' Sartre, however, does not concern himself with 'consciousness of the fact that . . .'; his whole focus is 'consciousness *of . . .*' objects and their qualities: of the jam, of its sticky coldness, of Pierre, of his just asking for a punch on the nose. Sartre's assertion that every consciousness is consciousness *of* something provides a further wrinkle to his claim that consciousness is nothing: it is not a thing but, rather, a relation. It is a relation between a subject and an object, though a note of caution is required: the subject is neither Husserl's transcendental ego nor Descartes's immaterial mind but a body-subject (see Chapter 5); the object is neither a representation in consciousness nor an isolated physical object but a meaningful whole within a field of perception and action (see below and Chapter 6).

The phrase 'to be conscious of something' sounds vague; we should rather think of it as generic: hearing a skylark, seeing a mushroom, being angry with Pierre, being afraid of penury, imagining his touch, remembering a *faux pas* and so on are all ways of being conscious of something, each with its own peculiarities, its own essence ripe for phenomenological investigation. Much of what Sartre says in the Introduction to BN where his conception of consciousness is introduced is easiest to understand in the context of *perception*: seeing something, hearing something, etc., and I will largely concentrate on this modality.[3]

Thus far, our reconnaissance mission has centred on consciousness of objects *other than consciousness*. But to his assertion that every consciousness is consciousness of something Sartre adds the claim that every consciousness is conscious of *itself*. This rather peculiar expression is often rendered into English as 'self-consciousness', but it has little to do with the ordinary English use of the phrase 'self-conscious', which generally means something like 'the embarrassment exhibited by persons . . . who are anxious about the opinions held by others of their qualities of character or intellect' or, we might add, clothes, physical appearance, athletic prowess and so on (Ryle 1949: 156). Although Sartre is acutely aware of this dimension of human experience – he will describe this as awareness of oneself as an object in the eyes of others, and it is central to his analyses both of what he calls 'being-for-others' and of the body – it is not at all what he means when he says that every consciousness is conscious of itself, and I suspect that the rendition of this as 'self-consciousness' is a source of some misunderstandings. Rather, the claim that every consciousness is consciousness of itself is the claim that to be conscious of, say, the stickiness of the jam is at one and the same time to be *conscious of being conscious* of the stickiness of the jam – though this assertion is hardly self-explanatory.

In the remainder of this chapter, we will look briefly at the distinction between being-in-itself and being-for-itself, in more detail at the implications of the claim that every consciousness is consciousness of something, and then finally at the difficult claim that every consciousness is conscious of itself.

Being-in-itself and Being-for-itself

Consciousness is central to human reality, according to Sartre, not simply because human beings are necessarily conscious but because a full exploration of consciousness entails explorations of its subject, its objects and its modalities, and these ultimately yield a fully rounded description of the being of human beings as what Heidegger called Being-in-the-world: embodied free subjects embedded in an intersubjective world of meaningful and value-laden objects. This helps to explain why at times Sartre uses the terms 'consciousness' and 'human reality' interchangeably, and why his technical term 'Being-for-itself' seems sometimes to refer narrowly to consciousness and sometimes to human being in general.

Why, apart from the historical precedent of Hegel, does Sartre choose these particular terms 'being-for-itself' and 'being-in-itself'? The very fact that all consciousness is consciousness *of* something is one guiding thread through this labyrinth.[4] Being-in-itself, Sartre tells us, *is in itself*, being-for-itself is not (BN xli–xlii). From the fact that consciousness is *of* something, we can infer that consciousness is neither a *thing* nor a *container:* 'consciousness has no "inside". It is just this being beyond itself' (IFI 5). As a *relation* between a subject and an object, consciousness can no more exist without an object than the relation 'Smith is taller than . . .' can 'exist' without something to fill in the blank. Sartre sometimes therefore characterizes consciousness as a 'perpetual lack'. Beings-in-themselves, by contrast, are 'complete in themselves'; they lack nothing. Even if we sometimes describe or experience physical objects as 'lacking' or 'missing' something – 'The moon is lacking a quarter', 'That chair is missing a leg' – such descriptions and experiences are always relative to the projects and purposes of conscious beings (BN I.1).

Intentionality

The claim that all consciousness is consciousness of something is the claim that all consciousness is 'intentional', a technical term which Sartre takes from Husserl.[5] The language of Sartre's short and colourful article 'Intentionality: a fundamental idea of Husserl's phenomenology' exhibits that same excitement which the idea of making philosophy out of an apricot cocktail had produced in him upon his first encounter with phenomenology. The explicit focus of this little article, and likewise of the discussion of intentionality in the Introduction to BN, is the alleged anti-idealist – and hence anti-Husserlian – implications of the notion of intentionality, and we look at his arguments below. Yet much of what the French phenomenologists found so attractive in Husserl was the vocabulary he gave them for describing the objects of consciousness such as the die, a vocabulary supplemented by the Gestalt psychologists.

Intentionality and its objects

In addition to 'intentionality', Sartre gets from Husserl a series of related terms: 'posit', 'positional' and 'thetic'. The claim that every consciousness is consciousness of something can also be expressed by saying that every consciousness 'posits' an object, or that every consciousness is a 'positional', equivalently 'thetic', consciousness of an object.[6] A first shot at explaining these terms might involve words such as 'attention' or 'focus', but these are of limited use. Firstly, they gloss over the question of whether positing an object involves conceptualization; and secondly, they may encourage a misleading picture of the object of consciousness as isolated.

Pre-conceptual vs. conceptual. A distinction that some – including Merleau-Ponty – have held to be of great importance is that between 'pre-conceptual' and 'conceptual', and the notion of attending to or focusing on simply glosses over this distinction.[7] Is my paying heed to the spotty cat on the cushion my *applying the concept* 'spotty cat' to the object of my perception? Do I, in Fingarette's phrase, 'spell out' this feature of the world to myself? Spelling-out is the exercise of a learned skill that, although it may not involve my actually saying anything or writing it down, is nonetheless 'modelled' on so doing (1969: 38–9); other philosophers might speak of spelling-out in terms of 'exercising conceptual capacities'. Merleau-Ponty argues that our most basic perceptual awareness of the world is pre-conceptual, it does *not* involve spelling-out; on the contrary, our pre-conceptual perceptual consciousness of things in the world precedes and underpins our ability to conceptualize and form judgements about them. Merleau-Ponty will point to the impossibility in practice of *fully* spelling out what one is perceiving: not just 'a spotty cat' but a particular small, slim cat whose dominant colour is a sort of dove-grey, whose spots are dark brown and cover her back and sides, and whose coat contains not just spots but stripes, along her shins and radiating over her forehead. And he will call attention to the fact that the concept expressed by the word 'spotty' may seem far more determinate than the relevant feature of the perceptual object before me. For example, I cannot say exactly how many spots I see; the dark-brown patches contain hairs which are paler; moreover, because each hair has a certain length, the edges of the darker patches are jagged, and they change if the cat stirs, so that her spottiness is a *furry* spottiness, etc.[8]

Merleau-Ponty in fact associates Sartre with the opposite view: he sees Sartre as in the grip of a *prejudice* in favour of the conceptual over the pre-conceptual, and supposes that Sartre's term 'posit' in his claim that every consciousness posits an object is equivalent to 'conceptualize' or 'spell out'. It is far from clear that he is right to do so, however; although Merleau-Ponty is undoubtedly more explicit than Sartre is about the distinction between pre-conceptual and conceptual, there seems to be no reason why Sartre cannot acknowledge the points that Merleau-Ponty makes.

Backgrounds and horizons. To gloss 'positing' in terms of 'attending to' or 'focusing on' is misleading if it is taken to imply that one is conscious of only the object upon which one is focusing, in isolation from what Husserl calls its 'horizons' including its background. We need to understand that every positing (positional, thetic) consciousness of an object is *at the same time* a non-positing (non-positional, non-thetic) consciousness (of) that object's background and horizons; I here follow Sartre's convention of putting the 'of' of non-positional consciousness in parentheses.[9] This parenthesizing signifies two things: first, this non-positional consciousness of the background is not an act of consciousness *additional* to the positional consciousness of the object, and second, the '(of)' of non-positional consciousness is not the 'of' of positing intentionality: the background is inextricably part of the perceptual experience of the object being focused upon but is not that object.

The phenomenologists took from Husserl the idea that every perception of an object has a 'zone of *background intuitions*' (*Ideas* I §35), and from gestalt psychology the related idea that the minimal unit of perception is – not an atomic sensation but – a figure-on-a-background. There is, they suggest, a sort of unintelligibility in the idea of a perceptual experience of, say, a spotty cat against *no* background (a bit like the idea of the grin without the cat!). If we understand the object of, say, a perceptual consciousness as what one attends to or focuses upon, that object is then the 'figure': what I am looking at is the spotty cat. Yet part of that perceptual experience is the literal background: the cushion upon which the cat is curled, the sofa upon which the cushion is placed, etc.; my perceptual experience of that same spotty cat on a different cushion, or on the same cushion having been placed on the floor, would be a different experience. If these things are part of our perceptual experience, then we are conscious (of) them, yet *ex hypothesi not* focusing on them: the things in the background were 'also "perceived", perceptually there, in the "field of intuition" . . . yet were not singled out, were not posited on their own account' (*Ideas* I §35).

In Sartrean language, to be positionally conscious of the cat is at the same time to be *non*-positionally conscious (of) the cushion. This non-positional consciousness is potentially a positional consciousness: all I need to do to actualize the potentiality is to shift my attention from the cat to the cushion she is lying on. To say that my positional consciousness of the cat is at the same time a non-positional consciousness (of) the cushion is to say that there is an *internal relation* between the figure (the cat) and the ground (the cushion). This is revealed in the fact that if I were to shift my attention to the background, I cannot but be aware that my positional consciousness of the cushion is not something wholly new relative to my earlier positional consciousness of the cat; indeed, my positional consciousness of the cushion, once I have shifted my attention to what was formerly the background, is at the same time a non-positional consciousness (of) the cat, which has now become background to the cushion. Background and figure thus form a synthetic unity, an organized whole.

This background is part of what Husserl calls the 'outer horizons' of an object; but objects have 'inner horizons' as well. For example, as the Gestalt psychologists too recognized, 'there belongs to every external perception its reference from the "genuinely perceived" sides of the object of perception to the sides "also meant"' (Husserl, CM §19). The ashtray or the lamp as we perceive it is, in Sartre's terms, 'opaque' or 'transphenomenal'. Granted that I 'see' only one side of the lamp; the other sides – what Husserl terms 'profiles' (*Abschattungen*) – are hidden from me. But in Merleau-Ponty's words, '[t]he hidden side is present in its own way'. It is not simply that I know or infer that it is there; rather, the object as a whole appears through 'a kind of practical synthesis: I can touch the lamp, and not only the side turned toward me but also the other side; I have only to extend my hand to hold it' (PrP 14), or 'the unseen side is given to me as "visible from another standpoint"' (PrP 15; cf. BN 322).[10] Sartre puts it that the hidden sides are 'indicated' by the sides actually seen (BN 322).

Hence to be conscious of the lamp is to be positionally conscious of the side of the lamp turned toward you and at the same time non-positionally conscious (of) the hidden sides. Again, these non-positional consciousnesses are potentially positional consciousnesses that can be actualized by my walking around to the other side of the lamp. And again, there is an internal relation between the various profiles of the lamp. The object itself, the lamp, is an organized whole, a synthetic unity of its profiles: the object 'is given as the infinite sum of an indefinite series of perspectival views in each of which the object is given but in none of which is it given exhaustively' (PrP 15–16; cf. BN xxiii).

Here too, intellectual prejudices may interfere with our description of perceptual experience. In the first place, our perception of the lamp includes our consciousness (of) its absent sides or profiles, and those in the grip of the prejudice in favour of the existent will object to the reality of absences. Indeed such thinkers may argue that the absent profiles could not be part of my perceptual experience of the lamp, on the grounds that perception is a causal process, that the hidden sides are out of the line of sight, hence such that light rays reflected from it could not strike my retina, and hence such that they could not possibly play a causal role in producing my perception. This supplementary argument exhibits the prejudice in favour of external relations. Moreover, as we have seen, there are internal relations between the background and figure and between the various profiles of the object, and the prejudice in favour of external relations will impede acknowledgement of these.

Clearly enough, these prejudices would join forces to impoverish our perceptual experience if we allowed them to hold sway. We would be left with a world of 'objects' that were isolated from their surroundings – with no sense of continuity when we shifted our attention from, say, the cat to the cushion or from one profile of the lamp to another – and a world, moreover that was two-dimensional, like one of those façades on the film-sets of Westerns. This is not the world which we as living human beings inhabit.

The philosophical importance of intentionality

It may be tempting to suggest that the intentionality thesis is trivial: as long as we are focusing on the transitive use of the verb 'to be conscious of' (or *avoir conscience de*), then it is simply a grammatical fact that all consciousness is consciousness of something – hardly worth elevating into an exciting philosophical discovery. Yet Sartre evidently thinks of the claim that every consciousness is consciousness of something as immensely philosophically important and fruitful. So what in his view is so revolutionary about this idea?

To say that consciousness is 'intentional' is to say that 'there is no consciousness which is not a positing of a transcendent object' (BN xxvii). We have talked already about the term 'positing'; the term 'transcendent' is multiply ambiguous in Sartre's philosophical writings, although all of his uses have the same root meaning of 'going beyond'. Two usages are immediately relevant here.[11] In one, 'transcendent' is equivalent to 'transphenomenal': such that the perceived object goes beyond any one phenomenon or appearance. We have seen already that the perceived object, for example the lamp, is transcendent in this sense, a sense for which Sartre also uses the term 'opaque'. 'Transcendent' in another usage is contrasted with 'immanent' or 'contained within'; and in saying that every consciousness posits a transcendent object, it is clear that Sartre means 'transcendent' in *this* sense: every consciousness 'transcends itself in order to reach an object' (BN xxvii).

On the face of it, Sartre infers 'transcendent' in the second sense from 'transcendent' in the first:

> The existence of the table is in fact a centre of opacity for consciousness; it would require an infinite process to inventory the total contents of a thing. To introduce this opacity into consciousness would be to refer to infinity the inventory which it can make of itself, to make consciousness a thing, and to deny the *cogito*.

Hence the table 'is not *in* consciousness – not even in the capacity of a representation. A table is *in* space, beside the window, etc.'[12] And then the rallying-cry: 'The first procedure of a philosophy ought to be to expel things from consciousness and to re-establish its true connection with the world' (BN xxvii).

We will come back to this argument in a moment. Sartre's conclusion that the table 'is not *in* consciousness – not even in the capacity of a representation', if true, has wide-ranging philosophical implications. It immediately undermines both idealism (including Husserl's) and one popular form of realism, so-called 'representational realism' – both versions of the stultifying 'digestive philosophy' in which he was educated. Both outlooks, Sartre observes, reduce the objects of consciousness to *contents* of consciousness, that is, to representations, as it were mental pictures of objects. The representational realist holds that what we directly perceive are representations caused by external objects which we thereby indirectly perceive, the idealist that there *are* no external objects beyond these representations. The idealist will offer a sceptical challenge to the representational realist to prove that there are such external objects, and this challenge has dogged representational realism throughout its history. Note that representations are not transcendent in either of the relevant senses. They are by definition *immanent in consciousness*, and they are *not transphenomenal*: a representation does not have unseen profiles, hidden perspectives which you could see if you were to go around to the other side. Thus if Sartre is right that the objects of consciousness are not immanent in it, then we can reject both representational realism and idealism, and we are in a position to sidestep the whole issue of scepticism about the external world.[13]

We can begin to see how the claim that every consciousness is consciousness of something escapes the charge of triviality. When fully developed, it implies that 'consciousness and the world are given at one stroke' (IFI 4). 'To say that consciousness is consciousness of something is to say that it must produce itself as a revealed-revelation of a being which is not it and which gives itself as already existing when consciousness reveals it' (BN xxxviii). In other words 'consciousness is born supported by a being which is not itself' (BN xxxvii). So scepticism about the so-called 'external world' cannot arise, and consciousness puts us directly in contact with that external world. For Sartre, it was a tremendous liberation to be able to say: 'You see the tree, to be sure. But you see it just where it is: at the side of the road, in the midst of the dust, alone and writhing in the heat' (IFI 4). Consciousness 'reaches all the way out to the world'![14]

What of the argument quoted above, apparently inferring non-immanence from transphenomenality? It seems both obscure and perfunctory. Rather than either taking Sartre to task for its defects or trying to remedy those defects on his behalf, it may be better to ask: why *is* it so perfunctory? I am inclined to suggest that it is because he doesn't think that its conclusion needs argument: that consciousness reaches all the way out to the world, that when we see a tree at the side of the road *we see a tree at the side of the road* – these are *lived certainties*. Hence the question we must ask is not: what is the *basis* of our certainty? but: how – in the grip of what intellectual prejudices – have philosophers talked themselves into doubting or denying it?[15]

Consciousness of Consciousness

Sartre affirms not only that every consciousness is consciousness of something other than itself, but also that 'every positional consciousness is at the same time a non-positional consciousness *of itself*' (BN xxix, italics added). This consciousness of consciousness may be either *positional* (thetic) or *non-positional* (non-thetic). Positional consciousness of consciousness he calls 'reflection', and of course every positional consciousness *of consciousness* is also non-positionally conscious of itself.[16] When he speaks of *non*-positional consciousness of consciousness, he puts the word 'of' in parentheses, as we did with the non-positional consciousness of backgrounds and horizons; and our earlier exposition of backgrounds and horizons will help to clarify Sartre's admittedly difficult conception of non-positional consciousness of consciousness.

Motivations for the distinction

The distinction between positional and non-positional consciousness of consciousness is required, Sartre argues, partly in order to avoid a philosophical conundrum: it is clear from experience that we *can* reflect; yet we cannot always be reflecting, on pain of infinite regress: I would need to be conscious *of* being conscious *of* being conscious . . . (BN xxvii). Non-positional consciousness of consciousness does not to lead to such a regress.

An unprejudiced description of experience also reveals the existence of non-positional consciousness of consciousness, and shows moreover that it is prior to reflective consciousness. If I am absorbed in counting the cigarettes in a case and someone asks me what I am doing, I unhesitatingly reply that I am counting, this expression of my reflective consciousness of consciousness bringing together not just the immediate consciousness ('eleven') but those that have preceded it ('. . . nine . . . ten') and those that are to come. This shows that I must have been conscious of each of the earlier stages in the counting *as counting consciousnesses*, so that these apparently separate consciousnesses are internally related to one another by virtue of having counting as their 'unifying theme'. In fact when I reach eleven, the '. . . nine . . . ten' and the '. . . twelve . . . thirteen' form the *temporal horizons* of the present consciousness. To be positionally conscious of 'eleven' in the context of counting is to be non-positionally conscious of 'ten' as just past and of 'twelve' as about to come. This is why I am able to reply to the question 'What are you doing?' so unhesitatingly. Yet this consciousness of the stages of counting as counting consciousnesses was *not positional*, because at the moment I was interrupted, what I was attending to was just: 'Eleven'. If I had been speaking aloud what I would have said was 'Eleven', not 'I am counting my cigarettes and I have just got to eleven.' Thus 'it is the non-reflective [non-positional] consciousness [of consciousness] which renders the reflection possible' (BN xxix).[17]

Non-positional consciousness of consciousness and the 'pre-reflective *cogito*'

Note that what appears in the verbal expression of reflective consciousness is not just the explicit reference to the theme which unifies the individual acts, i.e., 'counting', but also the word 'I'. This 'I' is revealed in the consciousness reflected-on only *through reflection*; as Sartre puts it, 'there is no *I* on the unreflected level. When I run after a streetcar, when I look at the time, when I am absorbed in contemplating a portrait, there is no *I*. There is consciousness *of the streetcar-having-to-be-overtaken*, etc., and non-positional consciousness of consciousness' (TE 48).

This, however, sounds unnecessarily mysterious. Consider the following relevant analogy, which will prove to be not just an analogy but an instance of non-positional consciousness of consciousness. Perceived objects, those figures-upon-backgrounds with their horizons of unseen profiles, occur within what the phenomenologists, following the Gestalt psychologists, call a *field*. That is, they are ordered and oriented: the streetcar is *on* its tracks, just *beyond* the café, up *ahead* and to the *right*. These orderings and orientations imply a centre, and that centre is the body-subject (see Chapter 5). Although the centre is no part of what is perceived, i.e., we are not conscious of the centre when focused on an object in the field of perception, nonetheless everything within the field of perception refers to or indicates or is oriented toward that centre: '[t]he location of my eyes floods through the visual world, organizing it and giving it sense as the vanishing point organizes every brushstroke of a Renaissance painting' (Leder 1990: 12). And not only are we are conscious (of) the centre of the perceptual field, this consciousness (of) the centre is an instance of or at least an aspect of non-positional consciousness of consciousness, since that centre is *us*, the subject of consciousness, the body-subject (cf. BN 330).

Thus Sartre's assertion that 'there is no *I* on the unreflected level' is a little misleading:[18] it is not, as Detmer supposes, that the 'I' is 'brought into being by an act of reflective consciousness' (1988: 22); one might as well say that there *is* no centre in one's visual field while one is focusing on objects within the field. What Sartre means is that there is *no positional consciousness* of the centre, no positional consciousness of the subject of consciousness, the 'I', in a positional but unreflected-on consciousness of the streetcar; but nonetheless my positional consciousness of the streetcar is simultaneously a non-positional consciousness of *my* being conscious of the streetcar as having-to-be-overtaken. This aspect of non-positional consciousness of consciousness Sartre refers to as the 'pre-reflective *cogito*', 'which is the condition of the Cartesian *cogito*' (BN xxix).

We might here consider an objection which has been made to Sartre's claim that consciousness is always conscious (of) itself. A pathological phenomenon called 'blindsight' has occupied philosophers of mind ever since Weiskrantz published his study of the phenomenon in 1988. Blindsighted patients have suffered lesions to their striate cortex which cause restricted regions of 'blindness' in the visual field. 'Patients typically say that they do not see lights or patterns projected into such a "blind" region of their fields', but 'if required to respond by forced choice to visual stimuli projected [there, they] can discriminate those stimuli, even though they may fervently deny that they "see" them' (quoted in Wider 1997: 98). 'When told of the high degree of accuracy of their answers, these people express surprise and many claim to have thought they were simply guessing' (ibid.: 98–9). Wider wants to describe blind-sighted people as perceptually conscious *of* objects but not con-scious (of) that consciousness, and hence uses the phenomenon as an objection to what she calls Sartre's 'self-consciousness thesis'.[19]

Why should we accept that blindsighted patients are perceptually con-scious of objects, however? The sole reason for saying this was that they could, if pressed, point to or discriminate between them. Yet perceptual consciousness itself entails far more than this. Unless, as seems highly doubtful, it can be made plausible that these objects are presented as figures-on-a-background with horizons of unseen profiles, we cannot say that they are perceptually conscious *of the objects*, in which case blindsight is not a counterexample to Sartre's claim. And if the objects *are* presented as figures-on-a-background, etc., then they are organized into a field which is oriented toward a centre; in which case the blind-sighted patients are conscious (of) this centre, and again blindsight is no longer a counterexample.

Our analogy between non-positional consciousness of consciousness and non-positional consciousness of the centre of the perceptual field, though valuable, may also serve to underscore some bewildering fea-tures of *positional* consciousness of consciousness. Whereas the back-ground can become the figure by a simple shift of perceptual attention, the same is not straightforwardly true of our non-positional conscious-ness (of) the centre of the perceptual field. I cannot *literally* look at the centre of my own perceptual field; as Sartre sometimes puts it, 'the eye cannot see itself'. But the real quandary arises from the consideration that it is the *subject* at the centre of the perceptual field: the subject is precisely not an *object*. Even if the eye could see itself, 'the eye cannot see itself *seeing*'. We need to examine positional consciousness of con-sciousness, i.e., reflection.

Positional consciousness of consciousness (reflection)

Ryle lambastes the philosophical concept of introspection, which, he claims, is presupposed by most philosophers and psychologists (1949: 11); it denotes 'a special kind of perception' by means of which a person can take 'a (non-optical) "look" at what is passing in his mind' (1949: 14). He raises two problems with this notion which may seem to have ana-logues in reflection:

(1) If I am looking at the cat – i.e., if I am positionally visually con-scious of the cat – and reflect on this perceptual consciousness, I am, it seems, conscious *of* being conscious *of* the cat. Would this not somehow require a *divided* consciousness, one to go with each 'of', so to speak? Would I not need to 'attend twice at once', as Ryle famously puts it (1949: 165)?

(2) Ryle's solution to his version of problem (1) *seems* very natural: he argues that much of what we call introspection is really retrospection (1949: 166f.): we introspect at time t_2 on a consciousness that occurred some time before, at time t_1.[20] We pay a price for this solution, however: retrospection 'will not carry many of the philosophically precious or fragile parcels' for which 'introspection has been nominated for the porter' (1949: 167), in particular its alleged infallibility. Sartre raises this problem himself *vis-à-vis* reflection: 'Will [reflection] keep its certitude if the being which it has to know is past in relation to it?' (BN 150). This question, as Sartre observes, seems to threaten the whole phenomenological enterprise: 'since all our ontology has its foundation in a reflective experience, does it not risk losing all its laws?' (BN 150).

To respond to these difficulties, we need to make some distinctions: between reflection and memory, and between reflection and introspection. The real problem with reflection will turn out not to be either of Ryle's problems: it is the threat of bad faith which what Sartre calls 'impure' reflection carries.

Reflection vs. memory: A superficial reading of Sartre might lead us to think that he himself sees reflection as memory. Reflection (at least pure reflection; see below) does possess certitude, and Sartre claims that this extends 'to the [future, not-yet-realized] possibilities which I *am* and to the past which I *was*' (BN 157). This is apt to be understood as the claim that reflection incorporates both anticipation and memory; yet since he is here making a claim about the *certitude* of reflection, this cannot be what he is saying. He cannot be claiming that our memories of our past, and also our anticipations regarding our future, are infallible. We have seen already that the present is not an infinitesimal instant; it has temporal horizons. For example, my positional consciousness of 'eleven' while counting the cigarettes is at the same time a non-positional consciousness of 'ten' as just past and 'twelve' as about to come. By the same token, though reflection – in contradistinction from both memory and anticipation – confines itself to the present, it is *not* thereby 'limited to the infinitesimal instant' (BN 156). If I reflect while I am counting the cigarettes, having just reached eleven, my reflective awareness might be expressed as: 'I have *reached* eleven *so far*'; the word 'reached' *indicates* the past and the phrase 'so far' *indicates* the future, but without focusing on them; thus in reflection, the past and the future 'haunt' the present in 'non-thematic form' (BN 157). And thus understood, reflection is certain: it brings nothing to the positional consciousness of the number of cigarettes that was not already there horizontally. By contrast, memory and anticipation are respectively positional consciousnesses of past and future – and they, unlike reflection, are open to error by their very nature.

This shows that Sartre cannot accept any solution to problem (1) that construes reflection as memory. By the same token, however, he is not forced to pay the price which such a solution carries, namely, giving up the certitude of reflection (problem (2)). We have yet, however, to see how he *does* avoid problem (1).

Reflection vs. introspection. We have seen reasons already for distinguishing between reflection and introspection (Chapter 1), but another is pertinent here. The philosophical notion of introspection is modelled on the notion of perception; it is imagined as a kind of 'looking within oneself'. If reflection were thus understood, however, this would immediately render the relation between the consciousness reflecting and the consciousness reflected-on *external*. But this is precisely *not* true of reflection (at least pure reflection). Just as my non-positional consciousness of the cushion was a potential positional consciousness that could be actualized by a shift in my perceptual attention, my non-positional consciousness of consciousness is a potential positional consciousness that can be actualized, as reflection, by a shift in attention. And just as there was an internal relation between figure and the background, such that my positional consciousness of the cushion is given as not wholly new relative to my positional consciousness of the cat, so too reflection, i.e., *positional* consciousness of consciousness, is not to be understood as a 'new consciousness, abruptly appearing, directed on the consciousness reflected-on' (BN 150).[21] As always, internal relations are characteristically articulated paradoxically: 'it is necessary that the reflective simultaneously be and not be the reflected-on' (BN 151), or, equivalently, 'the reflective is separated from the reflected-on by a nothingness' (BN 153).

It follows that Sartre does not run into Ryle's problem (1): there is no attending 'twice at once' because there are not two separate, externally related consciousnesses here.

Pure vs. impure reflection. What of the problem we posed earlier, the concern that reflection, as positional consciousness of consciousness, creates an object not only of that consciousness but of the subject, the 'I' which is revealed in reflection? Sartre insists that as long as the reflection is what he calls *pure* reflection, the consciousness reflected-on 'is not wholly an object but a quasi-object for reflection' (BN 155), and correspondingly it is not knowledge of the consciousness reflected-on but 'quasi-knowledge' (BN 162)[22] – unhelpful terms, to be sure, but perhaps to be expected in the realm of internal relations.

Yet most reflection is impure. Impure reflection bears more than a passing resemblance to what *in ordinary life* we might call introspection; it 'seeks to determine the being which I am' (BN 170). When I ask myself about which 'faults, virtues, tastes, talents, tendencies, instincts, etc.' (TE 71) I possess – am I jealous, industrious, irascible, clever with my hands? – or when I ascribe states to myself – I hate Pierre, I love my job – my reflection is impure. It has constituted 'psychic objects' within me, 'interiorized' and 'objectivated' (BN 160), which I suppose to engage in quasi-causal relations with one another (I love my job *because* I am industrious, I hate Pierre *because* I am a jealous person; cf. BN 169). Pure reflection, Sartre explains, 'keeps to the given without setting up claims for the future'. If, for example, I say to Pierre in anger 'I detest you' and then catch myself and say 'It is not true, I do not detest you, I said that in anger', the first reflection is impure, the second pure (TE 64). In the impure reflection, I go beyond the reflected consciousness of anger to that psychic object 'hatred', which I suppose to have existed 'in me' for some time and will continue past the moment of anger well into the future.

As will become clear in the next chapter, impure reflection is in *bad faith* (BN 161). And it is this, not mere error as would be introduced by memory, that is the real danger to reflection.

notes

1 Cf. Augustine on the question 'What is time?', quoted in PI §89.
2 Part of the reason why Sartre talks of consciousness rather than mind (*esprit*) may be that the term 'mind' (likewise *esprit*) is a noun with no immediately connected verb. Obviously in English there is the verb 'to mind', meaning variously 'to look out', 'to look after', 'to dislike' and so on, but none of these meanings are tightly connected to the meaning of the noun 'mind'. Minds seem ripe for reification.
3 Readers interested in exploring other modalities more fully may like to read Sartre's two books on the imagination and his *Sketch for a Theory of the Emotions*, all relatively approachable; memory and anticipation are touched on below, and the emotions are touched on in Chapter 6.
4 Sartre sums up the contrast in three formulae; only the first is discussed here. The other two are:

   (i) Being-in-itself *is what it is (and is not what it is not)*, whereas being-for-itself *is what it is not and is not what it is* (BN xli; see Chapter 4).
   (ii) Being-in-itself *is*, i.e., it does not possess what logicians call 'modal' characteristics: possibility and necessity – Sartre sometimes expresses this by saying that being-in-itself is 'superfluous' (*de trop*) – whereas '[t]he possible is a structure of the for-itself' (BN xlii; see Chapter 8).

5 Husserl took the term 'intentionality' from Franz Brentano, and Brentano himself was self-consciously reviving a scholastic concept. Sartre elaborates Husserl's notion of intentionality in ways which Husserl would arguably not have recognized; every phenomenologist pays tribute to Husserl in his own unique way.

6 No doubt Sartre's expectation that his readers will be familiar with Husserl explains why he feels no need to define them. Commentators often propose their own terms to try to clarify them. For example, Catalano (1974) tends to use 'direct' and 'indirect', McCulloch (1994) offers 'explicit' and 'implicit', etc.; each has its advantages and disadvantages, and I will stick with the terms Sartre uses.

7 Merleau-Ponty's distinction, taken from Husserl, between 'operative intentionality' and 'intentionality of act' (PP xviii; cf. PP 12 and PrP 36) is the distinction between pre-conceptual and conceptual consciousness of something.

8 Whether these points imply that my perceptual experience is pre-conceptual obviously depends heavily on what one counts as a concept or as exercising a conceptual capacity. The notion of 'non-conceptual content' has occupied some analytic philosophers, e.g., Evans 1982; Peacocke 1983; McDowell 1994. See Bermudez 1995 and Carman and Hansen's (2005) introduction for attempts to bring the analytic and Continental traditions together on this matter.

9 He does this in his treatment of non-positional consciousness *of consciousness*. Sartre himself says rather less than one would have liked about non-positional consciousness of horizons, and the Sartre literature tends to elaborate the notion of non-positional consciousness only in connection with consciousness of consciousness. I foreground non-positional consciousness of things *other* than consciousness both to bring out the richness of perceptual experience and because I think it can help to illuminate non-positional consciousness of consciousness; see below.

10 I here gloss over the distinction made by Kelly (2005) between the hidden sides being 'hypothesized but sensibly absent' and their having a positive presence, as indeterminate, in our perceptual experience; he ascribes the first understanding to Husserl, the second to Merleau-Ponty.

11 See P. S. Morris 1985b. The third usage – in which 'transcendence' is contrasted with 'facticity' – plays a prominent role in much of the remainder of BN; see Chapter 4.

12 As Detmer points out (1988: 19), Sartre's argument against the Husserlian transcendental ego is exactly parallel.

13 Many analytic philosophers see the notion of intentionality as *entailing* the notion of representations: to be *of* something is to have a content, and that content is widely seen as a representation. For Sartre, by complete contrast, the fact that consciousness is intentional implies that it does *not* have a content (BN xxvii), i.e., that nothing, including in particular representations, is immanent in consciousness.

14 Taylor (2005: 26) credits Merleau-Ponty with 'undo[ing] the state of thraldom' exercised by what he terms 'mediational epistemology': 'an understanding of the place of mind in the world such that our only knowledge of reality comes through the representations we have formed of it within ourselves'. Clearly *Sartre* has done much to undo that particular state of thraldom.

15 Detmer's interpretation (1988: 14ff.) is subtly but importantly different. He sees Sartre's argument as a kind of inference to the best explanation: the non-immanence of objects provides a better explanation of their transphenomenality than idealism can provide.

16 Many commentators use the term 'pre-reflective consciousness', although Sartre himself uses it only once in BN (76); confusingly, commentators use this term sometimes for non-reflective (non-positional) consciousness of consciousness, sometimes for an unreflected-on positional consciousness *of an object*. I will avoid the term 'pre-reflective' altogether except in the one context in which Sartre regularly uses it, namely, 'pre-reflective *cogito*'.

17 There is much disagreement among commentators about how to understand Sartre's notions of positional and non-positional consciousness of consciousness, and this passage in BN is notoriously difficult. It can be read quite differently, as implying not that non-positional consciousness of consciousness is a prerequisite for reflection but that positional consciousness of *objects* is a prerequisite for reflection. (This is true, but the issue is whether this is the point being made here.) From this perspective, what stops the threat of infinite regress is that it has a beginning: if we think of reflection on the analogy of a reflection in a mirror, and reflection on reflection as a second mirror, etc., for reflection to reflect anything there must ultimately be an object. By contrast, my interpretation has it that what stops the threat of infinite regress is that it has an end: although one is non-positionally conscious of any positional consciousness – and hence non-positionally conscious of reflecting – one is not non-positionally conscious *of being non-positionally conscious* of something, so there is no regress. Additionally, from this perspective, Sartre's claim that it is 'non-reflective consciousness which renders the reflection possible' is to be read as 'it is consciousness of objects other than consciousness which renders reflection possible'. Although I have no doubt that Sartre would *embrace* the claim that consciousness of objects is prior to reflection, I can't see that this reading of this sentence fully makes sense of the discussion of counting cigarettes.

18 It seems to have misled Caws (1979: 55ff.), who takes Sartre's arguments against the transcendental ego to be arguments against there being a subject of consciousness.

19 One might also consider sleepwalking, or Wider's example of 'sleep-driving'.

20 Cf. P. S. Morris, who implicitly accepts not only the equation of introspection with reflection (see below) but Ryle's analysis of introspection as retrospection (1976: 33–4).

21 *Pace* Detmer (1988: 18), who says that 'this is, of course, an entirely new act of consciousness'.

22 This leads Wider to complain that the relation between the (pure) reflective consciousness and the consciousness reflected-on is, on Sartre's characterization, neither cognitive nor non-cognitive (1997: 88ff.). Yet there is no contradiction in this; moreover, especially in light of Sartre's characterization of reflection as recognition rather than knowledge (BN 156), it seems right.

bad faith

F rom time to time people 'lie to themselves', as we say. Although
Sartre's examples are very much of his time – a woman on a date
with a man pretends to herself that his interest in her is purely intellectual (BN 55–6); a man who has deserted from the army tells himself
he is really a hero seeking the opportunity to display his courage in a different way (*No Exit*); a homosexual insists that he has simply never
found the right woman (BN 63ff.) – we can all think of similar instances.
Such lies to oneself or self-deception are, roughly speaking, what Sartre
calls 'bad faith', although, as we will see, many human phenomena –
neuroses such as inferiority complexes, prejudices such as anti-Semitism
– are at bottom bad faith.

Sartre's treatment of bad faith plays a pivotal role in BN. The question
that guides his chapter is: what must human reality be if man is to be
capable of bad faith? It has a triple importance: first, the answer to this
question reveals human reality to be far more complex and ambiguous
than most theorists recognize; second, it emerges that the ambiguous
nature of human reality is so anxiety-provoking that bad faith, as an
attempt to avoid facing it head-on, is a permanent threat to all of our projects, including philosophical ones.[1] Hence the third layer of importance: how, if at all, can we – as human beings, and as philosophers or
psychologists attempting to understand human beings – avoid falling
into bad faith about ourselves and others?

Sartre begins by bringing out the apparently paradoxical nature of bad
faith: bad faith can be called a lie to oneself, yet this notion is conceptu-
ally problematic. He goes on to consider, and dismiss, the Freudian solution to these paradoxes. Through a careful investigation of examples of
bad faith, he provides an – apparently even more paradoxical! – answer to
his guiding question: the condition for the possibility of bad faith is that
human reality *is what it is not and is not what it is*. We can make sense
of this via his notion of a *duality*; against this background, we can then
describe bad faith, motivated by the anguish which, Sartre claims, is our
consciousness of our ambiguous freedom. I try to make more explicit
than Sartre himself does how his conceptions of human reality and of

faith itself allow one to avoid the paradoxes with which the chapter begins. I end by considering what is perhaps the most urgent question: how, if at all, bad faith is escapable.

Paradoxes of Bad Faith

The very idea of self-deception may seem paradoxical.[2] Consider:

(1) In ordinary lying, the liar knows or believes one thing, but tries to bring it about that his victim believes the opposite; yet *self-deception* appears to require that one and the same person both believe something and not believe it. As Sartre puts it, 'I must know in my capacity as deceiver the truth which is hidden from me in my capacity as the one deceived' (BN 49).

(2) We only speak of 'lying' if the untruth-telling is intentional; otherwise it is merely a mistake. But if the intended victim realizes that the liar is intending to deceive him, the deception is bound to fail. In the case of self-deception, however, we once again appear to lack the 'duality of the deceiver and the deceived' which is a condition for the possibility of the successful lie. If I intend to lie to myself, I must be conscious of this intention, since intending is a modality of consciousness and every consciousness is conscious of itself (Chapter 3). Surely therefore my lie must 'fall back and collapse beneath my look' (BN 49); attempted self-deception couldn't possibly succeed.

We have at the moment a purely logical difficulty: experience tells us that self-deception does occur; yet paradoxes such as those sketched above seem to render its occurrence impossible. 'Our embarrassment then seems extreme since we can neither reject nor comprehend bad faith' (BN 50). Most people these days, including most philosophers, are likely to turn first toward some version of a broadly Freudian account: they will have recourse to unconscious beliefs and intentions or speak of one part of the person, say the id, deceiving another part, say the ego. Sartre is critical of such accounts on a number of grounds.

Sartre's Critique of the Freudian 'Solution'

Sartre's argument against the Freudian account of self-deception[3] is basically two-pronged.

On the one hand, the Freudian account is internally inconsistent. On the face of it, it reintroduces the duality of deceiver and deceived, which appeared to be necessary to make sense of the notion of a lie, into the individual self-deceiver. At first sight, this appears to be a split, not into two 'people' but into an id – an 'it' (the term 'id' often means 'it' in Latin), a collection of drives and instincts which 'can be reached only by more or less probable hypotheses' – and an ego which is *me*. Since what is deceiving me here is an 'it', on this reading 'psychoanalysis substitutes for the notion of bad faith, the idea of a lie without a liar' (BN 50–1). Closer inspection reveals that psychoanalysis does not consistently maintain this view of the id.[4] The id seeks to *express* its drives, the id must be *aware* that these drives have been repressed by the censor, it embarks on a *project* of disguise in order to get this expression past the censor. So in fact the id is not an 'it' at all. In that case psychoanalysis has substituted for bad faith not the idea of a lie without a liar but the idea of an everyday lie: self-deception is really *other*-deception writ small; Freud has 'split the psychic whole in two'. Sartre's argument is *not* the question-begging one that Freud has thereby explained away, rather than explained, self-deception, as commentators have occasionally maintained. It is rather that this split is inconsistent with Freud's own theories of unconscious symbolism. If id and ego really were two separate conscious beings, there would be an irredeemable obscurity in the fact that the symbolism with which the one conscious being, the id, cloaks its expressions comes to pervade the gestures and conduct of another conscious being, the ego. How could a woman's tickly cough, of which her ego is conscious, *symbolically express* the desire for an illicit love affair belonging to another entirely separate conscious being, the id (see BN 53–4)? Thus the Freudian account is incoherent.

On the other hand, Sartre continues, it is clear from descriptions of many psychoanalytic cases that in fact patients must be aware of that of which they are allegedly unconscious, since they exhibit 'acts of conduct which are objectively discoverable, which they cannot fail to record at the moment when they perform them'. Sartre takes the case of a 'pathologically frigid' woman who gives 'objective signs of pleasure' during sex, but 'fiercely denies them'. Such women 'apply themselves to becoming distracted in advance from the pleasure which they dread; many for example at the time of the sexual act, turn their thoughts away toward their daily occupations, make up their household accounts'. She does this '*in order to prove to herself that she is frigid*'. There is no question of an unconscious here; it is *bad faith*, with all its paradoxes (BN 54). Sartre's example frequently provokes derision from my female students: has he never heard of faking orgasms? Yet the woman who fakes an orgasm is not in bad faith; she behaves in this way in order, for example, to please her partner or avoid confrontation, but will also *tell* her partner that she experienced pleasure: her actions and her words cohere with each other. This is a straightforward 'cynical lie' (BN 67), no matter how altruistic the motive. But the woman described here vehemently and apparently sincerely *denies* to her husband that she feels pleasure, despite the objective signs of pleasure which she exhibits during sex. Thus we are left with the problem of bad faith; psychoanalysis has got us nowhere.

Human Reality: Dualities and their Internal Relation

We might express the logical problem in the form of a dilemma: if self-deception involves just one person, we inevitably run into the paradoxes outlined earlier. Yet if self-deception involves two people, then not only is it not *self*-deception, but we really cannot make sense of the phenomena of bad faith. Sartre's first step toward a solution is ingenious, if a little startling: self-deception involves just one person, but people *are not self-identical*: 'the principle of identity [i.e., self-identity, a = a, taken by logicians as a basic logical principle], far from being a universal axiom universally applied, is only a synthetic principle enjoying a merely regional universality': it applies only to *things* and not to human beings (BN 58). In fact 'human reality [is] a being which is what it is not and which is not what it is' (BN 58).[5]

Out of the frying pan, into the fire? Sartre apparently sees the road to the solution of one set of paradoxes, the paradoxes of self-deception, as leading via another, the claim that human reality violates logical laws!

We *can* make sense of this, however. To grasp his claim, we need the notion of a duality.[6] In broad outline, Sartre describes human reality as having multiple double aspects, in virtue of which human reality is not self-identical; but the two halves of these double aspects are internally related, so that in distinguishing them, Sartre is not 'cutting the psychic whole in two'.

Human reality by its very nature involves 'a double activity in the heart of unity' (BN 53). Sartre identifies several such dualities (BN 57–8):

1 *facticity*: factual conditions, such as having been born in such-and-such a place, to these parents, being a bourgeois, being in Oxford – vs. *transcendence*[7] – going beyond factual conditions towards *values*, e.g., wanting to distance oneself from one's birthplace or parents, embracing or rejecting bourgeois individualism. The term 'facticity' comes from Heidegger. Recall ('Sartre's Life', above) that for Heidegger human reality is Dasein, i.e., 'there-being'; facticity expresses our 'thrownness' into our particular 'there' (BT 135). The values by which we transcend this 'there' where we were thrown are central to the 'essence' of a human being, that essence which, according to the defining axiom of Sartrean existentialism, is posterior to existence,

and the choice of which is the choice of his fundamental project (see Chapter 8);

2 *being-in-the-midst-of-the-world* – 'our inert presence as a passive object among other objects' – vs. *being-in-the-world*: 'the being which causes there to be a world by projecting itself beyond the world toward its own possibilities';

3 *temporal dualities*, especially *past actions* vs. *future possibilities*;

4 *being-for-others* – very roughly, the second-person perspective – vs. *being-for-itself*: very roughly, the first-person perspective.[8]

In his chapter on bad faith (BN II.ii) Sartre spends most time on the facticity/transcendence duality, as do most commentaries; he also often uses the terms 'facticity' and 'transcendence' rather more broadly, to encompass the other dualities. It would be pointless to trouble ourselves overmuch about how many dualities there are, or whether they are distinct, or whether any have escaped Sartre's notice. We must also not allow ourselves to become confused by his use of the term 'being-for-itself' in the fourth duality; in this context it refers specifically to the first-person perspective. Just as he uses the term 'consciousness' sometimes to refer narrowly to the relation between the body-subject and its objects and sometimes more widely to human reality in its totality, he sometimes uses 'being-for-itself' to refer to human reality in its totality, and sometimes writes it, in this usage, as 'the For-itself'. So we can say that the For-itself encompasses *both* being-for-itself and being-for-others.

The first term in each duality indicates a respect in which human reality is in a sense object-like, even thing-like, whereas the second term indicates a respect in which human reality is not object-like. In his paradoxical-sounding formula 'Human reality is what it is not and is not what it is', the phrase 'what it is' refers to the first term in each of these dualities: facticity, being-in-the-midst-of-the-world, past actions, being-for-others. The phrase 'what it is not' refers to the second term: transcendence (values, which *are not* facts), being-in-the-world (which *is not* passive and inert, like a thing), future possibilities (which *are not* actualities), being-for-itself (which *is not* the me-as-object which the look of the other person brings into being). To say that human reality 'is not what it is' means, therefore, that human reality is not confined to the first terms in these dualities; it is not *only* what it is. To say that human reality 'is what it is not' is to say that it includes the second terms in each duality. For example, the individual's essence – what he *is*, we might say – is his fundamental project, which, as a choice of values, refers to the non-factual, hence to something *he is not*, or even something which *is not*, such as future possibilities that do not yet exist.

Moreover, the two terms in each duality are internally related to one another. For example, *my* facticity is internally related to *my* transcendence, *my* past actions to *my* future possibilities, and so on. I could not wish to distance myself from, i.e., transcend, my working-class background – part of my facticity – unless I had a working-class background, and indeed the very working-class background I in fact had. Again, what makes my possibility of becoming a philosophy professor *my* possibility and not merely '*a* possibility' is a certain lived trajectory extending from my past – my having been a philosophy student – through my present and projecting into my future. I could become a bricklayer – that is *a* possibility – but it is not *my* possibility. It could *become* my possibility if I were to re-evaluate the relative importance of money through a change in my fundamental project and recognize that I could double my income while maintaining my flexible working hours by re-training. At the moment it is not.[9]

Sartre's assertions that the principle of identity does not apply to human reality and that human reality is what it is not and is not what it is do indeed sound paradoxical; but there are reasons for this. There are, as we know, formidable prejudices which may interfere with our grasp of human reality. One is the prejudice in favour of external relations; and as we have observed, the linguistic expression of internal relations is almost bound to sound contradictory. A second is the prejudice in favour of the existent: the refusal to acknowledge that absences, potentialities and possibilities are real. Sartre takes a majestic stand against both prejudices when he states that human reality is what it is not and is not what it is: the existent and the non-existent are internally related, and the non-existent lies coiled at the heart of the existent – like a worm (cf. BN 21).

This is no more than a sketch of the ambiguities inherent in human reality. It takes Sartre the remainder of the book to draw out the implications of these various 'double activities at the heart of unity' which, he claims, are the condition for the possibility of bad faith. But, granted this as outline, what does bad faith now look like?[10]

Bad Faith, Freedom, Anguish and Ambiguity

Just as a lie is not a lie unless it is intentional, bad faith is not bad faith unless it is motivated. What motivates it is, according to Sartre, 'anguish' in the face of our freedom (BN 29). This characteristically Sartrean claim, that consciousness of freedom is deeply anxiety-provoking, may seem bizarre: surely freedom is something we all desire and value. Sartre's conception of freedom, however, is rather wider than many ordinary ones, and he manages to give some plausibility to the claim that consciousness of freedom entails anguish.

Since 'to be is to be free', freedom has the same dual structure as human reality itself (see Chapter 8). So too, correspondingly, does anguish. Sartre brings out a temporal duality in anguish: it may be either forward-looking or backward-looking; but presumably a full account of anguish would exhibit it as participating in all the dualities of human reality.

I may feel fear at the edge of a precipice; fear is the apprehension of myself as a destructible object in the midst of objects, one whom a sudden gust of wind or a landslip could cause to tumble to the bottom of the gorge (BN 30). Fear, however, is not yet anguish: anguish is manifested in vertigo, which is the recognition that '*nothing* prevents me from precipitating myself into the abyss' (BN 32). This is 'anguish in the face of the future'. And is there not something in this? Just think: I could swerve into the oncoming traffic; I could stay on the train until the next stop and miss that crucial job interview; I could make love to this man and destroy my marriage in an instant, cf. the young bride who 'was in terror, when her husband left her alone, of sitting at the window and summoning the passers-by like a prostitute' (TE 100). Do we not sometimes feel a terrifying 'vertigo of possibility' (ibid.) at the edge of a metaphorical as well as a literal abyss?

Now imagine that I had climbed up to the precipice having taken the resolution to end it all, to throw myself off. When I arrive, when I allow my gaze to slide down to the bottom of the abyss, I see all my resolutions melt away: I apprehend the 'total inefficacy of the past resolution . . . I am not subject to it, it fails in the mission I have given it'. This Sartre describes as 'anguish in the face of the past', the anguished recognition that I am not bound by my past decisions (see BN 32–3). Again, is there not something to be said for this description? Though we all joke about the inefficacy of New Year's resolutions and might be reluctant to dignify our 'agonizings' at our failure to lose that last kilo with the title 'anguish', where the decision is more serious, so too is the feeling which accompanies the recognition that it is still *up to us* to carry out our decision. It could also be argued that there is another type of anguish in the face of the past, an anguish in the face of responsibility, as when, having fulfilled my project of launching myself off the precipice but without succeeding in killing myself, I am forced to acknowledge that I am answerable for this paralyzed body.

Bad faith is, then, a response to anguish in the face of freedom, that is, in the face of ambiguous human reality. It is often represented in the literature on Sartre as taking two basic forms: either 'fleeing transcendence' or 'fleeing facticity'. But even if we agree to use these terms in their wider sense which encompasses the other dualities, this still oversimplifies: since each duality consists of an internally related pair, to flee one *is* to flee the other, and hence to 'find oneself abruptly faced with the other' (BN 56).

Thus the man who has run away from danger and confrontation on a number of occasions in the past may say 'I am *not* a coward', meaning thereby *not* that his past actions do not constrain his future, which would be true, but that the past is water under the bridge, his past actions have nothing to do with *him*; or meaning that the pattern which others see in his actions is not a pattern from his own perspective – on each occasion there is a different, perhaps a more noble, explanation: he was on his way to Mexico to launch a pacifist newspaper when he was caught deserting from the army (*No Exit*; cf. BN 63). On the face of it he is fleeing his past actions and acknowledging only future possibilities, or fleeing his being-for-others and acknowledging only his being-for-himself. But the very idea of future possibilities – those possibilities that are *his* rather than mere possibilities in the abstract – cannot be dissociated from his past actions; his actions form a temporal trajectory which projects into the future. This is not of course to say that he cannot change that trajectory; there is always the possibility of a 'radical conversion' (see Chapter 8); but that is not the case we are imagining here. So he is fleeing his future just as much as he is fleeing his past. Presumably a parallel argument applies to the notion that he is fleeing his being-for-others.

Saying 'I am not a coward' is not the only way for this man to be in bad faith; he may equally be in bad faith in saying 'I *am* a coward'. If he says it meaning thereby that the pattern of his past conduct fits the definition of a coward, what he says is true (cf. BN 64). But he is in bad faith if he is offering this by way of excuse – meaning that cowardice is a fixed part of himself, a character trait for which he bears no responsibility and which causes him to run away from danger; he has constituted his cowardice as one of those 'psychic objects' with which impure reflection fills the ego. Or again he may be saying 'I am a coward' as a confession, by way of being 'sincere'. As Sartre argues, however, sincerity – at least on his conception[11] – has exactly the same essential structure as bad faith (BN 65). The impossible ideal of sincerity is 'being what one is', where this means: being wholly identified with one's facticity, i.e., 'what one is' in the sense that human reality 'is *not* what it is' (BN 66). Sincerity is the declaration that 'I am what I am, I admit it'. But '[w]ho can not see that the sincere man constitutes himself as a thing in order to escape the condition of a thing by the same act of sincerity?' (BN 65). By its very nature, a confession is both an admission of responsibility for those acts and a demand to receive credit for one's sincerity, and is thus an implicit recognition of transcendence.

However, in the previous two paragraphs, I, like many commentators and even Sartre himself on occasion, succumbed to the temptation to express the bad-faith beliefs under scrutiny as 'I am a coward' or 'I am not a coward'. Although this simplifies our exposition, it embodies two assumptions that need to be queried:

(1) First, to express these beliefs in *sentences* seems to presuppose that beliefs, including beliefs in bad faith, are necessarily conceptualized or explicitly articulated. Sartre's examples by and large would be hard to fit into this pattern, however. For example, he describes a coquettish woman on a rendezvous with man: 'She is profoundly aware of the desire which she inspires, but the desire cruel and naked would humiliate and horrify her. Yet she would find no charm at all in a respect which would be only respect.' But then he takes her hand:

> This act of her companion risks changing the situation by calling for an immediate decision. To leave the hand there is to consent in herself to flirt, to engage herself. To withdraw it is to break the troubled and unstable harmony which gives the hour its charm . . . We know what happens next: the young woman leaves her hand there, but she *does not notice* that she is leaving it. (BN 55–6)

There are multiple layers of bad faith in this example, which Sartre analyses at length, but one lies in her treatment of her hand as a mere thing, a 'being-in-the-midst-of-the-world', rather than as part of her expressive body-for-itself (Chapter 5). We might say of her that 'she believes that her hand is a mere physical object which expresses nothing'; yet surely we do not need to imagine her as explicitly assenting to that proposition. The point here is not that she could not express her belief; after all, a belief is a consciousness and every consciousness is conscious (of) itself. It is rather that she need not reflect on her belief, i.e., her consciousness (of) her belief may remain non-positional, and if perception begins as pre-conceptual (Chapter 3), we ought to be open to the possibility that belief, prior to reflection, might do so as well.[12]

(2) Secondly, we know that as soon as we introduce the word 'I', we are on the plane of reflection: 'the *I* never appears except on the occasion of a reflective act' (TE 53). The point in drawing attention to this is *not* that a bad-faith belief cannot be reflected on; reflection may after all be impure. The man who *says* 'I am a coward', *meaning* thereby that his actions have been caused by a state of himself, cowardice, is reflecting impurely: he is constituting his cowardice as a psychic object. But bad faith may be exhibited at the non-reflective level as well, as the example of the coquette demonstrates.

We now have most of the materials we need to show how Sartre evades the paradoxes of bad faith.

Avoiding the Paradoxes

The 'faith' of bad faith and the paradox of belief

Our first paradox of bad faith was this: that I in my capacity of deceiver must believe something which I in my capacity as the one deceived do not believe. The key to Sartre's solution to this lies in his claim – characteristically expressed paradoxically – that 'To believe is to be conscious that one believes, and to be conscious that one believes is no longer to believe' (BN 69).[13] 'To believe is to be conscious that one believes': this just expresses the universal consciousness (of) consciousness. But why is 'being conscious that one believes' 'no longer to believe'? Plausibly, the 'consciousness of consciousness' *here* is positional rather than non-positional; this would then say that *reflection* transforms belief into non-belief: 'belief, by becoming belief for itself, passes to the state of non-belief' (BN 69). Or rather – since 'bad faith is *faith*' (BN 67) – reflection transforms faith into non-faith. Sartre distinguishes between two senses of the word 'belief': it may 'indicate the unwavering firmness of belief ("My God, I believe in you")' or something 'disarmed and strictly subjective ("Is Pierre my friend? I do not know; I believe so")' (BN 69). If we label these two senses 'faith' and 'opinion' respectively, the claim would be that reflection transforms faith into opinion: '[i]f know that I believe, the belief appears to me as a pure subjective determination' (BN 69).

The reason for this must surely relate to the fact that 'the object [of faith] is not given or is given indistinctly' (BN 67),[14] and this object is therefore by its very nature not open to what Sartre calls 'persuasive evidence'.[15] It is, precisely, a 'matter of faith' or a 'matter of opinion', and – because human reality is ambiguous – these 'matters of faith' include aspects of human reality. Garçin's facticity, his past history of running in the face of danger, provides 'evidence' or a reason for saying that he *is* a coward; yet his transcendence, his having *chosen* to run away on those occasions in the service of a not-yet-existent project, provides a reason to say that he is *not* a coward – not at any rate in the way that a table, a mere thing-in-itself, is, say, made of beech. 'The condition under which I can attempt an effort in bad faith is that in one sense, I *am not* this coward which I do not wish to be' (BN 66). It still requires a 'leap of faith' – past, so to speak, the sense in which I *am* a coward – to *believe* that I am not a coward. Once I say to myself 'I *believe* that I am not a coward', my faith appears to me as a mere opinion. At the same time, the consequences of this transformation from faith to opinion will depend on whether the reflection in question is pure or impure. Impure reflection will leave me complacent: 'that's my opinion and I'm sticking to it'; pure reflection may initiate a whole sequence of further reflections on the grounds for my opinion.

How, then, do we get around the paradox of belief which lying to oneself seemed to invite – my believing that I am a coward and at the same time not believing? Sartre's answer: that *every* belief is at the same time non-belief: '[t]o believe is not-to-believe' (BN 69)! We have seen how to make sense of this: it is not *exactly* that I believe and don't believe, but that my faith is vulnerable to being transformed by reflection into non-faith, i.e., mere opinion. Yet it seems to raise further questions. First, it seems to intensify the concerns around the second paradox, the paradox of intention; and second, it prompts the question: if this analysis applies to *all* beliefs, is there any difference between good faith and bad faith?

Reflection and the paradox of intention

Our second paradox was this: a lie is intentional, and yet to intend is to be conscious of intending; how could I lie to myself if I am conscious of my intention to deceive myself? The problem must be modified somewhat in light of the previous considerations: the intentional project of bad faith is now a project of believing something which is by its very nature a 'matter of faith' and which if reflected on will be revealed as mere opinion. Sartre's claim is that bad faith *exploits* the nature of faith: bad faith 'is resigned in advance to not being fulfilled by this evidence . . . It stands forth in the firm resolution not to demand too much, to count itself satisfied when it is barely persuaded, to force itself in decisions to adhere to uncertain truths' (BN 68). The intention in question, then, is not exactly the intention to deceive oneself, but the intention to set the standards of evidence low, with one eye on the fact that faith does not in any case admit of *persuasive* evidence: 'The original project of bad faith is a decision in bad faith on the nature of faith' (BN 68). But surely to be conscious of *this* intention would itself endanger the project of bad faith? It would indeed, if our consciousness of the intention were *positional* consciousness, i.e. reflection. Sartre, however, makes it clear that 'there is no question of a reflective, voluntary decision' (BN 68). Consequently we can maintain bad faith precisely as long as we do not reflect on this project, or to be precise, as long as we do not reflect purely.

Good faith and bad faith

All faith, whether 'good faith' or 'bad faith', is vulnerable to reflection, since reflection transforms faith into mere opinion. And one could from this perspective argue that since faith, as belief, involves taking a stand where *no* stand is fully justified, 'it is indifferent whether one is in good or in bad faith' (BN 70 n. 9). But even if faith by its very nature does not admit of conclusive evidence, there are surely better and worse ways to deal with the evidence, just as there are *opinions* which are more or less well grounded. And Sartre indicates as much when he refers to 'the norms and criteria of truth as they are accepted by the critical thought of good faith' (BN 68). If the project of bad faith is a non-reflective 'decision in bad faith on the nature of faith', i.e., a decision to *exploit* the nature of faith by setting the standards of evidence low, we can say that there is also a project of good faith: a 'decision in *good* faith on the nature of faith', which vows to examine the evidence critically (cf. Catalano 1996: 105). Sartre even provides a model of such an attitude:[16] the homosexual who asserted 'I am not a homosexual'

> . . . would be right actually if he understood the phrase, 'I am not a homo-sexual' in the sense of 'I am not what I am.' That is, if he declared to himself, 'To the extent that a pattern of conduct is defined as the conduct of a homosexual and to the extent that I have adopted this conduct, I am a homosexual. But to the extent that human reality can not be finally defined by patterns of conduct, I am not one.' (BN 64)[17]

The good-faith decision to treat the evidence critically amounts to the decision to engage in pure reflection: to, for example, rid oneself of those illusory psychic objects like cowardice, hatred or homosexuality which are imagined as fixed states of oneself which cause feelings and behaviour. Such an attitude presumably characterizes what Sartre terms 'authenticity': the 'radical escape' from bad faith whose possibility he indicates but 'the description of which', he disappointingly informs us, 'has no place here' (BN 70 n. 9; see 'Postscript', below). This attitude is difficult to attain and difficult to sustain: bad faith 'tends to perpetuate itself . . . Once this mode of being has been realized, it is as difficult to get out of it as to wake oneself up' (BN 68). Grounded as it is in the ambiguity of human reality and motivated by the anguish brought by consciousness of our ambiguous freedom, bad faith represents an 'immediate, permanent threat to every project of the human being'.[18] In the final section, we go through an example that both illustrates the difficulties of achieving good faith and displays some therapeutic techniques for helping someone to do this.

Achieving Good Faith: an Example

It will scarcely be controversial to assert that rational argument, for example, pointing out the epidemiological evidence that demonstrates the dire health consequences of tobacco – is seldom sufficient to get smokers to quit. The problem is not so much with persuading smokers to *want* to quit, at least in the sense of persuading them that they *ought* to quit and even getting them to *try* to quit; most reasonably well-educated smokers accept that smoking is bad for their health. The problem is with getting them actually to quit.

Both smokers and health workers are apt to speak of 'addiction'; they see themselves or their patients, not as choosing to smoke, but as being unable not to. This term 'addiction' seems to them to explain the difficulty of quitting – it is envisaged as a state of oneself that causes irresistible urges to smoke – and here is one area which has scope for bad faith: addiction is one of those psychic objects created by impure reflection. This is not to deny that people who try to give up smoking may experience physical discomfort, find it difficult to concentrate, become anxious and irritable. But this, the phenomenologists may contend, simply illustrates the fact that habits are *embodied*: our choices – to smoke, to run away from danger, to turn off the alarm and go back to sleep – become, when frequently repeated, 'sedimented' in the body, to use Merleau-Ponty's term (PP 441–2). The notion of addiction, at least in this context, is itself a device of bad faith. Another device is the notion of 'will power'. The smoker may admit that it is not an addiction, 'not like heroin', but say that he simply 'lacks the will power' to quit, conceiving of will power as a *property* which one either has or lacks, through no fault of one's own. Once again, however, what he is calling 'lack of will power' is nothing more than the sedimented habit of giving in to temptation.

Yet the smoker will insist, *in all sincerity*, that he wants to quit – even that he is desperate to quit. There are further layers of bad faith concealed here. Sartre writes:

> Some years ago I brought myself to the decision not to smoke any more. The struggle was hard, and in truth, I did not care so much for the taste of the tobacco which I was going to lose, as for the meaning of the act of smoking. A complete crystallization had been formed. I used to smoke at the theater, in the morning while working, in the evening after dinner, and it seemed to me that in giving up smoking I was going to strip the theater of its interest, the evening meal of its savor, the morning work of its fresh animation . . . in the midst of this universal impoverishment, life was scarcely worth the effort. (BN 596)

Many smokers will recognize Sartre's description of the meaning of the act of smoking: his metaphor of crystallization is acute.[19] Note what follows: to the extent that the idea of not smoking appears as a 'universal impoverishment' in the face of which life seems 'scarcely worth the effort', there is some sense in which despite his decision to quit, Sartre did not *want* to quit. Who would want to forgo what gives life its savour and interest? Those smokers who recognize their own case in this description must then have been in bad faith in saying that they wanted to quit; desire being a modality of consciousness that exhibits many of the ambiguities of human reality, they do and they do not want to quit.[20]

In addition, however, the smoker is apt to be in bad faith about this very desire. Once he has been brought to confess that there is a sense in which he does not want to quit, he is apt to say that he *can't help* having that desire. And we can grant that, *given* that smoking imparts to the theatre its interest, the evening meal its savour, and the morning work its fresh animation, one cannot but want to continue smoking. Indeed there is an internal relation between the qualities imparted to life by smoking and the desire to smoke. The issue is: in virtue of what does smoking impart those qualities to the theatre, the evening meal, the morning work? What is the source of this crystallization of meaning? Sartre's answer is: the smoker's own non-positional choice of values, his fundamental project.

And if the smoker did the crystallizing, he can decrystallize: '[i]n order to maintain my decision not to smoke, I had to realize a sort of decrystallization; that is, without exactly accounting to myself for what I was doing, I reduced the tobacco to being nothing but itself – an herb that burns' (BN 597). This signals that prior to this decrystallizing, he had, non-positionally, seen the *tobacco* as something *more than itself*: our chosen values humanize the world, objects and their qualities become ambiguous, as human beings are, and this is at the heart of this last layer of bad faith. The smoker who supposes that he can't help wanting to smoke is in bad faith about the qualities of tobacco: it seems to him that it is a fact about *it* – not the product of his own values – that it gives life its savour and animation.

This analysis identified three layers of bad faith:[21] the notion that smoking was an addiction, alternatively that the difficulty of quitting was due to lack of will power; the notion that the smoker unambiguously wanted to quit; and the notion that the smoker could not help wanting to smoke, itself grounded in the notion that tobacco possessed qualities in itself that were in fact reflections of the smoker's own chosen values. So what therapeutic techniques might we employ to remove these multiple layers of bad faith?

First, given that anguish in the face of freedom is the motive for bad faith, we might expect a good deal of resistance to giving up the notions of addiction and of lack of will power, where 'resistance' is to be understood as including the adduction of counter-arguments and counter-evidence. The smoker may, for example, back up his claim with statistics and the latest scientific research into 'addictive personalities'. We will have to engage with these arguments, and he will no doubt come up with rejoinders. He may or may not get to the point where he asks himself:

why am I so hooked on the notion of *addiction*? This is the first step toward pure reflection.

Persuading him that there was a sense in which he did actually *want* to smoke may depend on his recognizing something like his own experience of the world in Sartre's description of the meaning of tobacco in his life.

We might expect the smoker to resist, once again, having the responsibility for this desire pinned upon him. Here, I think, there are at least two stages in helping him past this point: (1) he has to recognize that the meaning which tobacco has for him isn't a meaning which the tobacco possesses in-itself; and (2) he has to recognize that the meaning it has for him is grounded in his own values.

Sartre's tale about his own attempt to give up smoking seems to recommend decrystallization as the way to achieve (1). But, be it noted, Sartre did not give it up until aged 71, many years after writing this passage! Evidently this momentary decrystallization was not sufficient to prevent those meanings from recrystallizing around the tobacco. My own suspicion is that a recrystallization around a *different* meaning would be more effective than a total decrystallization. When Sartre finally gave up tobacco, being under medical advice that his circulation was so poor that he might have to have his toes amputated if he did not, Beauvoir asked him ' "Doesn't it make you sad to think you're smoking your last cigarette?" "No, to tell you the truth I find them rather disgusting now." No doubt he associated them with the idea of being cut to pieces little by little' (AFS 102). Again, my mother sometimes claimed that what persuaded her to quit smoking was a friend's comparison between cigarette butts and bird droppings. Tobacco changed its meaning for her from something that allowed her to concentrate on her work to something revolting, like faeces. Recrystallization is easier than total decrystallization precisely because – as the phenomenologists are the first to stress – humans are meaning-giving creatures.

Bringing someone to the stage (2) recognition that the meaning that tobacco has for him coheres with his own values will clearly require an exploration of those values, perhaps even existential psychoanalysis, to bring to light his fundamental project. Plausibly, the analogy between cigarette butts and droppings took hold of my mother and motivated her because her own fundamental project placed a high value on fastidiousness. We would likewise need to explore Sartre's own fundamental project to understand why the precise image of being cut to pieces little by little gripped him sufficiently to bestow a new and motivating meaning on the tobacco.

It is, needless to say, no accident that the strategies for freeing someone from bad faith are largely analogous to the strategies for freeing someone from an intellectual prejudice – and no more guaranteed to succeed.

notes

1 I have here described the recognition of *ambiguity* as the source of anguish (Bell (1989: ch. 2) is a rare commentator who does the same); Sartre asserts that recognition of *freedom* is the source of anguish. But these, as should become clear, amount to the same thing.

2 Sartre lays out these paradoxes very clearly, in a manner that Anglo-American philosophers recognize and appreciate; anthologies on self-deception often reprint Sartre's chapter on bad faith. It is the only text of Sartre regularly read by analytic philosophers. Catalano suggests that it seems easy to take this chapter out of context because of its striking language and easily intelligible examples; as he notes, however, this chapter 'is not a tract on bad faith as such, but a progression in a reflection' (1998: 158).

3 On Sartre's interpretation; I make no attempt to assess its accuracy.

4 Sartre's best-known argument here, involving the attribution of bad faith to the 'censor', is the hardest to make plausible and I omit it in this exposition. (See also McCulloch 1994: 55.)

5 Elsewhere, e.g., BN 70, virtually identical passages refer to 'consciousness' rather than to 'human reality'; see Chapter 3.

6 Hazel Barnes translates *duplicité* as 'duplicity'; this is not incorrect but potentially deeply misleading given the dominant meaning of 'duplicity' in English. My own term 'duality' is somewhat misleading as well, since a duality in this sense has a duality/unity structure.

7 This term has multiple meanings (see Chapter 3), though all with the root meaning of 'going beyond'.

8 Commentators often speak of the '*third*-person perspective' here; yet Sartre's pivotal image of being-for-others involves one person looking at a second: the second-person singular pronoun 'you' captures this better than the third-person singular pronouns 'he' or 'she'.

9 *Pace* McCulloch 1994: 36 and 64ff.

10 The main lines of this section and the next were developed in K. J. Morris 1996a.

11 Santoni (1995: ch. 1) argues, rightly, that Sartre's discussion of sincerity involves an equivocation on the expression 'being what one is', and that the ideal of sincerity as 'being what one is' understood as being one's *facticity* is Sartre's own peculiar conception, rather than 'being what one is not and not being what one is'. I am inclined to think that one can acknowledge this without damage to Sartre's argument.

12 Cf. the distinction made in Chapter 1 between two conceptions of belief: practical commitment vs. assent to a proposition. Fingarette (1969: 92) evidently takes Sartre's use of the word 'belief' in the sense of assent to a proposition, despite his recognition that this is a fruitless way to analyse self-deception.

13 Sartre uses the word 'know' rather than 'to be conscious', but immediately admits that he has 'forced the description' with this word.

14 Thus the term 'belief' in Sartre's usage covers a narrower range than it tends to in Anglo-American philosophy. Anglo-American philosophers are often happy to speak of belief in connection with empirical propositions – e.g., 'The cat is on the cushion', and even mathematical propositions, e.g., '$2 + 2 = 4$' – whereas Sartre limits the word 'belief' to cases where nothing would count as persuasive evidence.

15 Sartre's use of the word 'evidence' is a little strained here; I will often use 'reason to believe' or 'reason to say'.

16 P. S. Morris's otherwise illuminating article (1980) unfortunately stops here when it comes to the question of escaping bad faith.

17 Sartre actually uses the word 'paederast' in this passage.

18 Catalano (1996: esp. ch. 2) distinguishes between two senses of bad faith, weak and strong, and claims that bad faith in the weak sense is inescapable. But what he understands by 'bad faith in the weak sense' is, it seems, nothing more than the ambiguity of human reality together with our tendency to flee it. These do make bad faith a permanent *threat*, but why call the threat of bad faith 'bad faith in the weak sense'?

19 Bob Solomon suggested (personal correspondence) that this image of crystallization came from Stendhal's essay 'On love'; this seems immensely plausible.

20 A full discussion of this point would take us into the issues surrounding *akrasia* or 'weakness of will'.

21 I don't mean to imply that these layers are wholly separate. Nor do I mean to imply that these layers are exhaustive, even in the case described; or that every smoker is in bad faith; or that every bad habit can be analysed similarly.

part II

All of the aspects of human reality to be elaborated in Part II have already been touched upon in Part I. Consciousness is a relation between a subject and an object; the subject of consciousness is the body-subject (Chapter 5), which is the centre of the field of perception in which the objects of perceptual consciousness appear. This field, and the objects within it, are inextricably intertwined with the field of *action* so as together to constitute life-space (Chapter 6). Action is by definition free action, so that freedom itself is manifested in life-space, a structure of what Sartre terms a 'situation' (Chapter 8). Moreover, the body-subject is also an object (Chapter 5), and an important dimension of its objectivity is revealed by the undeniable fact of being with other human beings (Chapters 5 and 7); others as objects of perceptual consciousness are also importantly different from all other perceived objects (Chapter 7), and social life involves an ongoing negotiation between my freedom and that of other subjects (Chapter 8).

Even this cursory sketch of the interconnections between the various aspects of human reality makes it clear that the body is central. This is one reason for beginning Part II with the chapter on the body. Despite the fact that Sartre tucks his own chapter on the body in BN somewhat out of sight in Part III ('Being-for-others') – and despite the fact that important aspects of the body are hidden away in chapters on other topics – I share with Catalano (1998) the conviction that BN III.2 should be seen as the pivotal chapter.[1] Another reason for placing this chapter so prominently is as a bit of Sartrean therapy. Sartre's treatment of the body in BN has tended to be invisible to those admirers of Merleau-Ponty who take *him* to have discovered the lived body; and to those admirers of Foucault who fail to see Sartre's observations on the body as the background to Foucault's renowned 'docile body' (1979). Finally, however, the body – to be precise, the lived body, one's own body as one 'exists' it everyday – is itself buried under multiple layers of 'invisibility'. This may be part of the reason why it has until recently been invisible to Anglophone philosophers.[2] Many Anglophone books on the philosophy of mind barely mention the body, despite the fact that the so-called 'mind/body problem' is one of the key issues in the field.[3] But although blindness to the invisible is perhaps intelligible, one might also suspect the operation of intellectual prejudices.

At the same time, despite its manifest centrality to Sartre's thinking, I have placed the chapter on freedom at the end of Part II, as Chapter 8. Although this positioning was not strictly necessary, it seemed to me, first, that Sartre's conception of freedom as freedom *in a situation* could best be understood against the background of two central and representative structures of the situation, namely life-space or 'my environment' and others or 'my fellowman', which are treated in Chapters 6 and 7 respectively. And secondly, it struck me that the body and freedom, understood as the facticity and the transcendence of consciousness respectively, constitute appropriate 'bookends' for Part II.

the body

'Look at a stone and imagine it having sensations . . . How could one so much as get the idea of ascribing a *sensation* to a *thing*?' (Wittgenstein PI §284). Yet it is precisely as a *thing* that many philosophers conceive the human body: an anatomical/physiological object 'composed of a nervous system, a brain, glands, digestive, respiratory, and circulatory organs whose very matter is capable of being analyzed chemically' (BN 303). This way of conceiving the body raises 'insurmountable difficulties' when we try to reunite this thing with consciousness (BN 303).[4]

'And now look at a wriggling fly and at once these difficulties vanish' (PI §284).[5] Wittgenstein's fly is not just a thing that moves, it is a living body trapped, let us imagine, in a spider's web, desperately trying to escape. If we reflect in an unprejudiced manner on our own experience of encounters with the bodies of other people, we recognize that the body we normally encounter is not an anatomical/physiological object but a *meaningful* object, an *expressive* object, one that *raises its arm in greeting*, or *clenches its fists in anger*, in a certain *context*. And thus described, our 'insurmountable difficulties' with uniting the body with consciousness dissolve.[6]

We experience not only the bodies of others, however, but our own bodies. Strange as it may seem, first-person experiences of the body are often neglected by philosophers; one symptom of this neglect is the widespread claim that so-called first/third-person asymmetry is 'the mark of the *mental*': 'Mental concepts are unique in that they are ascribed in two, seemingly very different, sorts of circumstances: we apply them to ourselves on the strength of our "inner" awareness of our mental states . . . and we also apply them to others on the strength of their "outer" manifestations in behaviour and speech' (McGinn 1997: 6). Yet many rather similar things could be said of bodies:[7] I have to *look* to see whether your legs are crossed or whether you are standing upright, but I don't normally have to look to find that out about my own limbs or orientation.[8] The fact that philosophers considering the body have seemingly forgotten their own bodies does not necessarily suggest a prejudice. Our own bodies are, as we will see, ordinarily 'invisible' in multiple respects.

Even on those rare occasions when philosophers do think about their own bodies, they tend to bring to bear what we have called the prejudice in favour of knowing over living. They ask 'How do I know the position of my own limbs?' or 'How do I know that I'm standing upright?' or 'How do I know that I'm moving?', and such questions render one's own body into something known rather than something lived or 'existed', into an object rather than a subject. Again, once we describe our experience of our own bodies correctly, there *is* no problem in uniting the body with consciousness.

We have already indicated several aspects of the experience of the human body.

(1) We *can* encounter bodies, whether our own or others', as physiological, anatomical or physical objects. If I am a doctor I may see the body of my patient, or even my own body on occasion, as a physiological thing which has a brain and a liver and endocrine glands, just as a corpse does (BN 303). The artist attempting to capture the model's stance on canvas may look at the body on the podium, in part, in terms of its anatomy and musculature, and may look at his own body from this standpoint if attempting a self-portrait. When I push my way through a crowd to catch my train I may encounter others' bodies as purely physical obstacles, and when the current sweeps me along I may experience the pure physicality of my own body.[9] Sartre says rather little about these ways of encountering bodies, for two reasons: first, because he considers that excessive focus on these aspects of the body immediately renders unintelligible the relation between consciousness and body; and second, because this is by no means the usual aspect under which either the body of another person or our own body appears.

(2) We normally encounter others' bodies as *meaningful* objects; the body of the Other is normally given as 'a body *in situation*'. It is not perceived as a thing among things, 'as if it were an isolated object having purely external relations with other thises . . . The Other's body . . . is immediately given as the center of reference in a situation which is synthetically organized around it' (BN 344).[10]

(3) Our own body as we normally experience it is often referred to as 'the lived body', one translation of the German term *Leib*. This term, as used by German phenomenologists such as Husserl and Max Scheler (1970), is contrasted with *Körper*, sometimes translated in this context as 'the thing-body', which corresponds to the physiological/anatomical/physical body described above. The core aspect of the lived body is what Sartre calls 'the body-for-itself' and what others call 'the body-subject': the *unperceived* and *unutilizable* centre of reference in a situation. As we will see, the body-subject is intertwined in complex and equivocal ways with the body considered as a thing.

(4) Other modalities of the lived body arise out of our intersubjectivity. For example, when I am aware of appearing within the perceptual field of another human being, I live my *own* body in an 'alienated' state.

This chapter concentrates on the lived body. I begin by setting out Sartre's description of the body-for-itself, exhibiting its multiple layers of invisibility, calling attention to some refinements which Sartre himself did not elaborate, and developing the more intersubjective aspects of the lived body. I then return to the bad-faith descriptions of the lived body referred to earlier to try to highlight the intellectual prejudices that underlie them.

The Lived Body

The body-for-itself

Heidegger's term for human reality was *Dasein*: literally, 'there-being'. Sartre begins his discussion of this dimension of the body by reminding us that '[f]or human reality, to be is to-be-there; that is, "there in that chair", "there at that table", [etc.]' (BN 308). The body is the 'thereness' – the core aspect of the facticity – of the For-itself.[11] Since the facticity and the transcendence of the For-itself are internally related, the very idea of a disembodied consciousness is eliminated at a stroke.

The body as it is lived in everyday dealings with the world is the unperceived centre of the field of perception and the unutilizable centre of the field of action. We have encountered this body-as-centre already as that our non-positional consciousness of which is an aspect of the pre-reflective *cogito*. These fields of perception and action of which the lived body is the centre, and which constitute our *life-space*, will be enlarged upon in Chapter 6. We will also discover that these are not two fields but one, since perception and action are internally related.

What Sartre refers to as 'the system of seen objects' is *oriented*; there is a field of vision in which objects appear as 'thises' against a ground (BN 316). 'It is necessary that the book appear to me on the right or on the left side of the table.' Moreover, objects always appear 'all at once – it is the cube, the inkwell, the cup which I see' but at the same time always 'in a particular perspective' (BN 317): 'objects may never show me more than one of their facets' (Merleau-Ponty, PP 92). These orientations, this ordering, this perspectivity refer to a centre of the field, and that centre is my body. We sometimes say that my body is my 'point of view' on the world, but this is misleading; it suggests an external relation between me and my body. When we think of a point of view we are likely to think of a traveller contemplating the landscape *from* a belvedere; but the traveller sees the belvedere as well as the landscape, the columns of the belvedere come between him and the landscape, he can move to get yet a better point of view, etc. But all these are precisely *not* true of my body. My body is 'the point of view on which I can no longer take a point of view' (BN 329), or in Merleau-Ponty's terms, that without which there could not *be* points of view (PP 92).

Just as an investigation of perception reveals the system of seen objects as constituting a perceptual field oriented around a centre, an investigation of action shows that objects appear to us in a field of action, 'at the heart of a complex of instrumentality in which they occupy a determined place . . . Each instrument refers to other instruments, to those which are its keys and those to which it is the key' (BN 321). Again, just as the orientation of the perceptual field indicates a centre, so too does the organization of this instrumental complex. And this centre, once again, is my body. It might be tempting to say that my body is the instrument to which all other instruments 'refer': the letters on the page I am writing refer to the pen and the pen 'refers to the hand and the arm which utilizes it' (BN 323). Again, however, this seems to make my relation to my body *external*. In fact, 'I do not apprehend my hand in the act of writing but only the pen which is writing; this means that I use my pen in order to form letters but not *my hand* in order to hold the pen' (BN 323). Sartre puts this point by saying that my body is the instrument which I cannot utilize; in more Merleau-Pontyan terms, it isn't an instrument at all, but *that by which instrumentality is possible*.

Yet we might wonder whether to designate the body-for-itself as the centre of the field of instrumentality does not treat *instruments* too instrumentally! Heidegger brings out a kind of invisibility manifested by tools and instruments. A hammer is in the first instance encountered as what he calls 'ready-to-hand'; it is something which is *for* pounding in nails. Although it is also a *thing* with a certain physical constitution and weight, this aspect disappears behind its readiness-to-hand (BT 67ff.). Building on this celebrated treatment, Merleau-Ponty considers the body which has accommodated itself to a piece of equipment through having acquired a motor habit; he observes that

> [a] woman may, without any calculation, keep a safe distance between the feather in her hat and things which might break it off. She feels where the feather is just as we feel where our hand is. If I am in the habit of driving a car, I enter a narrow opening and see that I can 'get through' without comparing the width of the opening with that of the wings, just as I go through a doorway without checking the width of the doorway against that of my body . . . The blind man's stick has ceased to be an object for him, and is no longer perceived for itself; its point has become an area of sensitivity, extending the scope and active radius of touch . . . To get used to a hat, a car or a stick is to be transplanted into them, or conversely, to incorporate them into the bulk of our own body. (PP 143)

'Incorporation' is to be taken literally: it means 'taking within the body [*corpus*]'; thus '[h]abit expresses our power of dilating our being-in-the-world, or changing our existence by appropriating fresh instruments' (PP 143).[12] The boundaries of the body-subject are therefore somewhat fluid: they do not precisely coincide with the boundaries of the body as a physiological thing, i.e., the skin.

This suggests that Sartre's claim that I apprehend the pen in the act of writing is not strictly correct: the pen too disappears, like the hand which is holding it, as it is surpassed towards the words appearing on the page. This seems not so much to contradict as to nuance his claim about bodies and instrumentality; tools and instruments may become *in a sense* part of the body, and to the extent that they do, they are no longer tools but part of the inapprehensible and unutilizable centre of the field of instrumentality, i.e., the body-for-itself.

The invisibility of the body-for-itself

The body-for-itself is, we might say, at least trebly invisible: it is by its very nature invisible, and that very *invisibility* is invisible for at least two reasons.

First, '[w]hile in one sense the body is the most abiding and inescapable presence in our lives, it is also essentially characterized by absence' (Leder 1990: 1).[13] The body-for-itself, as the *unperceived* centre of the perceptual field and the *unutilizable* centre of the field of action is by its very nature 'invisible' (BN 324); to be precise, our consciousness of objects in the perceptual field is non-positional consciousness of the centre of the field. A great deal of living actually requires that this consciousness remain non-positional. When one is reading – as opposed to, say, proofreading – the black marks on a page disappear behind the meaning, and if they did not we should find ourselves unable to read. And in somewhat the same way, our body disappears in our orientation toward the world. If we were positionally conscious of our limbs, we would find ordinary uninhibited fluent action impossible. Consider the difficulties met with by the philosopher Brian O'Shaughnessy: even when engaged in 'the most familiar and typifying of deeds' (1995: 178), e.g., playing tennis, we still, he says, *perceive* the position and movement of our limbs. He cashes 'perceive' out in terms of 'attending to', i.e., what Sartre will call *positional* perceptual consciousness. Thus, since O'Shaughnessy conceives of attention in quantitative terms – 'we have at any instant only so much attention to go around' (ibid.) – he supposes that our attention must be divided between our limbs and the approaching ball: 'some small measure' of our attention must be directed toward the movement of the hand or arm, even though most of it is apportioned 'ahead of the actively intervening limb' (p. 179).[14] *We* might suggest that anyone who attends, even in 'small measure', to the position of his limbs while playing tennis is at the least going to play tennis badly.

Second, this very invisibility is invisible as every familiar, taken-for-granted phenomenon is invisible; we need to suspend our unastonishment in order to notice it at all. Sartre's descriptions put into words something that is seldom made explicit.

Third, the invisibility of the body-for-itself is invisible in part through lack of contrast; and a Merleau-Pontyan strategy for enabling us to suspend our unastonishment through providing a contrast would be to describe neuropathological cases of human beings who had lost aspects of their body-for-itself as the taken-for-granted centre of their situation. It is only relatively recently that such cases have entered the popular consciousness, via Oliver Sacks's account of his patient Christina, who, suffering from an acute polyneuritis, suddenly found herself unable to stand unless she looked at her feet. 'When she reached out for something, or tried to feed herself, her hands would miss, or overshoot wildly . . . She could scarcely even sit up – her body "gave way" ' (1985: 44). 'She could at first do nothing without using her eyes, and collapsed in a helpless heap the moment she closed them . . . Her movements, consciously monitored and regulated, were at first clumsy, artificial.' Gradually, with practice, 'her movements started to appear more delicately modulated, more graceful, more natural (though still wholly dependent on the use of her eyes)' (1985: 47). Again, Cole and Paillard's patient IW had to concentrate so hard in order to walk that sneezing, which disrupted his concentration, made him fall over (1995: 250). Patients like Christina and IW demonstrate that everyday fluent action requires the body to remain invisible, by their very inability to perform everyday actions effortlessly. Although their bodies may remain – to a degree – the centre of their perceptual fields, they are no longer exactly the centre of their fields of action; one almost wants to say that these patients no longer *possess* fields of action. Thus the abnormality of such tragic cases may serve throw the normal situation of our own bodies into sharp relief.

At the same time, one might resist the drawing of a sharp contrast between the normal case where our body is the unperceived centre of our everyday dealings with the world and abnormal cases like Christina's. This point has both a general bearing – there are other instances where we may feel that an artificially rigid normal/abnormal dichotomy is being imposed – and a more specific one, which we turn to next.

Body as subject and body as object

Schusterman observes that the 'simple polarity' between normal and pathological 'obscures the fact that most of us so-called normal, fully functional people suffer from various incapacities and malfunctions'; I may, for example, be able to write or to play tennis or to drive a car but do so badly or clumsily (2005: 166). Leder's concept of 'dys-appearance', referring to the body's tendency to *appear* – to obtrude itself – in pain or illness, but also when one stumbles or delivers a poor backhand, might usefully be invoked here. Heidegger brings out not just the invisibility we have already alluded to, but also a special kind of visibility, manifested by tools and instruments: when the hammer breaks or goes missing it obtrudes its 'presence-at-hand', its thingness, upon us (BT 67ff.). Leder's dys-appearance is explicitly modelled on this notion (1990: 83ff.). And a similar dys-appearance prevails in the process of acquisition, as well as the process of refinement, of a motor skill: before the skill becomes fully 'incorporated' (Leder's term: 1990: 30ff.) – before the hat, the car or the tennis racket become capable of being 'incorporated' within the body (in Merleau-Ponty's sense, above) in the exercise of the motor skill – my body is in the equivocal position of being not only the *centre* of my fields of action and perception, but partially *within* those fields.

Sartre acknowledges that my own body *can* be something which I myself perceive or use as I would an instrument. I *can* 'see my hands, touch my back, smell the odor of my sweat' (BN 304). I can also utilize parts of my body as tools, e.g., I can use my hand just as I would a hammer, 'for example, when I hold an almond or walnut in my left fist and then pound it with my right hand' (BN 357). Sartre speaks of this appearance of the body as 'aberrant', in part in order to distance himself from the tradition which regards the body as an 'instrument handled by a soul', and devotes no more than two pages to it.[15] Yet Sartre arguably overshoots the mark in his enthusiasm for playing down this appearance of the body.[16]

He makes the unaccountable claim that 'this appearance of the body does not give us the body as it acts and perceives [i.e. the body-for-itself] but only as it is acted upon and perceived' (BN 358). He seems to have forgotten his own descriptions of his examples, e.g., 'I hold an almond or walnut in my left fist and then pound it with my right hand.' Here the left hand is no doubt being acted upon, it 'forms a part of the world' (BN 357), but the right hand is surely acting. Such cases thus bespeak the body's ambiguous status as both subject and object. The phenomenologically influenced sociologist Nick Crossley has done interesting work in exploring what he labels 'reflexive body techniques', 'whose primary purpose is to work back upon the body, so as to modify, maintain or thematize it' (2005: 9). These techniques are a special case of what the social anthropologist Marcel Mauss (1935) called *techniques du corps* ('body techniques'; see below). They include routine body maintenance practices – combing one's hair with one's fingers or using one's hands to apply moisturizer to one's face – as well as body modification practices such as scarification. Although Crossley is anxious to stress gender and class differences and although he focuses on their nature as *social* techniques, he sees such techniques as exhibiting the fact that 'we both *are* our bodies and we *have* a body' (2005: 2). Sartre's allegedly aberrant appearances of the body do precisely the same.

Sartre does, of course, fully *endorse* the claim that 'we both *are* our bodies and we *have* a body'; but he sometimes speaks in terms that may appear to invite the charge of a kind of 'body/body' dualism. In his treatment of the standard example of 'the toucher touching', Sartre will say that when I touch my right hand with my left, I, insofar as I am my left hand, am a body-subject; when I feel my right hand touched by my left, I am a body-object. But he continues: 'To touch and be touched . . . these are two species of phenomena which it is useless to try to reunite by the term "double sensation" '; 'we are dealing with two essentially different orders of reality' (BN 304). It may be felt that Merleau-Ponty expresses an entirely different and clearly *non*-dualistic view in this passage: 'in passing from one role to the other [from touching to being touched], I can identify the hand touched as the one which will in a moment be touching' (PP 93); its 'equivocal status as touching and touched' is one of the '*structural* characteristics of the body itself' (PP 95). This may seem to suggest that the body-as-subject and the body-as-object are not 'two essentially different orders of reality', but rather that the body is something which is neither subject nor object but a *subject-object* (PP 95).

In fact these two views are not incompatible. Sartre might put it that to be a subject (touching) is still necessarily to be a *potential* object (touched), and to be an object (touched), at least a body-as-object, is to be a *potential* subject (touching). He could even add that my positional consciousness of being touched is at the same time a *non*-positional consciousness of the hand's potentiality for touching, and that my positional consciousness of touching is simultaneously a non-positional consciousness of the hand's potentiality for being touched, so that the subject-role and the object-role of each hand are internally related. From this perspective, whereas Merleau-Ponty uses the terms 'subject' and 'object' to refer to the *potentiality* of touching and being touched respectively, Sartre uses these terms to refer to the *actualization* of these potentialities. This would allow Sartre to agree that the body is a subject-object, a kind of ontological duck/rabbit (see figure).

But where Merleau-Ponty's language stresses the ambiguity – the picture *can be seen* either as a duck or as a rabbit – Sartre's stresses the impossibility of being both at once: the picture *cannot be seen simultaneously* as a duck and as a rabbit. Thus there is no incompatibility between saying that the body is both subject and object and saying that the body can never be subject and object at the same time.

Duck/rabbit

This instantly dispels the charge of body/body dualism; yet this resolution seems too simple. Neither Sartre's nor Merleau-Ponty's description fully makes sense either of motor skill acquisition and refinement or of reflexive body techniques. If I am trying to learn how to swim or to improve my backhand, we would be hard pressed to say which *part* of my body is in the subject role, which in the object role, even at any given moment. And if we consider again Sartre's example of using the right hand to crack a nut held in the left, although our initial hunch was that the right hand is 'subject', it is more equivocal than that. It is acting as a hammer to crack the nut in the left hand; thus it seems to be both object (tool) and subject (tool-user). Likewise with the hand applying moisturizer to the face, which is both object used and subject using.

What all these considerations show is that the body is even more ambiguous than Sartre had allowed for; the body-for-itself is thoroughly intertwined with the body considered as a thing, and the boundary between the centre of the fields of perception and action and objects within those fields is somewhat fluid.

The lived body and other human beings

There are several further aspects of the lived body that arise from our living as human beings with other human beings.

(1) The body of the Other is a meaningful, situated object; the body-for-itself is the unperceivable and unutilizable centre of perception and action. But if the Other's body is a meaningful object within my field of perception, *my* body is a meaningful object within *his* field of perception, and my awareness of being such a meaningful object points to a new mode of being for the body.[17] Sartre has a lengthy description of this experience in BN III.1, focusing on shame, where it functions to illuminate our certainty of the Other's existence and the meaning of being looked at (see Chapter 7). His description in the chapter on the body (BN III.2) is very short; it focuses on the lived bodily experience of being looked at, and contains this remarkable description of shyness:

To 'feel oneself blushing', to 'feel oneself sweating', etc., are inaccurate descriptions which the shy person uses to describe his state; what he really means is that he is vividly and constantly conscious of his body not as it is for him but as it is *for the Other* . . . We often say that the shy man is 'embarrassed by his own body'. Actually this expression is incorrect; I can not be embarrassed by my own body as I exist it. It is my body as it is for the Other which may embarrass me . . . I seek to reach it, to master it . . . in order to give it the form and the attitude which are appropriate. But it is on principle out of reach . . . Thus I forever act 'blindly', shoot at a venture without ever knowing the results of my shooting. This is why the effort of the shy man after he has recognized the uselessness of these attempts will be to suppress his body-for-the-Other . . . he longs 'not to have a body any-more', to be 'invisible'. (BN 353)

The experience he describes so poignantly here will resonate not just with shy people but with sufferers of the psychiatric condition called 'body dysmorphic disorder', a distressing preoccupation with a non-existent or negligible defect in appearance.[18] Sartre himself suggests that this 'constant uneasiness' 'can determine psychoses such as ereuto-phobia (a pathological fear of blushing); these are nothing but the hor-rified metaphysical apprehension of the existence of my body for the Others' (BN 353).

One could be forgiven for thinking that this description of shyness is meant as a generalizable description of the lived-body-for-others, and one might well wonder whether the lived bodily experience of being looked at is always and necessarily as alarming as this description makes it sound.[19] Not everyone is shy; some manage, seemingly effortlessly, to give their bodies 'the form and the attitude which are appropriate'; some appear to have no 'longing to be invisible', but on the contrary seek to exhibit their bodies to others and find the experience of being looked at pleasurable.

There is little doubt that Sartre has a tendency to illustrate his discus-sion with unpleasant experiences and to use negative-sounding language to describe features of experience which are not necessarily negative. In fact Sartre uses similarly negative language in connection with the body-*for-itself*: a 'dull and inescapable nausea perpetually reveals my body to consciousness' (BN 338); we might begin to suspect something patholog-ical in his own psychological makeup! These negative-sounding terms can, however, be understood at two levels: the empirical and the onto-logical.[20] For example, 'nausea' may mean what we ordinarily mean, what he calls 'concrete and empirical' nausea, produced, for example, by spoiled meat or excrement; in another, it simply refers to our implicit awareness of our own body-for-itself, *whether or not* that awareness is unpleasant (cf. BN 338–9). Nausea at the ontological level describes an ontological dimension of this body, of which empirical nausea is just one characteristic manifestation. By the same token, his use of the term 'alienation' in connection with the lived-body-for-others (BN 353) refers at the empirical level to the *embarrassed* or *horrified* awareness of being looked at. Ontologically, alienation means the awareness, *whether pleasant or unpleasant*, of being looked at by an Other: note that the Latin root of 'alien', *alius*, just *means* 'other'.

(2) In his chapter on freedom, Sartre develops an aspect of the human body that seems to achieve no explicit recognition in his chapter on the body. He spotlights what he calls 'collective techniques' which 'determine my belonging to collectivities'. Such collectivities include the human race; '[b]elonging to the human race is defined by the use of very elementary and very general techniques: to know how to walk, to know how to take hold . . .' (BN 512). There are also smaller collectivities which dictate the precise *ways* in which I walk, grasp things and the like:

> to be a Savoyard is not simply to inhabit the high valleys of Savoy; it is, among a thousand other things, to ski in the winters, to use the ski as a mode of transportation. And precisely, it is to ski according to the French method, not that of Arlberg or of Norway. . . . In fact, according to whether one will employ the Norwegian method, which is better for gentle slopes, or the French method which is better for steep slopes, the same slope will appear as steeper or more gentle exactly as an upgrade will appear as more or less steep to the bicyclist according to whether he will 'put himself into neutral or low gear'. (BN 513)

Had the description of the French method of skiing but been more detailed, this passage could have been written by Marcel Mauss, whose lectures at the Collège de France Sartre and Merleau-Ponty attended (Hayman 1987: 237), although I make no claim for influence here.[21] It seems a classic example of one of Mauss's 'body techniques' (1935), a term which Mauss employed to refer to the ways in which culture influenced the manner in which human beings walk, run, swim . . . Sartre's concern in the chapter on freedom is to show that collective techniques in general, including for example language, are brought into being and kept in existence by a dialectical interplay between individuals and society, so that others are not thereby limiting the individual's freedom. But with this body-centred example, Sartre acknowledges, with Mauss, the body's essential capacity to be 'at once thoroughly natural and thoroughly cultural' (Casey 1998: 208).

(3) In his chapter 'Concrete relations with others' (BN III.3.ii), Sartre has a lengthy and celebrated discussion of sexual desire, which he defines as

'[m]y original attempt to get hold of the Other's free subjectivity through his objectivity-for-me' (BN 382). Sexual desire and sexual repulsion are not, he argues, merely a 'contingent accident bound to our physiological nature' but 'fundamental structures of being-for-others' (BN 383–4). Desire is sometimes compared to hunger or thirst; like hunger, sexual desire has physiological manifestations. But whereas 'hunger is a pure surpassing of corporeal facticity' – 'the For-itself flees it toward its possibles; that is, toward a certain state of satisfied-hunger' (BN 387) – sexual desire '*compromises* me': 'one ceases to flee' this corporeal facticity, 'one slides toward a passive consent to the desire'. Thus 'desire is not only the revelation of the Other's body but the revelation of my own body' (BN 388).

The expression of sexual desire – an expression which Sartre compares to the expression of thought by language – is the caress: 'in caressing the Other I cause his flesh to be born beneath my caress, under my fingers . . . [I] *incarnate* the Other' (BN 390). 'By each caress I experience my own flesh and the Other's flesh through my flesh, and I am conscious that this flesh which I feel and appropriate through my flesh is flesh-realized-by-the-Other' (BN 396). Indeed, the whole *world* is transformed, and the relation of my body to the world: no longer is my body the unutilizable centre of a field of objects to be utilized: 'A contact with them is a *caress* . . . In my desiring perception I discover something like a *flesh* of objects . . . the warmth of air, the breath of the wind, the rays of sunshine, etc.; all are present to me n a certain way, as . . . revealing my flesh by means of their flesh' (BN 392).

This experience of my own body as flesh is very different from my living it as the unperceived and unutilizable centre of the fields or perception and action; and this experience of the Other's body as flesh is very different from my perception of that body as such a centre. Although Sartre insists that sexual desire thus described is a bad-faith relationship, one might think that on the contrary his phrase 'double reciprocal incarnation' (BN 391) perfectly expresses a moment of authentic intertwining.

The body, then, although it *is* a thing, is also not *simply* a thing. Its subjectivity and its objectivity commingle in complex ways; and its relations to others' bodies, likewise comminglings of subjectivity and objectivity, introduce further ambiguities and complexities.

Intellectual Prejudices Regarding the Lived Body

Non-phenomenological philosophers tend to misdescribe the experience of the body-of-the-other as the experience of a physiological, anatomical or physical thing (see Chapter 7). They also tend to ignore our experiences of our own bodies. In this case, their blindness to the lived body is perhaps sufficiently explained by its normal invisibility in everyday life. However, when they do pay our own bodies some mind, they tend to treat them as objects; and here one must suspect the operation of intellectual prejudices.

Although the body-for-itself 'is *lived* and not *known*' (BN 324), on those rare occasions when one's own body is thematized in the philosophical literature, it tends to be thematized as an object of knowledge; the usual focus is on knowledge of the movement and spatial disposition of the limbs relative to one another or to other objects. The first/third-person asymmetry of the body, when it is recognized by Anglo-American philosophers, is all too· frequently accommodated by the invention of special types of sensation or special perceptual modalities. Such philosophers will say that we know that we are moving through 'kinaesthetic sensations',[22] or that we know the position of our limbs and the orientation of our bodies through 'proprioception', an alleged sixth sense in addition to the traditional five (sight, hearing, touch, taste and smell).[23]

Consider again Sacks's patient Christina, whose body – according to our phenomenological diagnosis – is no longer exactly the centre of her field of action and who might almost be said no longer to have a field of action. Sacks's verdict is rather different: he asserts that Christina has lost her proprioceptive capacity; she is 'proprioceptively blind'. And this notion of proprioception is one onto which many philosophers and psychologists have latched. It appears to offer a way of saying that, rather than *living* our body's position and orientation, we *know* where our limbs are and whether we are upright through the senses – usually proprioception, but if we lose that, then we need to use our other senses. And yet if we press this story, it is hard to make it fit the phenomena.

That there is something just a bit eccentric about proprioception as a sense-modality is indicated by the fact that it was not 'discovered' until the nineteenth century. Sherrington, credited with this discovery, called it 'our secret sense', Sacks calls it 'our hidden sense' (1985: 42). Cole and Paillard ascribe its hiddenness simply to the lack of awareness of people in whom it was absent (1995: 246), but Sacks adverts to its operations being 'automatic and unconscious' (1985: 42). Yet given that perception is a modality of consciousness, there is a peculiarity in the very idea of *perceiving* automatically and unconsciously.

Again, we might be struck by Christina's own gloss on Sacks's interpretation of her condition: 'This "proprioception" is like the eyes of the body, the way the body sees itself. And if it goes, as it's gone with me, *it's like the body's blind*.' She reasons, 'So I have to watch it – be its eyes' (1985: 46). Her gloss amounts to a recognition that proprioception is *not* simply another sensory modality: she wants to say that *she* sees, hears, feels, tastes and smells, but it is her *body* that proprioccepts – or used to, prior to her neurological disaster. Equally noteworthy is the fact that Christina's body becomes an object of perception for her only after she has lost her proprioceptive capacity. Moreover, she experiences herself as disembodied – hence the title of Sacks's case study: 'The disembodied lady' – when her body becomes an object of perception. That is, when her body becomes an object of perception it is no longer fully a body-*subject*, no longer *her*.

Philosophers wanted proprioception to answer the question 'How do we know the position of our limbs and the orientation of our body?' At first sight, understood as a perceptual modality, it seemed tailor-made to do so. Yet the phenomena themselves, it seems, resist this understanding. All of our difficulties vanish if we say, as the phenomenologists do, that we normally *live* rather than know our own bodies, and that it is this capacity to live her body that is impaired in Christina. From this perspective, it was only the prejudice in favour of knowing over living that induced philosophers to *ask* 'How do we know?' and to embrace proprioception as the answer.

There are many other directions in which Sartre's analysis of the lived body has been and might be extended and enriched; he has already taken us almost unrecognizably beyond the idea of the human body as a physiological, anatomical or physical thing, and has gone a considerable distance toward undermining the prejudice in favour of knowing over living.

We have seen that the lived body is the centre of the fields of perception and action. In the next chapter we find that these two fields are inseparable, and explore the life-space which is constituted by these fields.

notes

1 At the same time, his hiding away his main treatment of the body in the Part on being-for-others, and scattering other aspects of it elsewhere, demands explanation: possibly a little bit of bad faith?

2 Exceptions – apart from those Anglophone philosophers who are self-consciously continuing the phenomenological tradition – include Evans 1982, Campbell 1995, the authors in Bermudez et al. 1995, and recent discussion of so-called 'embodied cognition' (e.g., Haugeland 1995; Clark 1998) which stress notions such as 'embeddedness' and 'ongoing agent-environment interactions'. Many of these remain wedded to the vision of the body as an object and of these interactions as causal.

3 In fact the mind/body problem is typically explained as '[t]he question as to the relation between mental phenomena and physical states of the body, specifically of the brain' (McGinn 1997: 17). Thus the mind/body problem has mutated into the mind/*brain* problem.

4 These are exacerbated when the body is displaced in favour of the brain: 'How could this grey and white gook inside my skull be conscious?' (Searle 1984: 15)

5 This remark may seem to encourage a certain form of behaviourism. If behaviour is understood as mere physical movements, then our difficulties do *not* vanish; for this to happen, it must be understood as action , i.e., as internally related to consciousness; see Chapter 7.

6 This is not Sartre's point in the passage in BN 303; his concern there is the misguided effort to 'unite my consciousness not with *my* body but with the body of *others*'. Sartre, I think, gets tangled in his own terminology: his use of the word 'object' is highly promiscuous. It covers aspects of the body which he himself sees as radically distinct: he is keen to separate the sense in which the body of the Other is a meaningful, situated object and hence radically *different* from mere things, physiological objects, or tools, and yet the term 'object' covers all of these.

7 Cf. Evans, who observes that many bodily properties exhibit what he, following Strawson, calls 'immunity to error through misidentification'; as he notes, 'many philosophers give the quite mistaken impression that it is only our knowledge of our satisfaction of mental properties' which give rise to this immunity (1982: 216).

8 In fact McGinn's example in this very passage – a headache – might naively strike us as another splendid example of the *body's* exhibiting first/third-person asymmetry! There are many intellectual prejudices in this neighbourhood. See K. J. Morris 1996b.

9 Cf. Monasterio (1980), who thinks, wrongly in my view, that Sartre positively *excludes* this aspect. It is this aspect to which Sartre refers when he defines one term of one of the basic dualities of human reality as 'being-in-the-midst-of-the-world'. It is, moreover, implicit in his account of freedom. Freedom is only possible in a 'resisting world'; but the world can resist only if the *body* resists; e.g., the walls are only an impediment to my escape from prison given that my body is such that it cannot simply go through them.

10 I postpone detailed treatment of the body of the Other, or the Other-as-object, to Chapter 7.

11 It seems remarkable that Heidegger himself did not see the need to discuss the body in BT.

12 Sartre makes a partially parallel point here: spectacles or magnifying glasses 'can approach the body to the point of almost being dissolved in it . . . [they] become, so to speak, a supplementary sense-organ' (BN 329). Merleau-Ponty's examples involve more explicitly the notion of habit, which is undeveloped in Sartre.

13 Drew Leder, in a phenomenological study called *The Absent Body* (1990) which rapidly, and justly, became a classic, elaborated the invisibility of the lived body-for-itself in a number of directions.

14 In fact, he tells us that we don't attend to our limbs but to the *representation* of those limbs in our 'body image'.

15 '[I]f I apprehend my body as an instrument . . . it demands an instrument to manage it', which implies either an infinite regress or the 'paradox of a physical instrument handled by a soul, which . . . causes us to fall into inextricable

aporias' (BN 321). One can imagine Merleau-Ponty adopting the strategy of citing patients with neurological damage who *always* experience their own bodies as tools (see, e.g., Cole and Paillard 1995).

16 He even designates our ability to perceive and use our own body a ' "curiosity" of our constitution' (BN 357), one that we possess purely contingently.

17 Sartre's description of the lived-body-for-others focuses on the awareness of being looked at as a *psychic* object. It could be further developed through a consideration of the experience of being looked at as a physiological object – what Foucault (1975) would call the medical gaze.

18 See Phillips 1996. Morris 2003 connects BDD to this dimension of Sartre's lived body.

19 Cf. Dillon 1998: 137f. We will raise a parallel question about shame in Chapter 7.

20 Cf. Heidegger's distinction between the ontic and the ontological.

21 Sartre engages at length with Mauss's most famous essay, 'The gift' (esp. in *Notebooks for an Ethics*), but I have been able to find no explicit reference to Mauss's notion of *techniques du corps*.

22 Sartre does consider Maine de Biran's notion of a sensation of effort which informs us when we are *acting*; he claims that '[w]e never have any sensation of effort . . . We perceive the *resistance* of things. What I perceive when I want to lift this glass to my mouth is not my effort but the *heaviness of the glass*' (BN 324).

23 Neither Sartre nor Merleau-Ponty explicitly address the notion of proprioception; Merleau-Ponty, however, does engage with the notion of a body image that may play something of the same role (PP I.3). His discussion is a critique of contemporary psychologists' conceptions of the body image; e.g., empiricist psychologists try to see it as a kind of assortment of images derived from 'kinaesthetic and articular impressions' which keep track of positional changes of parts of the body (see K. J. Morris 1992). But such a compendium of sensations cannot explain, for example, how knowledge can be transferred from the right-hand side of the body to the left-hand side, e.g., in the minimal effort it takes to learn to shift the gear-stick on the other side when one shifts from a left- to a right-hand drive car. This implies that the two hands must, as wholes, be implicated in a 'comprehensive bodily *purpose*' (PP 98–9). But nor can we think of the body image intellectualistically, as a kind of mental representation which a person *uses* to 'plot the spatial relations between various parts of his body' (Campbell 1995: 11) or attends to in order to keep track of the movements of his limbs (O'Shaughnessy 1995). Some have preferred the term 'body schema' to 'body image' partly in order to distance themselves from these empiricist and intellectualist interpretations (e.g., Gallagher 1995). For Merleau-Ponty, to speak of the body image properly so called is to speak of the body 'being polarized by its tasks . . . of its collecting together of itself in pursuit of its aims: the body image is finally a way of stating that my body is in-the-world' (PP 101).

life-space

As we saw in the previous chapter, the lived body is the centre of the fields of perception and action. The space which is constituted by these fields – the space 'which is originally revealed to me' (BN 322) – is what is sometimes called 'life-space'; Sartre calls it the 'real space of the world' (BN 308).

Like the lived body, life-space is so utterly familiar as to be invisible. We are apt, if asked 'What is the human body?', to say that the body is an anatomical, physiological or physical object and thereby to forget our normal experiences of the bodies of our fellow human beings and indeed our own body. Similarly, the question 'What is space?' – even if we make it clear that we are talking, not about 'outer space', the space of astrophysics, but about the space in which we perceive and act – is apt to make us think in terms of the axes and coordinates of, say, maps and to forget about how we actually experience space, spatial locations and the things we encounter in these spatial locations. For example, I locate my coffee cup not by latitude, longitude and direction relative to the compass but as just *here* (imagine that I am reaching out) and, as in this example, such spatial locating is normally in the context of a project, such as the project of taking in some caffeine so as to facilitate the articulation of a particular sentence on the screen. And as this example portrays in miniature, although I have been speaking of the 'fields', plural, of perception and action, this is misleading: these fields are one and the same: 'perception and action are indistinguishable' (BN 322), that is, internally related.

Sartre's characterizations of life-space and of the objects of perception within life-space draw heavily on Gestalt psychology.[1] Although the phenomenologists have been critical of some Gestalt theories, many Gestaltist *descriptions* are far more phenomenologically accurate than that of their empiricist predecessors, and some of the terminology which enters into these descriptions captures something phenomenologically important. We begin with Sartre's description of life-space. Implicit in this description is a particular conception of the spatial location of objects within life-space; this is determined not by map coordinates but relative to 'axes of practical reference' (BN 321). Sartre's depiction is elaborated further by Merleau-Ponty; these elaborations also help us to see more clearly what it means to say that the lived body is the *centre* of life-space. Sartre's descriptions of the objects met with in life-space draw both on Gestalt psychology and on Heidegger, and illuminate the claim that perception and action are internally related.

Phenomenological Description of Life-space

Sartre describes life-space as 'hodological', a term for the invention of which he acknowledges the Gestalt psychologist Kurt Lewin;[2] this term derives from the Greek *hodos*, meaning 'way' or 'path'. Lewin took many of the central concepts which enter into his description of hodological space – 'vector', 'region', 'path', 'field' – from the then immature mathematical discipline of topology, partly with a view to putting psychology itself on a firmer scientific basis (1936: Preface); hence he called his approach 'topological psychology' or 'vector psychology'; it is also referred to as 'field theory'. He developed topological psychology in an effort to 'understand the forces which govern behaviour', and used the term 'hodological space' or 'life space' to designate 'the totality of facts which determine the behaviour of an individual at a certain moment' (1936: 12). Many of his case studies are of the life spaces of children, often in experimental settings.

In all of these respects, Lewin could not be further from Sartre, who has no interest in mathematics, no investment in the scientific status of psychology, and no awareness of children; moreover, the idea that life-space *determines* the behaviour of an individual at a given moment would seem to be utterly at odds with Sartre's conception of freedom. Yet, although the ends which structure life-space are *chosen*, we are not, by and large, explicitly conscious of having chosen our ends, and hence the life-world presents itself to us very much as Lewin described it (see Chapter 8).[3]

Objects within our 'psychobiological environment' are not motivationally neutral; they have 'valences'.[4] The Gestalt psychologist P. Guillaume freely renders this term in less technical-sounding language as, e.g., 'appeal', 'attraction', 'exigence', 'solicitation' (Guillaume 1937: 132).[5] Valences 'determine the direction of the behaviour' (Lewin 1935: 77), those with a positive sign effecting approach, those with a negative sign effecting withdrawal (p. 81). An object's valence 'usually derives from the fact that the object is a means to the satisfaction of a need, or has indirectly something to do with the satisfaction of a need'; since the state of satisfaction of a need may change from moment to moment, so too do valences (p. 78). Valences may also be 'induced': when, for example, an adult 'forbids or permits the handling of certain objects, characterizes behaviour as good or bad', the objects or behaviours may acquire negative or positive valences for the child accordingly (p. 98). Thus 'there is a *reciprocity* between the feelings of the subject and certain affective properties of objects in the phenomenal field' (Guillaume 1937: 132, italics added). Sartre puts it that 'the hodological field [is] maintained by desire' (NE 350).

Valences are one important type of force within the person's 'field of force', which Guillaume also calls the 'phenomenal field'; they are driving forces, but there are also restraining forces, or barriers, which define the boundaries of regions of freedom of movement (Lewin 1935: 80–1). Lewin delights in representing these forces diagrammatically with vectors, i.e., arrows – converging when the valence is positive, diverging when it is negative (see 1935: 91) – and in representing the 'locomotions' determined by the combination of forces in play within the field of force by paths, i.e., directed dotted lines in his diagrams. Guillaume offers some helpful illustrations: if I am simply lying tranquilly on the beach, the phenomenal field which extends around me is 'homogeneous, uniform'. 'But suddenly, a cry of alarm splits the silence, at some distance, to my left: the field is now centred on that point which becomes an attracting pole; it contains a vector directed from my position toward that point.' Again, a battlefield contains 'a gradient of danger and of difficulty'. On a playing field, 'in addition to its permanent orientation, the incessant displacements of the team of players give variable positive and negative values to different parts from moment to moment, creating zones of resistance and open zones which orient their efforts' (1937: 133).

As Mirvish notes, 'Lewin's notion of spatiality is very different from that of ordinary Euclidean space. For in the latter there is posited a fixed set of coordinates, independent of any particular subject, with respect to which objects . . . can be definitively specified as to their place at any given time.' By contrast, for Lewin, spatial coordinates vary not only from subject to subject but from moment to moment for any given subject (Mirvish 1984: 156–7). We are dealing here 'not with objective space, but with subjective or phenomenal space, filled with objects as they present themselves in the perception of a living being, with their negative and positive values, attractive objects, obstacles and barriers' (Guillaume 1937: 140).

Lewin is particularly interested in situations of conflict: for example, where the child 'stands between two negative valences': an unpleasant task on the one hand, a punishment if he fails to perform it on the other (1935: 91). The child's environment is full of 'demands and difficulties', the former arising from social forces, the latter from 'physical facts of the environment and the limitations of the child's own abilities: an object that he wants to lift proves too heavy, a staircase down which he wants to crawl proves too steep, or the pencil does not go over the paper as it should' (1935: 97). Any such conflict situation can give rise to an increase in the total state of tension, which leads to restless behaviour and may generate substitute behaviour, as happens when a child who wishes to draw when the supply of paper has run out may caress the pencil and watch other children drawing (1935: 96). If such a situation 'becomes *hopeless*', 'the child, despairing, *contracts*, physically and psychically, under the vectors coming from all sides' (1935: 94).

Sartre's explicit remarks on life-space are scattered; there is no one chapter in BN, for instance, devoted to it. One of his few sustained discussions occurs in STE; he refers to

> those exigences and those tensions of the world around us . . . we can draw up a 'hodological' chart of our *Umwelt*,[6] a chart that will vary in function with our actions and our needs . . . in a normal and well-adapted activity the objects 'to be realized' present themselves as needing to be realized in specific ways . . . the world of our desires, our needs and of our activities, appears to be all furrowed with strait and narrow paths leading to such and such determinate ends . . . [H]ere and there . . . there are pitfalls and traps.

This suggests a comparison of the life-world to 'one of those pin-tables where for a penny in the slot you can set the little balls rolling: there are pathways traced between hedges of pins, and holes pierced where the pathways cross one another'. 'This world is *difficult*', he says, and its difficulty 'is out there, in the world, it is a quality of the world given to perception (just as are the paths to the possible goals, the possibilities themselves and the exigences of objects – books that ought to be read, shoes to be re-soled, etc.)' (STE 61–3).

A full discussion of Sartre's account of the emotions is beyond the scope of the present book, but it is clear that his account explicitly owes a good deal to Lewin's discussions of conflict and of substitute behaviour; he quotes at length (STE 41–4) from Guillaume's exposition of a Lewinian experimental conflict situation, including one of Lewin's vector diagrams (see figure).

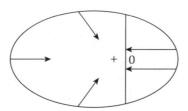

A vector diagram of a conflict situation, derived from K. Lewin

life-space

The core of Sartre's account is that an emotion is a transformation of the hodological world which we bring about when these paths become too difficult: 'All ways are barred and nevertheless we must act. So then we try to change the world; that is, to live it as though the relations between things and their potentialities were not governed by deterministic processes but by magic' (STE 63). He cites the 'sour grapes' story as an archetype of emotional conduct that would *be* emotion if the situation were more critical and the 'incantatory behaviour' more serious (STE 66):

> This little comedy that I play under the grapes, thereby conferring this quality of being 'too green' upon them, serves as a substitute for the action I cannot complete. They presented themselves at first as 'ready for gathering'; but this attractive quality soon becomes intolerable when the potentiality cannot be actualized. The disagreeable tension becomes, in its turn, a motive for seeing another quality in those grapes: their being 'too green', which will resolve the conflict and put an end to the tension. (STE 65–6)

Location of Objects in Life-space

If life-space is hodological, the spatial location of objects within life-space will likewise be given hodologically. According to Sartre,

> [o]bjects are revealed to us at the heart of a complex of instrumentality in which they occupy a determined place. This place is not defined by purely spatial coordinates but in relation to axes of practical reference. '*The glass is* on the coffee table'; this means that we must be careful not to upset the glass if we move the table. The package of tobacco *is on* the mantle piece; this means that we must clear a distance of three yards if we want to go from the pipe to the tobacco while avoiding certain obstacles. (BN 321)

It may not be entirely clear what he means. We would expect that to speak of 'axes' is to speak of spatial dimensions, i.e., length, breadth and depth; we might then expect axes of *practical reference* to be spatial dimensions which are in some sense centred on the body: 'up' and 'down', 'nearer' and 'further', 'ahead' and 'behind', 'left' and 'right' and so on. To locate an object in relation to such axes would seem to be to identify its place as, for example, 'there, to the left, a bit further than the table'. Yet Sartre seems to be going further. He is identifying the place of an object hodologically: in terms of potential *paths* to the object and in terms of *difficulties* and *obstacles* along those paths. To see what justifies this, it might be illuminating to look more closely at the axes themselves; Merleau-Ponty devotes a good deal of time to this, and his remarks will help to clarify what it means to say that the lived body is the *centre* of life-space.

I will focus principally here on what Merleau-Ponty says about 'up' and 'down'. 'Up/down' is a basic axis of the life-world, in the absence of which we are both literally and metaphorically disoriented: think of expressions like 'I don't know which way is up', 'Everything is topsy-turvy', 'My life has been turned upside-down'. Merleau-Ponty employs his favoured method of rendering the invisible-because-familiar: cases – on this occasion experimentally induced – where subjects literally 'don't know which way is up'. He describes the introspectionist psychologist G. M. Stratton's famous experiments from the end of the nineteenth century with so-called inverting spectacles and the Gestalt psychologist Max Wertheimer's experiments with a room which the subject only sees through a mirror which reflects it at an angle of 45 degrees. To Stratton's subjects, 'the whole landscape at first appears unreal and upside down' and 'the body is felt to be in an abnormal position'; actions miss their target. Gradually, over a period of several days, 'the body progressively rights itself', 'objects increasingly have a look of "reality"', and 'actions which were at first liable to be misled . . . now go infallibly to their objective . . . At the end of the experiment, when the glasses are removed, objects appear not inverted . . . but "queer", and motor reactions are reversed: the subject reaches out his right hand when it should be his left' (PP 244–5). The transformation in Wertheimer's subjects occurs much more quickly: they at first see the room 'slantwise': a man walking about in it appears to be leaning sideways, a piece of cardboard dropped appears to fall obliquely. 'After a few minutes a sudden change occurs: the walls, the man walking about the room, and the line in which the cardboard falls become vertical' (PP 248).

Merleau-Ponty's discussion of these experiments makes essential use of his language of 'inhabiting' and 'gearing'. For the world to be oriented *is* for one to inhabit it and for one's body to be geared to it. In Wertheimer's study, '[a]t first the mirror presents the subject with a room differently canted, which means that the subject is not at home with the utensils it contains, he does not inhabit it' (PP 250). 'At the beginning of [Stratton's] experiment, the visual field appears both inverted and *unreal* because the subject does not live in it and is not geared to it' (PP 251). To be at home in a room or to live in it is to *inhabit* it, that is, for one's *habitual* modes of action to be called forth by the valences of the objects in the room and for those objects to respond in the way one expects; this is what is meant by the gearing of one's body to the world. At the beginning of these experiments, a utensil like a cup or a pen does not call forth the habitual actions of lifting and drinking or of picking up and writing, and one's efforts to perform these actions result in spilled coffee and dropped pens. After several days, in the case of Stratton's experiment, or a few minutes in the case of Wertheimer's, I re-acquire 'a certain possession of the world by my body, a certain gearing of my body to the world . . . my perception presents me with a spectacle . . . as clearly articulated as possible, and . . . my motor intentions, as they unfold, receive the responses they expect from the world' (PP 250). Thus what accounts for the orientation of the spectacle is my body, but not my body 'as a thing in objective space, but as a system of possible actions . . . with its phenomenal "place" defined by its task and situations' (PP 249–50).

Merleau-Ponty also has a lengthy discussion of depth-perception, i.e., perception along the dimension 'nearer' and 'further'. He argues, contrary to a common dogma, that a man who is further away does not look smaller unless you alter the entire experience by isolating the man, say by peering at him through a tube or a hole in a screen (cf. also Köhler 1970: 71ff.). 'Otherwise he is neither smaller nor indeed equal in size . . . he is *the same man seen from further away*' (PP 261). What this means is that:

> the man two hundred yards away is a much less distinguishable figure, that he presents fewer and less identifiable points on which my eyes can fasten, that he is less strictly geared to my powers of exploration . . . the increasing distance . . . expresses merely that the thing is beginning to slip away from the grip of our gaze. (PP 261)

To be further away is thus to be less geared into my potentialities for action and exploration. Lewin makes an interesting additional observation about hodological distance: he introduces the idea of an ' "almost" situation', where the desired object is *just* out of reach, which, as Lewin notes, 'has an especially marked significance' (1935: 86). Sartre's too-green grapes might be an example: the importance of the difference between 'within reach' and 'just out of reach' is massively disproportionate to its difference in measurable space. Again, if I am cycling to see Pierre in the next village, the distance may be relatively short; 'Let my tire be punctured, and my distance from the next town suddenly changes; now it is a distance to be counted by steps and not by revolutions of the wheels' (BN 505).

Direction too is hodological. In situations which require a detour around a barrier in order to reach a goal, or which require fetching a tool or asking for help, we can observe a distinction between 'direction in the psychobiological field' and 'physical direction': although physically the person has turned away from the goal, hodologically he is still approaching it (Lewin 1935: 83–4). From this point of view, 'ordinary geometry appears as a particular case, privileged by its simplicity', for example, the case where the path between two points requires no detours around obstacles (Guillaume 1937: 141).

What Sartre called the axes of practical reference, therefore, are intrinsically hodological. If the dimensions of 'up' and 'down', 'nearer' and 'further', essentially refer to the gearing of our body to the valences of the world, then Sartre's hodological explication of the place of objects in relation to these axes makes perfect sense. And simultaneously we are enabled to see more clearly what it means to say that the body is the centre of life-space.[7]

The Objects of Perception in Life-space

Sartre's descriptions of hodological space and the lived body in BN are interwoven with a discussion of perception and its objects. First, like the Gestalt psychologists and like Merleau-Ponty, he argues against a conception of perception centred on the notion of atomic sensations or impressions caused by atomic stimuli.[8] Secondly, he shows that what we perceive is neither a sensation nor an atomic stimulus but what the Gestalt psychologists called a segregated whole, what Sartre calls a 'this', against a background and perspectivally, hence with inner and outer *horizons* (Chapter 3). Thirdly, he shows that these 'thises' refer to possible actions: they are in Heidegger's terms 'ready-to-hand'. Thus the things which we locate perceptually in relation to the axes of practical reference are themselves practical, they implicate potentialities for action. It follows that the fields of perception and action are the same field, and perception and action are internally related. We'll look at each of these stages in more detail.

Critique of introspectionist sensations and behaviourist stimuli

The Gestalt psychologists set themselves in opposition to the introspectionist psychology prevalent at the time, which had dominated the textbooks that Sartre and Merleau-Ponty read in their student days.[9] They simultaneously opposed behaviourism, which they viewed as sharing far more with introspectionism than the behaviourists would care to admit. Introspectionism was a form of empiricism; its proponents were eager to investigate sensory experience while retaining the right to call such investigations – *pace* the contemporary behaviourists – scientific. They operated on the assumption that 'local sensation depends upon local stimulation' (Köhler 1970: 97), that is, that pure sensations were caused by simple atomic qualities of things in the world, mediated by stimulation of, say, the retina, where the atomic qualities were to be understood as unaffected by their context and relations to other qualities and where the pure sensations were to be understood as unaffected by other processes such as learning, memory and emotional response. As Köhler argues, sensations thus conceived are 'only the first half of a reflex arc', so that introspectionism and behaviourism actually begin from exactly the same place (1970: 97).

The introspectionists insisted on the need for special training in order to access the 'bare sensory material' without its overlay of meaning and the effects of learning, and for special conditions of observation in order to exclude the confounding effects of context. On this basis they insisted that we do not strictly *see* a book, 'since this term involves knowledge about a certain class of objects' (Köhler 1970: 69). Again, the circular plate at the setting across the table does not look circular, as the untrained observer might say, but elliptical – 'once we have thought about their projection on our retina we shall have to admit that this is true' – and we can gain access to its true sensory shape by looking at the plate through a hole in a screen. 'With some training . . . anyone can see these real sensory facts, even without the screen, provided he assumes the right attitude, the attitude of introspection' (Köhler 1970: 73–4). Why are *these* held to be the real sensory facts? Because *they are what the introspectionist is led to expect by his theory*: 'one kind of experience is obviously given a higher value than another . . . [because] one experience agrees with what peripheral stimulation makes one expect, while the other does not' (p. 92). Thus Köhler neatly exhibits introspectionism as the product of intellectual prejudice, bringing out the perversity of the thinking that begins with a theory of what our perceptual experience *must be*, explaining away any discrepancies between its predictions and our actual perceptual experience by 'lack of training' or 'distraction by the sensory context' or 'contamination by knowledge or learning'.

Sartre too gently mocks the notion of sensation. He describes having volunteered for various experiments, presumably undertaken by psychologists of this introspectionist mould:

> I found myself suddenly in a laboratory where I perceived a more or less illuminated screen . . . Sometimes an inept experimenter asked me if 'my sensation of light was stronger or weaker, more or less intense' . . . his phrase would have had no meaning for me if I had not long since learned to use the expression 'sensation of light' for *objective* light as it appeared to me *in the world* at a given instant. (BN 311, italics added)

But this is not what the experimenter imagined he meant in asking the question; he took himself to be asking for a description of something subjective, a 'pure sensation', 'defined by the action on us by the stimulant through the intermediary of the sense organ' (BN 312). Worse yet, by 'subjective', he does not mean what he ought to mean, namely 'belonging to a subject', a being-in-the-world; he means that the sensation is an inert, passive object which inheres in an environment invented for the purpose called 'the mind' (see BN 313–14). Thus conceived, Sartre concludes, sensation is a 'pure fiction. It does not correspond to anything which I experience in myself or with regard to the Other' (BN 314). It is 'a hybrid notion between the subjective and the objective . . . a bastard existence . . . a pure daydream of the psychologist' (BN 315; see also PP Introduction, ch. 1).

The perception of *Gestalten*

If we do not perceive pure sensations or the simple atomic qualities which give rise to the local stimuli in the retina which are supposed to cause these sensations, what do we perceive? To understand perception, we have to acknowledge from the start that we are 'in the presence of the world and of objects . . . I apprehend only the green of this notebook, of this foliage and never the sensation of green' (BN 315). The green of the notebook, however, must not itself be understood as an isolated, atomistic quality, nor must the notebook itself be understood as an isolated object. The phenomenologists wholeheartedly embrace many of the concepts in terms of which the gestalt psychologists described our perceptual experience: the notions of a 'field'; of a 'segregated whole', i.e., a *Gestalt* (plural, *Gestalten*) – 'the contents of particular areas [of the visual field] "belong together" as circumscribed units from which their surroundings are excluded' (Köhler 1970: 137); of 'figure/ground' – objects in the perceptual field are articulated into figures, i.e., segregated wholes, framed by a background which is less distinct and detailed than the figure (cf. Koffka 1935: 185ff.); of various 'constancies' – of size, shape, colour and so on – so that, for example, the man who is further away looks roughly the same size as he did when he was closer (Köhler 1970: 71ff.).[10]

These notions of figure/ground and Gestalt, arrived at empirically by the Gestalt psychologists, tally with the Husserlian horizonal analysis of the objects of perception, arrived at through phenomenological reflection (Chapter 3). Since phenomenological reflection yields essences or meanings, the phenomenologists stress – *pace* the Gestaltists themselves – that these Gestaltist features are not merely contingent, the way we *happen* to perceive: 'these rules of appearance . . . are strictly objective and derive from the nature of things' (BN 317). Thus Sartre tells us that the perceptual 'revelation' of a thing 'implies the complementary constitution of an undifferentiated ground which is the total perceptive field. The formal structure of this relation of the figure to the ground is therefore necessary. In a word, the existence of a visual or tactile or auditory field is a necessity' (BN 3160); it is 'that without which a phenomenon cannot be said to be perception at all' (Merleau-Ponty, PP 4). Again, 'an object *must always appear to me all at once* – it is *the cube, the inkwell, the cup* which I see . . . this appearance always takes place in a particular perspective which expresses its relations to the ground of the world and to other thises' (BN 317).

What remains to be clarified is the implication that 'from this point of view action and perception are indistinguishable' (BN 323).

Gestalten and potentialities for action

The claim is not simply that perception is active – that perception is not merely the passive reception of sensory information from the environment – true though that is. Nor is the claim that perception *is action*; that would be nonsensical. On the contrary, 'action is presented as a future efficacy which surpasses and transcends the pure and simple perceived', whereas the perceived 'is revealed to me as co-presence' (BN 322). The claim is rather that perception is 'revealed only in and through projects of action': the thing perceived, though present, points towards the future, toward potentialities for future actions: 'The thing perceived is full of promises . . . each of the properties which it promises to reveal to me . . . engages the future'. So, for example,

> [t]he cup is there on the saucer; it is presently given to me with its bottom side which *is* there, which everything indicates but which I do not see. And if I wish to see the bottom side – i.e. to make it explicit – it is necessary for me to grasp the cup by the handle and turn it upside down.

Thus to say that the bottom of the cup is indicated, horizonally, by 'other structures of the cup' *is* to say that these other structures indicate the action of turning the cup upside down 'as the action which will best *appropriate* the cup for me' (BN 322).

Even this simple example brings us back to the idea that 'objects are revealed to us at the heart of a complex of instrumentality'. Lewin had said that objects are defined by their 'functional possibilities': 'The stairs are something that one can (or cannot yet) go up and down, or something that one climbed yesterday for the first time' (Lewin 1935: 77). These may serve as means for attaining desired objects: the stairs may serve as a means for attaining the toy on the landing, or for escaping from the intimidating visitor (cf. 1935: 102), and thereby acquire a positive valence. Sartre, as we have seen, identified hodological space with Heidegger's *Umwelt*, normally translated as 'environment', and it is in Heidegger's explication of what he calls 'environmentality' that he introduces a distinction between 'mere things', and 'equipment', the latter of which we encounter in our 'concernful dealings' (BT 68). 'The kind of Being which equipment possesses – in which it manifests itself in its own right – we call "ready-to-hand" ' (BT 69), a term which he contrasts with mere 'presence-at-hand'. His best-known example of a ready-to-hand piece of equipment is the hammer (e.g., BT 69ff.), which in his terms 'refers' to, i.e., is 'serviceable for', pounding in nails (BT 78). Sartre clearly has both Lewin and Heidegger in mind when he writes that for 'a purely contemplative consciousness',

> the hammer would not refer to the nails but would be alongside them; furthermore the expression 'alongside' loses all meaning if it does not outline

a path which goes from the hammer to the nail and which must be cleared. The space which is originally revealed to me is hodological space; it is furrowed with paths and highways; it is instrumental and it is the location of tools. (BN 321–2)

The properties of things are revealed as 'potentialities, absences, instrumentalities', and are perfectly expressed by those Latin gerundives of which Sartre is so fond: 'the nail is "to be pounded in" this way or that, the hammer is "to be held by the handle" ' (BN 322). Thus 'sense perception is in no way to be distinguished from the practical organization of existents into a *world*' (BN 321).

One might object that this picture of the perceptual-cum-instrumental field does not sufficiently take into account what the philosopher Gaston Bachelard calls the 'coefficient of adversity' in things,[11] the ways in which the world resists or threatens our instrumental projects: '[t]he bolt is revealed as too big to be screwed into the nut; the pedestal too fragile to support the weight which I want to hold up . . . the storm and the hail [are] threatening to the harvest, the phylloxera to the vine' (BN 324–5). Sartre had already long since acknowledged 'This world is *difficult*' (STE 62). His response to the objection is that 'the instrumentality is primary: it is in relation to an original instrumental complex that things reveal their resistance and their adversity' (BN 325). The very notions of '*too* big', '*too* fragile', and 'threatening' make sense only in the context of a project: of screwing a bolt, of supporting a vase, of growing crops. This, as we will see (Chapter 8), is a central strand in his discussion of freedom; he will urge 'that the coefficient of adversity in things can not be an argument against our freedom, for it is *by us* – i.e., by the preliminary positing of an end – that this coefficient of adversity arises' (BN 482) and indeed that 'the coefficient of adversity and its character as an obstacle . . . is indispensable to the existence of a freedom' (BN 484).

These notions of hodological space, of hodological location, and of perception as internally related to action are thus central not only to understanding the lived body and emotion, and to grasping Sartre's conception of freedom; they also, as we will see in the next chapter, have a role to play in his discussion of others and intersubjectivity.

notes

1 If this chapter is a little more historical and exegetical than the others, it is because the Gestalt background to Sartre's phenomenological descriptions is so seldom highlighted by commentators.
2 He introduced the term in 1934, in '*Der Richtungsbegriff in der Psychologie*', *Psychologische Forschung* XIX: 249–99. Guillaume (1937: 140) calls this 'a very curious article'.

3 'This apprehension of the means as the one possible path to the attainment of the end . . . may be called the pragmatic intuition of the determinism of the world' (STE 62).

4 The term 'valence' translates Lewin's term *Aufforderungscharakter*, rendered more literally by the Gestalt-influenced psychologist J. J. Gibson's term 'affordance'.

5 Guillaume was the foremost French Gestalt psychologist of his day; Sartre quotes at length from him in STE (41–4) and was clearly familiar with his 1937 book.

6 This is a Heideggerean term, often translated as 'environment', literally translatable as the 'world around' or 'the world about', but with the prefix '*um*' indicating not just 'around' or 'about' but 'in order to' (BT 65, tr. note).

7 It is worth contrasting this phenomenological account with a discussion of the topic by the analytic philosopher John Campbell, who argues that although our spatial frame of reference is 'egocentric', we *cannot* understand it as body-centred. But, first, Campbell takes for granted that 'body-centred frames of reference' are a subset of *object*-centred frames of reference (1995: 10), e.g., a frame of reference centred on, say, a pillar-box and defined by its 'natural axes'. The principal stumbling-block, once *that* is taken for granted, is that the 'spatial relations between various parts of his body' which we need in order to construct a body-centred set of axes must themselves be 'given in egocentric terms: one foot is presented as to the right of another, below the rest of the body, and so on'. Hence, he argues, we cannot non-circularly define the egocentric frame of reference as a body-centred frame (Campbell 1995: 10–12). If we think of the body, at least insofar as it is the centre of life-space, as a subject rather than an object, and of the axes as 'axes of practical reference' as just elucidated, all our difficulties vanish.

8 Sartre also argues that sense-perception thus conceived undermines any possibility of understanding sense-perception as giving us knowledge of the world. He offers a *reductio ad absurdam* of this conception of perception. First, '[i]n order to establish sensation we must proceed on the basis of a certain realism': the experimenter must presume that his subject's eyes, and his own instruments, exist in the world, i.e., are not simply an association of sensations; but secondly, 'on the level of sensation all this realism disappears': sensations are merely subjective affections of the mind; nevertheless, thirdly, 'it is sensation which I give as the basis of my knowledge of the external world. This basis could not be the foundation of a real contact with things' (BN 314). Merleau-Ponty is also concerned to attack the intellectualist conflation of perception with judgement (PP: Introduction, ch. 3; PrP).

9 I am grateful to Adrian Mirvish for this last point.

10 Gestalt psychology seems to have fallen out of favour; there are modern theorists such as Gibson who have substantial debts to Gestalt theories of perception, but Gibson himself tends to be treated as somewhat peripheral.

11 Bachelard (1884–1962) was a prominent though idiosyncratic figure in the generation preceding Sartre, writing about both science and poetry in almost equal measure, and creatively engaging with both psychoanalysis and phenomenology.

others

Sartre opens his chapter on the existence of others (BN III.1) by reminding us of a familiar experience: shame.

> Here we are dealing with a mode of consciousness which has a structure identical with all those which we have previously described. It is a non-positional self-consciousness, conscious (of) itself as shame . . . In addition its structure is intentional; it is a shameful apprehension *of* something and this something is *me*. I am ashamed of what I *am*. Yet . . . it is in its primary structure shame before somebody . . . I am ashamed of myself as *I appear* to the Other. (BN 221–2)

The consciousnesses we have described up to this point could be diagrammed with just two terms: subject and object. If we were to try to diagram shame, there would necessarily be *three* terms involved: *I*, the subject of the shameful apprehension, the one who is ashamed; *me*, the object of the shameful apprehension, that of which I am ashamed; and *the Other*, the subject before whom I am this shameful me-object. 'Thus shame is a unitary apprehension with three dimensions: "I am ashamed of myself before the other" ' (BN 289). This familiar type of experience is one in which *there can be no doubt* that there is a consciousness other than our own involved.

Yet just as philosophers are wont to ask questions like 'How do I know that the external world exists?', they may also ask 'How do I know that Others – i.e., other conscious beings – exist? How do I know that those bodies I see around me are not zombies lacking consciousness, or mere mindless automata?' I could argue on the basis of an analogy with the behaviour I myself exhibit when I am, for example, angry; I find that I clench my fists and I can see in the mirror that my face grows red, so when I see another clenching his fists and reddening, I hypothesize that he is angry and thus that he too is a subject. Or I could observe correlations which might allow me to *predict* his future behaviour: 'experience teaches us, for example, to interpret the sudden reddening of a face as the forewarning of blows and angry cries', and I might on this basis suggest that the hypothesis that the Other is angry, and hence a subject, is an inference to the best explanation. However, it should be clear that 'this procedure can only give us a *probable* knowledge' (BN 224).

Thus, if we define 'solipsism' as the idea that it is not *certain* that one's own consciousness is not the only consciousness there is, many philosophical ships founder on 'the reef of solipsism' (BN 223). And yet solipsism is 'impossible': 'nobody is truly solipsistic . . . my resistance to solipsism . . . is as lively as any I should offer to an attempt to doubt the *cogito*' (BN 250–1); 'Others exist' is as *certain* as '*I* exist'. Foundering on the reef of solipsism is symptomatic of philosophical bad faith.

Sartre identifies two basic modes in which we encounter Others: as objects, and as subjects, either as 'looked-at' or as 'looking', although Sartre also considers the 'us' and the 'we'. Each encounter is in its own way a potentially dramatic and explosive one. The philosophical reasoning that leads to solipsism makes two fundamental errors: first, it insists on *beginning* with the encounter with the Other-as-object, and second, it *misdescribes* that encounter. Each of these errors stems from intellectual prejudices, and a correct phenomenological description of these experiences of others enables us to identify the prejudices which have led philosophers, however unwillingly, into solipsism.

Up to this point, we will have dealt with a purely philosophical problem: solipsism. The existence of other subjects will have been revealed as certain. Yet those others with whom we indubitably share the world – and to whom, indeed, we are internally related – are at the same time potentially disturbing presences: there are human as well as purely philosophical problems connected with others. Sartre's notorious discussion of concrete relations with others may seem to imply that interpersonal relations are doomed to being futility and conflict. We end with a consideration of whether this gloomy view is inevitable.

The Other-as-object

Phenomenological description of the Other-as-object

We have already met the Other-as-object: the body-of-the-Other, that meaningful object, that situated object, *is* the Other-as-object (cf. BN 346).[1] Here as there, Sartre stresses the radical differences between this object and all others:[2]

> I am in a public park. Not far away there is a lawn and along the edge of that lawn there are benches. A man passes by those benches. I see this man. I apprehend him as an object and at the same time as a man. What does this signify?

If I were to think of him as being only a puppet, I should apply to him the categories which I ordinarily use to group temporal-spatial 'things'. That is, I should apprehend him as being 'beside' the benches, two yards and twenty inches from the lawn, as exercising a certain pressure on the ground, etc. His relation with other objects would be of the purely additive type; this means that I could have him disappear without the relations of the other objects around him being perceptibly changed. . . . Perceiving him as a *man*, on the other hand . . . is to register an organization *without distance* of the things in my universe around that privileged object. To be sure, the lawn remains two yards and twenty inches away from him, but . . . [i]nstead of the two terms of the distance being indifferent, interchange-able, and in a reciprocal relation, the distance *is unfolded starting from* the man whom I see and *extending up to* the lawn . . . instead of a grouping toward me of the objects, there is now an orientation *which flees from me*. (BN 254)

Although the Other is an *object* in this example in virtue of the fact that I am looking at him and not vice versa, he is perceived as a *meaningful* object around whom the world is organized: he – his body – is seen as a centre of his own fields of perception and action, and the space he inhabits is a life-space, it is *hodological*; thus the lawn is in front of *him* in a sense that it is not 'in front of' the bench; the man *faces* the lawn, the bench does not, etc.[3] This implies that to remove the man from the scene would be to change it in a way that removing the bench would not; he is a 'privileged object': because the man is a centre of his fields of perception and action, objects group themselves around him in a way in which they do not group themselves around, for example, the bench.

The final clause of this passage, it must be admitted, has a slight note of hysteria to it, which crescendos in subsequent paragraphs: the 'appearance of a man in my universe' is 'an element of disintegration in that universe . . . suddenly an object has appeared which has stolen the world from me' (BN 255)! It is the fact that the objects in the park group themselves around the man that is so potentially disturbing; until I saw him, objects were orienting themselves solely in relation to *me*. As Schroeder puts it, 'one is momentarily deposed: an alternative center challenges one's hegemony' (1984: 181).

Of course the description of the Other as 'stealing' my world is *sometimes* rather apt: there I am, gazing caressingly at that place in the river where it bends, where the willow overhangs it and the sun-kissed water lilies dot the stagnant surface like a Monet painting. I think I am alone and although I don't quite formulate the thought 'This is *my* river', if I suddenly notice someone a bit further up, gazing at the same scene, I might almost have the sense that he has stolen it from me. And yet is the experience necessarily unpleasant? Don't I sometimes think, not 'Oh no, I've got competition' but 'That's nice, I've got company'? This is a point we have observed on a number of occasions before: Sartre's tendency to focus on the unpleasant species of the genus in question. Life-space being hodological, people may differ in the valences they assign to things; this would come out very clearly should the person sitting further up the bank suddenly turn on his radio very loudly. Whereas for me silence has a positive valence and the noise of the radio a negative one, for him the valences are opposite (cf. Mirvish 1984: 168–9). But the assigned valences *need* not differ.

This, however, is not the only worry we might have. Does Sartre's image of 'stealing' not imply that each person's world is his alone? This worry is the basis of Merleau-Ponty's insistence that we must not 'conceive our perspective views as independent of each other; we know that they slip into each other and are brought together finally in the thing' (PP 353). The inner horizons of an object – e.g., the unseen profiles of the lamp, the non-positional consciousnesses of which are wound up with the positional consciousness of the seen side – indicate *other subjects* by whom the sides unseen by me are or might be seen. In short, the world is an intersubjective world, and although each of us has a different perspective on it, these perspectives 'gear into' one another. There is no reason why Sartre should not accept this; it does not undermine his point that each person is a centre of a perspective on the world and hence that to encounter another is – totally unlike encountering a mere thing – to become aware of a centre of perception and action other than oneself.

Intellectual prejudices regarding the Other-as-object

The philosophical outlook which ends up in solipsism conceives of the relationship between the Other's body and his consciousness as external (cf. BN 223), a consequence, in part, of the prejudice in favour of external relations which dogs a great deal of philosophy; and a direct result of this is a paradigmatic instance of what we have called 'the impoverishment of perceptual experience'.

The prejudice in favour of external relations. We know by now that the body is not merely a physiological object. Sartre's description of the body-for-itself already refutes the idea that my body and my consciousness are externally related. But his description of the body of the Other, i.e., the Other-as-object, does the same for the idea that the Other's body and his consciousness are externally related. Although the Other's body, that is, the Other-for-me, is indeed an object, it is a very special kind of object. As his description of the encounter with the Other-as-object showed, the Other is a *meaningful* object, and its meanings 'do not refer to a mysterious psychism . . . These frowns, this redness, this stammering, this slight trembling of the hands, these downcast looks which seem at once timid and threatening – these do not *express* anger, they *are* the anger' (BN 346, cf. PP 184).[4] This last claim seems open to the objection that someone might simply be putting on a show: it is not anger but 'only a pretended irritation' (BN 294). The response is that 'I am mistaken because I organize the entire world around this gesture differently than it is organized in fact' (BN 293). For example, I expect a blow which does not in fact occur: 'it is only in relation to other gestures and to other objectively apprehensible acts that I can be mistaken. I am mistaken if I apprehend the motion of his hand as a *real* intention to hit me . . . [i.e.] as the function of an objectively discernable gesture which will not take place' (BN 294). Thus in the first place I will discover my mistake when the expected blow does not happen, when Pierre laughs and claps me on the back instead. In the second place, whether the Other is angry or merely pretending to be angry, his gestures are the gestures of a meaningful object embedded in a context, so are the gestures of an object who is also a subject:

> In itself a clenched fist [or a frown, redness etc.] is nothing and means nothing. But also we never perceive a *clenched fist*. We perceive a man who in a certain situation clenches his fist. This meaningful act considered in connection with the past and with possibles and understood in terms of the synthetic totality 'body-in-situation' *is* the anger. (BN 346–7)

Thus our experience reveals the Other's body and his consciousness as internally related.

The perception of others and the impoverishment of perceptual experience. Moreover, the argument from analogy and the inference to the best explanation canvassed earlier rest on a presupposition: that '[w]hat I apprehend on this face is nothing but the effect of certain muscular contractions, and they in turn are only the effect of a nervous impulse' (BN 224). Thus is our perceptual experience impoverished: 'people too readily believe that all perceptions are of the same kind' (BN 347). In fact, since the body of the Other is a *psychic* object, it follows that 'my perception of the Other's body is radically different from my perception of things' (BN 345): 'the perception of it can not *by nature* be of the same type as that of inanimate objects . . . Thus it is not necessary to resort to habit or reason by analogy in order to explain how we *understand* expressive conducts. These conducts are originally given to perception as understandable' (BN 347). Thus such perfectly ordinary locutions as 'Her happiness shone forth in her eyes' or 'His face darkened in anger' are not, as these philosophers would have us believe, mere misleading *façons de parler*, but accurate descriptions of objects of perceptual experience.

Merleau-Ponty spells this out further; attuned in a way that Sartre never is to animals and infants, Merleau-Ponty notes first that 'my understanding of gestures' is for the most part 'confined to human ones': 'I do not "understand" the sexual pantomime of the dog, still less of the cockchafer or the praying mantis' (PP 184). He locates this ability to understand human beings in 'the reciprocity of my intentions and the gestures of others, of my gestures and intentions discernable in the conduct of other people'; to understand a gesture is to 'recapture' it via 'an act on the spectator's part' (PP 185). The body of the praying mantis is too unlike our own for us to imitate, and even if we could, this imitation would not carry bodily comprehension with it; nor would a purely intellectual understanding of the sexual purpose of its mating display suffice for this. Although in adults this recapturing of the gesture is suppressed or only incipient, an infant will visibly make the gesture:

> A baby of fifteen months opens its mouth if I playfully take one of its fingers between my teeth and pretend to bite it . . . its own mouth and teeth, as it feels them from the inside, are immediately, for it, an apparatus to bite with, and my jaw, as the baby sees it from the outside, is immediately, for it, capable of the same intentions . . . It perceives its intentions in its body, and my body with its own, and thereby my intentions in its own body. (PP 352)

This is not a matter of an intellectualist argument from analogy, but a kind of 'blind recognition' (PP 185). 'It is through my body that I understand other people' (PP 186).

The point can be further strengthened à la mode de Merleau-Ponty by considering abnormal experiences of others: the experience of those who suffer from autistic spectrum disorders such as Asperger's syndrome. Temple Grandin, one such individual, thinks of herself as 'an anthropologist on Mars' in her efforts to understand others.[5] She describes herself as having built up a library of mental 'videotapes' 'of how people behaved in different circumstances. She would play these over and over again and learn, by degrees, to correlate what she saw, so that she could then predict how people in similar circumstances might act' (Sacks 1995: 260). Grandin has to ' "compute" others' intentions and states of mind, to try to make algorithmic, explicit, what for the rest of us is second nature' – or possibly even first nature (p. 270). Other children participated in 'an exchange of meanings, a negotiation, a swiftness of understanding so remarkable that she [as a child] sometimes wondered if they were all telepathic'. She can now 'infer' social signals, 'but she cannot perceive them, cannot participate in this magical communication directly, or conceive the many-leveled kaleidoscopic states of mind behind it' (p. 272). Her perceptions of others are impoverished in just the way that the philosophers imagined *all* of our perceptions of others to be; she *does* have to argue from analogy and make inferences to the best explanation – and her very abnormality demonstrates that *we* do not.

Of course, here as elsewhere, we may think that the phenomenologists draw too sharp a dichotomy between the normal and the abnormal. For instance, rather as there are occasions when perfectly normal people treat their own bodies as instruments, as when they use one hand to crack a nut, there are occasions when normal people engage in calculating and predicting others' likely responses, as when they are engaged in a political campaign. Again, rather as the process of motor skill acquisition involves a period of adjustment during which the body occupies an ambiguous status of being both subject and object, moving to a new country often involves a period of adjustment during which one finds others' behaviour and responses opaque.[6] And, rather as there are human beings who are clumsy and for whom the body-for-itself is never wholly an invisible and intangible body-subject, there are human beings who are insensitive to others' thoughts and feelings, who never *wholly* participate in the 'magical communication' which was so inaccessible to Grandin. The conclusion ought to be not that the phenomenologists' descriptions are inaccurate but that they are incomplete: interpersonal human reality is even more ambiguous and nuanced than they allow.

Philosophers land up in solipsism in part because they misdescribe the experience of the Other-as-object. Even more fundamentally, however, their very question 'How do I know that other subjects exist?' implies beginning with the Other-as-object, because knowledge is by definition knowledge *of objects*; and this, Sartre urges, is the wrong place to begin one's philosophical inquiry into the existence of others. We must begin with the Other-as-subject, for only there will we find certainty.

The Other-as-subject

Phenomenological description of the Other-as-subject

Sartre's description of an encounter with the Other-as-subject is even more famous, or infamous:

> Let us imagine that moved by jealousy, curiosity, or vice I have just glued my ear to the door and looked through a keyhole. I am alone and on the level of a non-thetic self-consciousness . . . [My attitude] is a pure process of relating the instrument (the keyhole) to the end to be attained (the spectacle to be seen) . . . But all of a sudden I hear footsteps in the hall. Someone is looking at me! What does this mean? It means that I am suddenly affected in my being and that essential modifications appear in my structure . . . (BN 259–60)

Sartre's description of these modifications occupies several pages. The chief points to note are these:

1 'I now exist as *myself* for my unreflective consciousness' (BN 260). 'I *am* this being', the 'me' or Ego, the object which the Other sees (BN 261).
2 I am not the foundation of this object which I am; it is not even 'the indirect, strict effect of my acts as when my shadow on the ground or my reflection in the mirror is moved in correlation with the gestures which I make. This being which I am preserves a certain indetermination, a certain unpredictability . . . If it is comparable to a shadow, it is like a shadow which is projected on a moving and unpredictable material' (BN 261–2).
3 These characteristics stem 'from the fact that the other is free . . . the Other's freedom is revealed to me across the uneasy indetermination of the being which I am for him' (BN 262).
4 'I grasp the Other's look at the very center of my act as the solidification and alienation of my own possibilities . . . my transcendence [is] transcended' (BN 263).
5 This object which I am is *inapprehensible*: 'I cannot live [the qualities he confers on me] as my own realities . . . I accept the responsibility for this stranger who is presented to me, but he does not cease to be a stranger' (BN 274); 'I shall never have a concrete intuition' of my being-for-others (BN 275).

As with Sartre's description of the Other-as-object, a certain note of hysteria enters his description of the Other-as-subject: 'being-seen constitutes me as a defenseless being for a freedom which is not my freedom . . . I am a slave to the degree that my being is dependent at the center on a freedom which is not mine and which is the very condition of my being' (BN 267). Again, there *are* experiences to which such descriptions are strictly accurate: I once had a student who was an amateur stand-up comedian, and described the experience of 'dying' before an unsympathetic audience in shatteringly Sartrean terms. One can, however, remove the note of hysteria and retain an insightful description of the experience of being looked at. Like a shadow, my being-for-others depends in part on my actions and the way I move, and if it did not, the Other's judgement of me could never 'touch me to the quick'; but like a shadow projected on moving and unpredictable material, my being-for-others depends also on the Other's values and projects, i.e., his freedom.

Again, Sartre's choice of example – shame – may make it seem as though the awareness of being looked at is always unpleasant; and yet when he says that 'shame is only the original feeling of having my being outside' (BN 288), we are not to understand this as saying that we always feel ashamed when being looked at. As we noted in respect of nausea and alienation (Chapter 5), Sartre is using the word 'shame' in two senses: one empirical, where it refers to the *unpleasant* awareness of oneself as an object which arouses distaste in another; and one ontological, where it simply means the awareness of oneself as an object for another. In the ontological sense of the word 'shame', it equally covers the *pride* one feels when others are listening admiringly to one's brilliant viola performance – although even here, arguably, one's pride is affected at its heart by one's vulnerability before others; I may make a mistake for which they will not forgive me, or they may get bored.[7]

The exact meaning of item (4) may not be immediately apparent: the notion of 'the solidification and alienation of my own possibilities', which Sartre also spells out as 'my possibility becom[ing] a probability which is outside me' (BN 265). I want to suggest that we can make good sense of this via the notion of so-called first/third-person asymmetry, although 'first/second person asymmetry' might be more accurate in the context of the Look. Consider this bit of dialogue, which is meant to illustrate the process of my possibility becoming a probability: ' "I swear to you that I will do it." "Maybe so. You tell me so. I want to believe it." ' (BN 265). One can sense the mounting frustration of the first speaker, the Gallic shrug of the second. And yet, at bottom, all this dialogue invokes is the first/second-person asymmetry of expressions of intentions or promises: my saying 'I intend to do *x*' is in the language-game of certainty, whereas your saying of me 'You intend to do *x*' is in the language-game of knowledge; that is, whereas it makes no sense to speak of doubt in connection with my own intention, it does make sense for you to doubt that I so intend. And whereas it makes no sense to ask me 'How do you know that you intend to do this?' it makes sense to ask me 'How do *I* know that you intend to do this?' By the same token, because my expression of intention is for you within the language-game of knowledge, it gives you a basis, more or less firm, for predicting what I will do. Since my expression of intention is for me in the language-game of certainty, it does not give *me* a basis for prediction. My performing the promised action is, for you, at best probable; it is not probable for me (cf. Wittgenstein, PI p. 224). Such first/second-person asymmetry is inevitable.

As usual, Sartre's language – 'the alienation of my possibilities' – is negative-sounding language: as if there were something intrinsically horrible about the awareness of such first/second-person asymmetry![8] And his example is a distressing one: it is evidently a case in which the Other does not entirely trust you. One could say that first/second-person asymmetry carries with it the *possibility* of mutual distrust, and Sartre for his own reasons chooses to focus on cases where that possibility is actualized; this is consistent with adding, as Merleau-Ponty might wish to, that mutual *trust* is the basic case.

This interpretation of alienation also helps to make sense of item (5): the claim that my being-for-others is inapprehensible. It is not that I *cannot know* how the other person views me or responds to me; after all, he can tell me or otherwise communicate his views. If a member of the audience says that I'm hilarious, or laughs, or applauds, I *may* be able to conclude that my being-for-others is funny. Moreover, although in some circumstances we can say that the audience member may be lying – perhaps to spare my feelings, or to spur me on to make an even greater fool of myself – in other circumstances such knowledge *may* be 'infinitely probable'; if he is helpless with laughter at my jokes, I cannot doubt that he finds me funny. But even 'infinitely probable' knowledge is not certainty, and I could only attain certainty if I could literally be Other to myself – if I could find *myself* funny, or pathetic as the case may be (*pace* Schroeder 1984: 199ff.). Certainty is ruled out by first/second-person asymmetry.

Intellectual prejudices regarding the Other-as-subject

As we will see, the look of the Other reveals his existence as *certain*; but recognition of this is impeded by the prevalence of a prejudice in favour of knowledge over certainty. This is why philosophers raise the problem of the Other's existence as a problem of knowledge. The Look also reveals the relation between me and the Other as *internal*, a revelation which is only possible once we have rid ourselves of the prejudice in favour of external relations.

The prejudice in favour of knowledge over certainty. The experience of being looked at – shame, for example – reveals the existence of the Other-as-subject as *certain*: 'the Other's existence was experienced with evidence [i.e. certainty] in and through the fact of my objectivity' (BN 302). The certainty here is exactly the same as the certainty of one's own existence as revealed in the Cartesian *cogito*; indeed it is itself a kind of 'second *cogito*': '[i]f the other's existence is not a vain conjecture, a pure fiction, this is because there is a sort of *cogito* concerning it' (BN 251). Neither my own existence nor the existence of the Other is a logical or metaphysical necessity; these are what Sartre refers to as 'factual necessities': *given* the fact that I think, it is necessary that I exist; *given* the fact that I feel shame, it is necessary that others exist.[9] Nor is the existence of others derivable from the first *cogito*: we cannot say that given the fact that *I* think, it is necessary that *others* exist: 'It would perhaps not be impossible to conceive of a For-itself which would be wholly free from all For-others and which would exist without even suspecting the possibility of being an object.' But, again as a matter of factual necessity, it is 'indisputable' that 'our being along with its being-for-itself is also for-others' (BN 282, italics added).

The language-game of certainty does not permit the question 'On what basis are you certain?' Certainty, unlike knowledge, is not based on evidence, it does not permit questions of validation or invalidation. Sartre does however spell out more fully in what this certainty consists. The crucial point is that the transformations which I and my world undergo when I experience shame are transformations which I could not possibly bring about myself; only *another subject* could produce them. It may be tempting to say that I objectify *myself* when I look in the mirror; indeed many of the judgements which others make about us and which might naturally evoke shame are judgements that we sometimes make about ourselves in these circumstances: 'I am ugly', 'I am disgusting', 'I am clumsy' and so on. But such judgements don't *transform* me, or my world, in the relevant ways.

In the first place, if another ascribes such qualities to me, 'I can not live them as my own realities . . . I accept the responsibility for this stranger who is presented to me' – judgements like 'You are clumsy' or 'You are ugly' touch me to the quick – but this me-object 'does not cease to be a stranger' (BN 274). The object which I am for another is *alienated*, and 'in no case can I ever alienate myself from myself' (BN 275). Moreover, 'the Other does not constitute me as an object for myself but for *him*' (BN 275), so that even if I can be said to be an object *for myself* when I look in the mirror, this is precisely what does *not* happen when I am looked at by another. I am aware of being an object for a subject but not an object *for me*. This being-which-I-am-for-others is not in my control: 'If the Other sees one as ugly, one can do little either to sustain or to overthrow this judgment. One can argue, cut one's hair, or have plastic surgery; the Other may still insist on seeing ugliness' (Schroeder 1984: 209).[10]

In the second place, the look of the Other 'is not only a transformation of myself but a total metamorphosis of the world': under the look of the Other 'I am looked-at in a world which is looked-at', but *not by me* (BN 269). I am no longer the centre of my fields of action and perception, I am an object within another's fields of action and perception.

This second *cogito* is no more a proof of the existence of Others-as-subjects than the first *cogito*, Descartes's *cogito*, was a proof of his existence. The fact that Descartes *thought* did not give him a *reason for believing* that he existed, as if before the *cogito* he lacked certainty of his own existence and only afterwards did he possess certainty: 'Actually I have always possessed certainty that I existed, I have never ceased to practice the *cogito*. Similarly my resistance to solipsism – which is as lively as any I should offer to an attempt to doubt the *cogito* – proves that

I have always possessed certainty that the Other existed' (BN 251).[11]
This resistance 'is based on the fact that the Other is given to me as a
concrete evident presence which I can in no way derive from myself and
which can in no way be placed in doubt nor made the object of a phenomenological reduction' (BN 271). Even if we could, in accordance with
Husserl's demand, place the world in brackets, we would not thereby
place the Other-as-subject in brackets because he is *not an object*, he is
not an element of the world (cf. BN 272–3). Thus, '[j]ust as my consciousness apprehended by the *cogito* bears indubitable witness of itself and of
its own existence, so certain particular consciousnesses – for example,
"shame-consciousnesses" – bear indubitable witness to the *cogito* both
of themselves and of the existence of the Other' (BN 273).

The traditional 'problem of other minds' is that of justifying claims
to know of the existence of conscious beings other than oneself; we
seem unable to escape solipsism owing to inadequate answers to the
question 'How do I know that Others exist?' Sartre connects the notion
of knowledge with the notions of probability, validation and invalidation, and objects; and insofar as the objects in question are Others-
as-objects, the philosopher's question is therefore linked with the
second-person perspective.

Sartre argues that by beginning with the Other-as-object, as the traditional problem of knowledge of other minds necessarily does, we undermine any possibility even of attaining *probable* knowledge. Unless we
reveal the existence of the Other-as-*subject* as certain, our beliefs about
the Other-as-object have no foundation at all: 'if the Other on principle
and in its "For-itself" is outside my experience, the probability of his
existence as *Another Self* can never be either validated or invalidated . . .
[it] becomes a pure fictional conjecture'. Indeed it is worse than that:
unlike conjectures about, say, life on Mars, which will only remain con-
jectural 'so long as we do not have at our disposal instruments or scientific theories enabling us to produce facts validating or invalidating
this hypothesis . . . the structure of the Other is on principle such that
no new instrument will ever be able to be conceived, that no new theory
will come to validate or invalidate the hypothesis of his existence' (BN
250–1). Thus the certainty of the Other-as-subject is prior to knowledge
of the Other-as-object. We need to *begin* with the Other-as-subject: the
Other, claims Sartre, 'can not *at first* be an object' (BN 252, cf. BN 287).
Without certainty of the Other-as-subject, we cannot even perceive the
Other as a *meaningful* object.[12]

It will be retorted that whatever the merits in general of the distinction between knowledge and certainty, when it comes to this particular
question we really are stuck with the second-person perspective and
hence with the aim of knowledge rather than certainty – we are after all
inquiring about the existence of *others*. The only alternative would be to

attain a first-person perspective on the consciousness of the Other, and that would require us – impossibly – to *be* the Other. And if Sartre is right that without certainty regarding the Other-as-subject, the existence of the Other-as-object, i.e., as meaningful or psychic object, is not even probable, has not even the status of a fictional conjecture, then Sartre has exacerbated the problem of others far beyond our wildest nightmares.

Yet what is remarkable about Sartre's account of the experience of the look of the Other-as-subject is that it *is* a first-person account. It does not – of course – involve the impossible attainment of a first-person perspective on the consciousness of the Other, but it does rest on a first-person experience, namely shame. The reasoning just reviewed, which seemed to exacerbate the problem of other minds so drastically, rests on a crucial conditional: '*If* the Other on principle and in its "For-itself" is outside my experience . . .'[13] This, however, is precisely what the discussion of shame called into question: what I experience in shame is the Other-as-*subject*, as *For-itself*. What has blinded past philosophers to this possibility is a further prejudice: the prejudice in favour of external relations, here in connection to the relations between human beings, to which we now turn.

The prejudice in favour of external relations. The experience of shame reveals an internal relation – in fact, more than one. As we have seen, shame is a three-place relation: '*I* am ashamed of *myself* before the *Other*.' Each of the three terms is revealed as internally related to the others: there is an internal relation between I and myself, between I and the Other, and between myself and the Other. The first two of these relations are of a particular kind: what Sartre calls an 'internal negation'; thus the Look involves a 'double negation' (BN 284–5). An *external* negation would 'separate the Other from myself as one substance from another substance', as when we say that the table *is not* the inkwell; an internal negation is 'a synthetic, active connection of the two terms, each of which constitutes itself by denying that it is the other' (BN 252).

So, first, the negative internal relation between I and myself is the internal relation between the two poles of the duality between being-for-itself and being-for-others, and plays out the formula that human reality is what it is not and is not what it is. If my being-for-others – 'myself' in Sartre's terms – is as a coward or a voyeur, it can be said that I *am* a coward or a voyeur, just as aspects of my facticity – my having been born in such-and-such a place, my having such-and-such an occupation – allows me to say that I *am* from Quincy, Illinois or that I *am* a philosophy lecturer. But we transcend our facticity, so I am not (i.e., I transcend) what I am (these facts about me). And likewise, as we have just seen, I am not a coward or a voyeur *for myself* but for *others*. Thus I am not (for-myself) what I am (for-others).

Second, I and the Other are revealed as negatively internally related via the shame brought about by the Look: '[t]he Other must appear to the *cogito* [the shame-consciousness] as *not being me*' (BN 252). As we have seen, I cannot bring about in myself the transformations of myself and of my world which the Look produces; shame indubitably reveals the existence of another subject, an alien freedom, a conscious being who is of necessity not me.

Third, my being-for-others – myself – is internally related to the Other. I depend on the Other *in my very being*; I would not be what I am – for example, shameful, vulgar, ugly, beautiful, charming – if it were not for the Other. It is not simply that 'the Other teaches who I am' (BN 274). The Other *does* this, of course; I *find out* that I am charmless or funny or shameful because others tell me so or let me know through their responses, and this point is an important bulwark against the view that so-called self-knowledge is always unmediated and infallible.[14] But this is not Sartre's principal point here: it is that without the Other I would not *be* charmless or funny or shameful. It is the Other's look that transforms me, in my very *being*, from a person looking through a keyhole into a shameful voyeur (see Schroeder 1984: 235ff.).

The prejudice in favour of external relations conceals these multiple internal relations. Sartre's master-stroke – using first-person experience to reveal with certainty the existence of other subjects – depends on his recognition that human beings are internally related, that first/second-person asymmetry coexists with internal relations between the first-person and the second-person perspective.

Sartre has given acutely observed and vivid descriptions of our encounters with others as objects and as subjects. But are these really the only two modalities in which we encounter others? What about *us* and *we*?

The Us-object and the We-subject

Sartre acknowledges those 'concrete experiences in which we discover ourselves not in conflict with the Other but in community with him' (BN 413), experiences which he labels as the 'Us-object' and the 'We-subject'.[15] The former experience arises, for example, with 'communal work: when several persons experience themselves as apprehended by the Third [say, the foreman] while they work in solidarity to produce the same object' (BN 419); the object which they collectively produce, say a bottle-opener, is *for* a We-subject in the sense of a 'One-subject': *one* opens bottles with this instrument (BN 424).

Yet this is not, I think, what interests us; we want to know about the sort of We-subject to which Merleau-Ponty alludes in his description of dialogue: '[M]y thought and his are interwoven into a single fabric . . . we are collaborators for each other in consummate reciprocity. Our perspectives merge into each other, and we co-exist through a common world' (PP 254). Sartre does acknowledge an experience of the 'we' which is not an experience of the 'one'; but, he argues, this experience 'could not constitute a structure of human reality' since it is 'experienced by a particular consciousness; it is not necessary that *all* the patrons at the café should be conscious of being "we" in order for me to experience myself as being engaged in a "we" with them' (BN 414). In support of this last point he notes the sort of exchange that demonstrates the possibility of this experience of the 'we' being mistaken: ' "We are very dissatisfied." "But no, my dear, speak for yourself" ' (BN 414).

The essential point here is, once again, that first/second-person asymmetry is ineliminable. My awareness that you are dissatisfied is epistemologically and phenomenologically different from my awareness that I am dissatisfied; the first is in the language-game of knowledge, the second in the language-game of certainty. The question 'How do I know that you're dissatisfied?' makes sense, the question 'How do I know that I'm dissatisfied?' does not. My beliefs about your state of mind are open to validation and invalidation in a way that my certainty regarding my own state of mind just isn't; I may be mistaken about your sense of dissatisfaction in a way in which I cannot be mistaken about my own. And as Merleau-Ponty brings out, in a much more amiable example,

> in so far as I can, by some friendly gesture, become part of that grief or that anger, they still remain the grief and anger of my friend Paul: Paul suffers because he has lost his wife, or is angry because his watch has been stolen, whereas I suffer because Paul is grieved, or I am angry because he is angry. (PP 356)

Philosophy often lands up in solipsism willy-nilly; since solipsism is not a possibility which can be lived – since the existence of the Other is a lived certainty – we must suspect the operation of intellectual prejudices. Getting rid of prejudices in favour of external relations and in favour of knowledge over certainty clears the way for acknowledging Sartre's extraordinarily rich descriptions of encounters with the Other-as-object and the Other-as-subject, and undermine the unwitting urge to solipsism. But it is not only within philosophy that others are problematic.

Concrete Relations with Others

No exposition of Sartre on Others would be complete without some mention of his notorious descriptions in the first two sections of his chapter 'Concrete relations with others'. 'To transcend the Other's transcendence, or, on the contrary, to incorporate that transcendence within me without removing from it its character as transcendence – such are the two primitive attitudes which I assume confronting the Other' (BN 363). The subtitles of the sections in which he describes these two 'primitive attitudes' give us a foretaste: 'Love, language, masochism' and 'Indifference, desire, hate, sadism'. Love, we are told, is 'a contradictory effort' (BN 376), and our recognition of this may lead us to masochism – which 'is and must be itself a failure' (BN 378–9). Indifference – of whose 'inadequacy' one cannot but be aware (BN 381) – may give way to sexual desire, which 'stands at the origin of its own failure' (BN 398), and it is 'this situation which is at the origin of sadism' (BN 399), which also 'bears within itself the cause of its own failure' (BN 404). This circular movement from one attitude to the other 'with its abrupt reversals of direction constitutes our relation with the Other' (BN 408). It seems that that Other whose existence was so certain, that Other to whom I was so thoroughly bound via internal relations and internal negations that solipsism was out of the question, is a deeply troublesome creature with whom to have to share the life-world.

I won't follow all these circles, reversals and failures through in detail; a couple of cases in point will serve to illustrate the reasoning.

The aim of love, Sartre tells us, is 'to assimilate the Other as the Other-looking-at-me' (BN 365), hence to get hold of the Other's freedom. The lover's desire is not to enslave the beloved; he 'will then feel that both his love and his being are cheapened'. Nor, however, can he be satisfied with a 'free and voluntary engagement'. 'Who would be content with a love given as pure loyalty to a sworn oath?'; 'he wants to be loved by a freedom but demands that this freedom as freedom should no longer be free' (BN 367). He, the lover, must be 'the chosen one', not merely one chosen 'among others', which would be a merely contingent love. Yet he must be chosen as part of the beloved's original choice of being-in-the-world (see Chapter 8); this is the true meaning of expressions like 'being made for each other' or 'soul-mate' (BN 370).[16] Who cannot recognize this description? But

> [l]ove is a contradictory effort . . . I demand that the Other love me and I do everything possible to realize my project; but if the Other loves me he radically deceives me by this very love. I demanded of him that he should found my being as a privileged object by maintaining himself as pure subjectivity confronting me; and as soon as he loves me he experiences me as subject. (BN 376)

The despair provoked by recognizing this contradiction at the heart of love may give rise to a new project: 'causing myself to be absorbed by the Other and losing myself in his subjectivity', an enterprise 'expressed concretely by the masochistic attitude' (BN 377). This enterprise also fails, since '[e]ven the masochist who pays a woman to whip him is treating her as an instrument and by this very fact posits himself in transcendence in relation to her', and hence as a subject (BN 379).

Again, consider this description of the attitude of indifference, wherein I practise 'a sort of factual solipsism; others are those forms I pass by on the street'. 'I brush against "people" as I brush against a wall; I avoid them as I avoid obstacles . . . the ticket-collector is only the function of collecting tickets; the café waiter is nothing but the function of serving the patrons.' This *blindness* with respect to others', however, 'includes an implicit comprehension of being-for-others, that is, of the Other's transcendence as a look' (BN 380–1).[17] And the indifferent man's non-positional awareness of being in danger of the Other's look 'alienating me behind my back . . . can occasion a new attempt to get possession of the Other's freedom': sexual desire (BN 382), described earlier (Chapter 5).

Before we conclude that we would be better off living on a desert island, we must take note of one vital point: that the concrete relations Sartre describes in such resplendently recognizable and devastatingly bleak terms are bad-faith relations. They all rest on a failure to coordinate our awareness of the Other's facticity – his being-for-me – and his transcendence – that in virtue of which I have a being-for-him. A footnote at the end of §ii refers to the possibility of 'deliverance' from this circle of failure through a 'radical conversion' (BN 412 n.14). That same radical conversion of my bad-faith fundamental project (see Chapter 8) which allows me to escape bad faith with respect to myself allows me to have authentic concrete relations to others.

The freedom of the Other is at the same time one crucially important prima facie limit to our own freedom. In the final substantial chapter we turn finally to freedom.

notes

1 This is not to say that the Other *always* appears as a meaningful object; the body of the Other may appear as a physiological, anatomical or physical object (cf. Chapter 5 and Schroeder 1984: 181). But if one focuses solely on such encounters with the Other, then solipsism will seem inevitable.

2 We have already observed that Sartre uses the word 'object' extraordinarily promiscuously: he here stresses the differences between the Other-as-object and mere things like lawns and park benches. We have also already noted that although Sartre does not use Merleau-Ponty's phrase 'subject-object', it is clear that this is precisely how he thinks of human beings. However, his insistence that we always encounter the Other either as a subject or as an object, never both simultaneously, is no more tenable than his insistence that one's own body can never be experienced as both subject and object simultaneously (see Schroeder 1984).

3 See Mirvish 1984 for a discussion of the difference between instruments and Others-as-objects from the perspective of hodological theory.

4 Although, as Sartre is aware, this description might seem to open him up to the charge of behaviourism, the behaviourists have, he argues, lost sight of the fact that the Other is 'the object which is understood only in terms of its end'. Rather than reducing the Other's body to a mere object and reducing his anger to mere movement, '[t]he Behaviorist point of view must be reversed' (BN 294).

5 Oliver Sacks borrowed this phrase for the title and title essay of his 1995 book.

6 Merleau-Ponty does note that we may have difficulties in understanding the expression of emotion in 'primitive people or in circles too unlike the ones in which I move' (PP 184).

7 Sartre treats pride differently (BN 290–1); he equates it with vanity, and sees it as an 'attempt in my capacity as Object to act upon the Other. I take this beauty or this strength or this intelligence which he confers on me – in so far as he constitutes me as an object – and I attempt to make use of it in a return shock so as to affect him passively with a feeling of admiration or of love.' Although this is a recognizable use of the word 'pride', it does not seem to me to be the only use.

8 Schroeder is one of many who assume that alienation must be negative (1984: 193f.). Again, it may be helpful to remind ourselves that 'alienation' literally means something like 'othering'.

9 Schroeder refers here to a transcendental argument (1984: 202ff.); would he also regard Descartes's *cogito* as a transcendental argument?

10 This point is one that is apt to be concealed if one thinks of being-for-others simply as 'outside-view properties' (P. S. Morris 1976) or 'the social self' (Schroeder 1984), which seems to make being-for-others encompass character traits, including virtues and vices. But these one can ascribe to oneself, with no need for another to judge one as ungenerous or unkind, simply by being aware that one has transgressed a particular moral rule or fulfilled a particular set of criteria. But guilt is not shame (*pace* Schroeder 1984: 227f.); awareness of having transgressed a moral rule is not the same as awareness of being looked at. It follows that character-trait ascriptions are *not straightforwardly* part of our being-for-others. (In this connection, it is strange that Schroeder (1984: 209) cites ugliness as a character trait.)

11 Sartre uses the verb *savoir* where my translation refers to 'possessing certainty'; Barnes, perfectly correctly, translates this with 'know'. But since French uses both *savoir* and *connaître* – *connaître* being what he contrasts with 'possessing certainty' – and both can be translated as 'to know', this translation, however correct, is apt to cause confusion.

12 From this point of view we might be struck by Temple Grandin's lack of 'self-consciousness', in that ordinary sense of the term that goes along with notions like embarrassment and shame; although Sacks feels 'foolish and self-conscious' trying out her 'squeeze machine', she feels no such thing (Sacks 1995: 265).

13 Barnes's translation begins this sentence with 'Since', drastically altering the meaning.

14 P. S. Morris has developed this theme well, e.g., in 1985a.

15 Sartre's main point in describing these sorts of experiences is to deny that these reveal anything fundamental about human reality that has not already come out in his initial descriptions of our encounters with the Other-as-object and the Other-as-subject. The experience of the Us-object is simply an 'enrichment of the original proof of the for-others', and the We-subject reveals 'nothing in particular' (BN 429), since, he claims, unless we were *already* aware of the Other, we 'would in no way be able to distinguish the manufactured object from the pure materiality of a thing which has not been worked on' (BN 427). The 'we' involved in the misunderstanding 'could not constitute a structure of human reality' since it is 'experienced by a particular consciousness'. These concepts, given a social and historical dimension by Sartre's project in the *Critique of Dialectical Reasoning*, assumed a far greater importance in their new incarnations as 'seriality' and the 'group-in-fusion'.

16 'Essential love' was of course just how Sartre referred to his relationship with Beauvoir.

17 Schroeder's 'lived solipsist' (1984: 221ff.) is supposed to lack this implicit awareness; I find this difficult to make sense of except as a description of autism or Asperger's syndrome.

freedom

S artre's conception of freedom is regularly described as 'radical' or 'extreme'.[1] And it is true that he makes some seemingly extravagant claims about freedom and about responsibility, for example, that '[f]reedom is total and infinite' (BN 531), that 'the slave in chains is as free as his master' (BN 550), and that 'man being condemned to be free carries the weight of the whole world upon his shoulders; he is responsible for the world and for himself as a way of being' (BN 553). It is Descartes's view of freedom, that 'the will or freedom of choice . . . is not restricted in any way' (*Meditation IV*), or that the will 'can in a certain sense be called infinite' (*Principles* I.35), that Sartre sees both as the key to Descartes's whole philosophy and as his greatest insight. Descartes's only problem was that his courage failed him at the last possible moment; having recognized that it is in virtue of his unlimited will that man most resembled God, Descartes nonetheless put the choice and the definition of the ultimate end for man in God's hands, instead of in man's hands where it belongs (CF). As Sartre writes in criticism of one of Descartes's fellow rationalists, 'we are [according to Leibniz] free since our acts derive from our essence. Yet the single fact that our essence has not been chosen by us shows that all this freedom in particulars actually covers over a total slavery' (BN 538).

Once we understand Sartre's conception, however, we will see that it is not nearly as outrageous as it might seem at first glance.

First and most obviously, he is not saying that we are omnipotent![2] Not only would this be an absurd claim to make given that human beings are so manifestly *not* omnipotent, it would, according to Sartre, involve an absurd conception of freedom. There can, he argues, only be freedom in a *resisting* world; hence only an embodied and situated consciousness can be said to be free, and it follows that Descartes's omnipotent God, allegedly the possessor of absolute freedom, cannot be said to be free at all. Sartre draws from this the unexpected consequence that success is not important to freedom, at least on the conception he is developing here (BN 483). So the fact that I, as a slave in chains, am unlikely to succeed in breaking them does not make me less *free* than if I did stand a good chance. Only the absurd conception of freedom as omnipotence could suppose that failure compromises it.

Secondly, Sartre's conception stands in stark opposition to a certain public image of the existentialist free act as what the novelist André Gide called the *acte gratuit*, the gratuitous act: the act done on the spur of the moment, on a whim, capriciously, for no reason. Examples might include Meursault's shooting of the Arab on the beach because the sun was in his eyes in Albert Camus's novel *L'Étranger*, or Lafcadio's pushing a stranger off the train for no reason or motive in Gide's *Les Caves du Vatican*. But this is *not* Sartre's conception of the free act. Gide's ' "act" is one of pure caprice' (EH 48), says Sartre, and he puts the word 'act' in scare-quotes precisely because, as he argues, an action done for no reason is not an action at all. He sees the determinists as having got far closer to the truth than libertarians of Gide's ilk, although ultimately, he argues, both effectively deny that human beings *act* and so both are in bad faith.

It is often said by those seeking a more nuanced understanding that Sartre uses the term 'freedom' in two different senses: referring sometimes to *ontological freedom*, 'the sense in which freedom is the defining characteristic of human beings', and at other times to *freedom in a situation*, referring to the fact that the situation is a condition for, though not a limitation on, our freedom (Whitford 1982: 56–7; cf. Compton 1998; Stewart 1998b). To say that the *word* 'freedom' is ambiguous in Sartre's usage is not quite right, in my view; the important ambiguity in question is existential, not semantic,[3] and resides in the ambiguity of human reality itself, which 'is what it is not and is not what it is', i.e., is both facticity and transcendence in an inextricable internal relation. As the body may be said to be the facticity of consciousness, freedom is its transcendence; but just as the body as facticity is internally related to the For-itself's transcendence, freedom as transcendence is internally related to facticity. The picture of Sartrean freedom as 'extreme' ignores Sartre's treatment of the facticity of freedom, which occupies more than seventy pages of BN. His 'extreme' claim 'I am absolutely free and absolutely responsible for my situation' continues: 'But I am never free except *in situation*' (BN 509).

We look first at freedom as transcendence. Philosophers have sometimes made a distinction between 'negative freedom' and 'positive freedom', often crudely expressed in terms of 'freedom from' and 'freedom to'. We can see Sartre's account as having these two aspects, with his own characteristic twists. Negatively, to be free is to be free *from* determination by *what is*: although we may, and indeed must, speak of the *causes* of actions, these causes are, he argues, no part of what is; they are *négatités* – lacks, absences, etc. – which, moreover, refer to a not-yet-existent end. Positively, to be free is to have *chosen* those ends by choosing what Sartre calls a fundamental project, and to be free *to* choose new ends by undergoing a radical conversion of one's fundamental project; although contrary to popular opinion, 'reversing steam' (BN 465) in this way is anything but easy.[4]

We then examine the internal relations between facticity and freedom; this investigation addresses those common-sense objections which 'remind us of our impotence' in the face of the various structures of our situation: our place in the world, our past, our environment, our fellow human beings, and the fact of our own death. Sartre's responses to these objections clarify why most of these things are not to be understood as limitations on our freedom, precisely because freedom and facticity are internally related.

Freedom and Transcendence

'It is strange', Sartre observes, 'that philosophers have been able to argue endlessly about determinism and free-will . . . without ever attempting first to make explicit the structures contained in the very idea of *action*' (BN 433). Once we understand the idea of an action, we will see that no distinction can be drawn between an action and a *free* action. Consequently, to deny that human beings are free, to deny that they engage in free action, is to deny that human beings act, and this is something that can be denied only in bad faith. Both determinism and libertarianism in the forms that he addresses these doctrines deny that we act. It is in discussions of freedom that ordinary bad faith and philosophical bad faith come together most clearly. In ordinary bad faith, we consider ourselves either as utterly 'weighed down' – by the past, by our bodies, by our being-for-others, by present circumstances – or as totally 'weightless'. Philosophers discussing human beings are inclined to see them in the same seemingly opposed lights: determinists are aligned with the one form of bad faith, libertarians with the other.

We will see, first, that actions are caused. In this the determinists are correct; their problem is their failure to understand the notion of cause aright and ask the right questions about it. We will see, secondly, that not only is each action done towards an end, but that there is a unity, unique to each individual, to the ends toward which each person acts: the 'fundamental project'.

Negative freedom: actions, ends, causes, motives and reasons

The central point about actions is that they are intentional: an action is the intentional realization of a conscious project. In a general way we distinguish between things that we do and things that merely happen to us. Although tripping, belching, and bumping into something *can* be done intentionally, i.e., they *can* be actions, in the typical case they don't involve the intentional realization of a project. We also distinguish between things that we do and things which happen as an unintended consequence of what we do, for example, '[t]he careless smoker who has through negligence caused the explosion of a powder magazine has not acted', that is, he has not performed the action *of* blowing up the powder magazine. To act does not imply 'that one must foresee all the consequences of his act', and one has 'performed an act just in so far as he realized his project' (BN 433) (cf., e.g., Davidson 1980).

To say that an action is intentional is to say that it has an end – that towards which the action is aiming or projecting – and that it is to be understood in terms of a cause, i.e., a reason (*motif*) and a motive (*mobile*).[5] The 'tedious discussions between determinists and the partisans of the liberty of indifference' (BN 436) centre on causes.[6] The determinist holds that every act has a cause, the libertarian of indifference, by definition, that there are free acts and that to be free an act has to lack a cause, or to have causes of equal weight pointing in opposite directions.

Sartre agrees with the determinist; his complaint is that the determinist has not carried his inquiry far enough: he has not asked how a cause 'can be constituted as such' (BN 437), and as we will see, such an inquiry ultimately undermines determinism. Sartre has far less time for the libertarian of indifference. This libertarian looks for decisions 'for which there exists no prior cause, or deliberations concerning two opposed acts which are equally possible and possess reasons (and motives) of exactly the same weight' (BN 436). The only truly free act is that performed for no reason at all, or that performed in conditions like that of Buridan's ass who was presented with two bags of oats of precisely the same size and precisely equidistant – and presumably died of starvation because he lacked free will. The liberty of indifference described here is akin to the scholastic notion which Descartes castigates in *Meditation IV* as 'the lowest grade of freedom'; in contemporary terms it refers to Gide's 'theory of the *acte gratuit*'. Sartre dismisses this conception of liberty briskly: because intention and cause are internally related, '[t]o speak of an act without a cause is to speak of an act which would lack the intentional structure of every act' (BN 436–7). These libertarians therefore end up denying that human beings *act*. This is symptomatic of bad faith.

These are rather different targets from the determinist and the libertarian who figure in many analytic discussions of 'free will vs. determinism'. The issue there is often propounded as the question of whether human actions are caused or uncaused, i.e., 'outside the causal chain', 'counter-causal', 'undetermined', or 'random'. If the issue is so set up, libertarianism, 'far from restoring (the possibility of) freedom . . . removes its main prop' (McFee 2000: 58).[7] Although we *might* apply the word 'random' to Gide's *acte gratuit*, as in 'random violence' and 'random acts of kindness', it is not at all the contra-causal kind of randomness of the libertarian who figures in analytic thinking; a capricious or arbitrary act – 'random' in the one sense – might well be subject to causal laws and hence not be random in the other sense (cf. Wiggins 1973; Dennett 1978: ch. 15).[8] A determinist of the analytic persuasion could happily accommodate caprice.

Sartre's determinist, however, starts from the premise that every action has a cause, i.e., a reason and a motive. But, because he misunderstands these, he too is in bad faith about action. Sartre offers these initial explanations of reasons and motives, which might be given by a determinist of the sort with which he is engaging; by the time he is finished, they are radically modified, and hence the determinist's conception is shown to be inadequate:

> Generally by cause [*motif*] we mean the reason for the act; that is, the ensemble of rational considerations which justify it . . . [or] an objective appreciation of the situation . . . The motive, on the contrary, is generally considered as a subjective fact. It is the ensemble of the desires, emotions, and passions which urge me to accomplish a certain act. (BN 445–6)

Take a perfectly mundane action: my going to the shops for a pint of milk. The *reason* for my act might be my objective appreciation of the fact that there is no milk in my fridge, perhaps supplemented by the belief that milk is available at the shops, and the *motive* my desire for milk; these two operating in conjunction caused my action.[9] This sounds so straightforward as to be trivial; what could the problem possibly be?

If we press it, however, we find two important features of the story which are problematic for the determinist. The first is that in order fully to make sense of this reason and this motive in their relation to this action requires us to refer to those concrete nothingnesses which Sartre names *négatités*, whereas the aim of the determinist with whom Sartre engages is to explain all action in terms of factual existences or things that can be inferred from them. The second is that the action, its end, its motive and its reason are all revealed as internally related, whereas the determinist wishes to give a causal story which recognizes only external relations.

The role of négatités. Go back to the determinist's version of our story of everyday life. Consider first the reason offered, recalling that reasons are meant to be objective appreciations of the situation which justify the action. Well, clearly my objective appreciation of the non-presence of milk in the fridge does not, by itself, justify my act. After all, I may equally attain an objective appreciation of the non-presence of lard in my fridge, yet the recognition of that fact would not send me off to the shops. Nor will adding further objectively appreciated facts of this ilk get us one whit further. The only way of describing my objective appreciation of the situation that would begin to look like a *justification* of the act is: my noticing the absence or the lack of milk. The determinist will resist the thought that I could objectively appreciate an absence: lacks and absences are neither positive or factual existences like the presence of milk, nor inferable from positive existences, as the non-presence of milk is inferable from a complete inventory of the actual contents of my fridge, since '[n]o factual state can determine consciousness to apprehend it as a *négatité* or as a lack' (BN 435–6). But nor can we do without *négatités*: the condition of an action is 'the recognition of a "desideratum"; that is, of an objective lack or again of a *négatité*' (BN 433). No ensemble of objectively appreciated features of a situation can ever justify *any* action, as long as we confine what can be objectively appreciated to positive existences and what can be inferred from them.

Consider then the motive, here the desire for milk. On the face of it, if we were to combine this motive with the originally specified reason, we would have at least the beginnings of a justification of the act: the non-presence of lard in my fridge does not justify my action of going to the shops because I have no desire for lard; but I do have a desire for milk, and surely when this subjective fact is combined with my objective appreciation of the fact that there is no milk in the fridge, it justifies my going to the shops for milk! But what is a desire? What can it mean to call a desire a 'subjective fact'? '[H]ow can we explain desire if we insist on viewing it as a psychic state; that is, as a being whose nature is to be what it is?' Desire 'must by nature be an escape from itself toward the desired object . . . Desire is a lack of being. It is haunted in its inmost being by the being of which it is desire' (BN 87–8). My desire for milk is haunted in its inmost being by *milk*, but not present, existent milk, for then it would not be *desire*, but by milk as a pure present nothingness. Hence the determinist story goes wrong from the moment it describes desire as a subjective fact.

Thus in order to understand my going to the shops for milk, I must be understood as effecting a 'double nihilation': I must 'posit an ideal state of affairs [the end: having milk] as a pure *present* nothingness', *and* I must 'posit the actual situation [the absence of milk] as nothingness in relation to this [ideal] state of affairs' (BN 435). This is negative freedom indeed!

The internal relations between act, end, reason and motive. The determinist story saw external relations everywhere: the reason and the motive of the act were two externally related facts which combined somehow to cause the action, where the notion of cause is itself understood as an external relation. Closer investigation reveals that the reason is internally related to the motive and that the motive is nothing other than the project of the action, which refers to the *end* – which, as a non-existent, did not really figure in the determinist's story at all. Moreover, there are obscurities at the heart of the determinist's causal explanation of the action itself, obscurities which vanish when we recognize that the action is also internally related to the end or motive, and thus to the reason.

'In order to be a cause [of an action, as opposed to a phenomenon], the cause must be experienced as such' (BN 437); to experience the non-presence of milk as a cause or reason for acting – that which I objectively apprehend and which justifies my action – is to experience the non-presence of milk as an absence; and this is to experience it as *motivating*. This real, concrete *négatité* simultaneously moves me to action and justifies my action, and it can be characterized neither as subjective nor as objective in the way that the determinist understands these terms. The reason can 'act in the capacity of a cause' only if it is 'discovered by a *motive*' (BN 472). And the motive 'is not distinct from the project' (BN 449; cf. 472). Hence 'the reason, far from determining the action, appears only in and through the project of an action' (BN 448), i.e., the motive. And the motive refers to the end: if the motive, the project of the action, is to get some milk, the end is that not-yet-existent state of affairs, having some milk. Although we can describe the reason for an action as 'the objective appreciation of a situation', fully spelled out, what this comes to is this: 'the objective apprehension of a determined situation as this situation is revealed in the light of a certain end as being able to serve as a means for attaining this end' (BN 446). Reasons, motives, and ends form an 'unanalyzable totality' (BN 453).

And this unanalysable totality is internally related to the action itself. The concrete *négatité* the perception of which I might express as 'I'm out of milk' is not, as we have seen, a motivationally neutral property of the world: it is a property the perception of which makes *demands* on me; hodologically, it creates a vector: to perceive the fridge as having the property 'lacking milk' is to *project* the action of going to the shops for milk. Nor must we make this 'projecting of the action' into yet a further subjective fact – a 'volition', or an 'intention' – which itself then causes the action. To project the action *is* to act. The action performed may not be the action projected: I could get hit by a car on the way to the shops, so that the *success* of my action is, as Davidson has happily put it, 'up to nature' (1980: 59) and opportunity; or I might for now confine myself to writing 'milk' on the list. But that is not the point here; to project the action is to do something that, nature and opportunity allowing, will be the action projected.

In addition, there was an unnoticed obscurity at the heart of the determinist's account. Was it ever really clear how the objective fact – the non-presence of milk – and the subjective fact – the desire for milk – were supposed to combine forces to produce the action? 'Evidently we are dealing with two radically distinct layers of meaning. How are we to compare them? How are we to determine the part played by each of them in the decision under consideration? This difficulty . . . has never been resolved' (BN 447). Once we recognize that reason, motive, end and action are internally related, that they form an unanalysable totality, the difficulty vanishes.

Sartre's description has already made a good deal of progress in comparison to the determinist's. As long as the determinist sets his face against *négatités* as causes of action and as long as he holds on to the prejudice in favour of external relations, he cannot make sense of actions. But the reader may well be wondering: what exactly this all has to do with *freedom*? Where, for example, does the idea of *choice* get in? The answer will involve our looking more closely than we have done at *ends*. As we will see, we choose our ends, i.e., our values, what kinds of reasons will weigh with us; the *négatités* which motivate and justify our actions appear in the world through these chosen ends. As we will also see, the notion of choosing our ends contains some conceptual difficulties.

Positive freedom: ends and the fundamental project

What we have thus far described is negative freedom: it is freedom *from* determination by what is; but what about freedom *to*? We saw in Chapter 6 that 'the real space of the world' is hodological; and also that Lewin, from whom this term is derived, conceives of the positive and negative valences of things encountered in hodological space as determining the direction of behaviour. Precisely this may seem to be the case from everything that has been said so far: the fridge simply *presents* me with a property, albeit a special kind of property, a hodological property, that of 'lacking milk'; given that the fridge has this property, and given that to perceive this property is to see the world as making *demands* upon me, namely, to alleviate this lack by going to the shops, it may seem that I could not act in any other way. This seems troublesome given that the idea that 'I could have done otherwise' is often felt to capture a core aspect of freedom.

Sartre's notion of the 'fundamental project' both makes sense of this 'could have done otherwise' and downplays its importance, at least in day-to-day life. Even the mundane act of buying milk is to be understood in the context of a larger project, indicated by a series of 'towards-whiches'. My project of buying milk is towards that of making tea, which is towards that of being more alert . . . to work on my book . . . to finish my book . . . and ultimately a 'for-the-sake-of-which': for the sake of fame and fortune, let us say, or something yet more fundamental.[10] Thus the simplest everyday act indicates my fundamental project, and 'it is this original choice which originally creates all reasons and all motives . . . it is this which arranges the world with its meaning, its instrumental-complexes, and its coefficient of adversity' (BN 465). I *could have* done otherwise, because one *can* choose a new set of values, but choosing a new set of values is neither easy nor lightly undertaken. Because who we are is defined by our values, to choose a new set of values is, in effect, to choose to become a different person.

We've had enough of buying milk, I expect; let's take Sartre's story: 'I start out on a hike with friends. At the end of several hours of walking my fatigue increases and finally becomes very painful. At first I resist and then suddenly I let myself go, I give up, I throw my knapsack down on the side of the road' (BN 453). Now, why did I do what I did?

The determinist will attempt to explain my action by my objective appreciation of certain facts: that the hill is steep and my body is fatigued, combined with the subjective fact that I dislike fatigue. We know already that this description won't do; my reason for stopping, what I objectively apprehend, isn't simply a hill of gradient of, say, 10 per cent but a hill which is '*too* steep', and this property of the hill is a hodological property. Again, in apprehending my tiredness, I am not apprehending something that could be spelled out in terms of, say, levels of lactic acid: I apprehend my body as *too* tired. This apprehension of my body is internally related to the perception of the hill; to say that the hill is too steep and to say that I am too tired to go on are not really distinguishable. And my motive is simply the project of the action of stopping: to apprehend my body as too tired and the hill as too steep *is* to project the action of stopping, and that is, other things being equal, to stop.

So far, this is familiar territory, and it raises the same question: did I have a choice about stopping, given that the world was presenting me with a hill that was too steep to continue and a body that was too tired to go on? Could I have done other than I did? Sartre pursues this very point:

> Someone will reproach me for my act and will mean thereby that I was free
> – that is, not only was my act not determined by any thing or person, but
> also I could have succeeded in resisting my fatigue longer, I could have
> done as my companions did and reached the resting place before relaxing. I
> shall defend myself by saying that I was *too tired*.

This debate, Sartre says, is 'based on incorrect premises' (BN 453–4). Indeed both interlocutors are *in bad faith*. Why?

On the one hand, when I say 'I'm too tired', I seem to be suggesting that my fatigue, as an objective fact-in-itself, *causes* me to stop. This cannot be right. After all, 'my companions are in good health – like me;

they have had practically the same training as I . . . they are for all practical purposes "as fatigued as I am". How does it happen therefore that they suffer their fatigue differently? Someone will say that the difference stems from the fact that I am a "sissy" and that the others are not (BN 454–5).' But this gets us nowhere; 'to be a "sissy" can not be a factual given and is only a name given to the way in which I suffer my fatigue' (BN 455). The point is that I have *chosen* the way in which I suffer my fatigue; to this extent my reproachful companion is right.

But it is a choice only because it is to be 'explained within the perspective of a larger choice in which it would be integrated as a secondary structure' (BN 455). This 'larger choice' is the choice of a fundamental project, which constitutes the person's – totally individual and changeable – 'essence'. Sartre's autobiographical work *Les Mots* presents his own fundamental project as *being a writer*: 'I existed only to write and if I said: me – that meant the me who wrote' (W 97). It is not that his fundamental project is capturable in a single word; after all, a fundamental project is unique to the individual, and any number of very different individuals could have being a writer as their fundamental project. Rather, that word condenses into a single drop a cloud of meanings and values which will be entirely different for different writers. In Sartre's case, these include his relationship to his grandfather and his grandfather's evident pride in his own *Deutsches Lesebuch*, which prepared the young Sartre, still unable to read, 'to see teaching as a priesthood and literature as a passion' (W 30). They include compensation for his sense of his own insubstantiality and dispensableness: in his childish stories, Sartre himself rescued young maidens with his sword, and he was indispensable to every social situation: people said of him 'Someone's lacking here: it's Sartre' (W 72, cf. 58, 106). The single word 'writer' unites many aspects of his life, yet we cannot understand what that word means *in his case* without seeing in myriad detail what is thereby united.

More typically, Sartre characterizes fundamental projects in ways that are less immediately recognizable. In the case of the hiker, '[t]his way of yielding to fatigue and of letting myself fall down at the side of the road expresses a certain initial stiffening against my body and the inanimate in-itself'.[11] My companion who loves his fatigue, by contrast, lives it 'in a vaster project of a trusting abandon to nature, of a passion consented to in order that it may exist at full strength, and at the same time the project of sweet mastery and appropriation' (BN 455). Thus my act of throwing my knapsack down and stopping 'was not *gratuitous* . . . it had to be interpreted in terms of an original project of which it formed an integral part' (BN 464).

So we can say the following: (a) that the hiker could have done otherwise, as his companion rightly said; (b) that given his fundamental project, given that he has chosen himself as someone who, *inter alia*, lives his fatigue as unbearable and the hill as too steep, he *will not* do otherwise; and (c) that to do otherwise would be to initiate a radical conversion of his being-in-the-world, i.e., to choose a new fundamental project:

> we can not suppose that the act could have been modified without at the same time supposing a fundamental modification of my original choice of myself . . . I can refuse to stop only by a radical conversion of my being-in-the-world, that is, by an abrupt metamorphosis of my initial project, *i.e.*, by another choice of myself and of my ends. (BN 464)

Such a conversion is extraordinarily difficult, and this is partially justifies the hiker's assertion that he could not but have stopped.

Some puzzles about the fundamental project. Sartre often speaks as though our original choices of fundamental projects are 'genuine historically datable acts, decisions, or events' (Charmé 1984: 40), for example, that moment when a voice declared to Genet 'You're a thief' (SG 26). Yet what are we to say of the individual prior to this moment of choice? If my choice of fundamental project is a choice *of myself*, who chooses? Since actions are by definition intentional and hence directed towards an end, how can the individual act prior to his choice of end? We could sidestep these problems if we supposed that the project is chosen, say, at the moment of birth or earlier; but how can we speak of someone's choosing at an age when the very idea of choice, i.e., a choice for which one might be held responsible, seems inapplicable (Manser 1966: 122)? Moreover, there can never, it seems, be any reasons or motives either for choosing or for changing a fundamental project, since a fundamental project is *inter alia* a choice of what will *count* as reasons for one. Does this not render a choice or change of fundamental project gratuitous, in precisely the sense that the Gidean libertarian's acts were gratuitous?

It may help to concede straight away that the notion of choice here is clearly very different from any ordinary notion of choice; there is, for instance, no deliberation, no choosing between options. But there is a more subtle point to be made: whereas ordinarily Sartre equates choices with actions, the choice of fundamental project is not an action;[12] he also calls the project, perhaps more accurately, a 'fundamental attitude' (BN 570), a way of being-in-the-world. It is no more an action than an artist's style *is* any one of the paintings which he executes, to use an analogy which Sartre hints at (BN 50). If the original choice of a fundamental project is not an action, then questions about when it was made are out of place. Although in telling the story of someone's life – including one's own – a particular moment may stand out as that which crystallizes the meaning of that pattern, Charmé reminds us (1984: 40ff.; cf. P. S. Morris 1976: 54ff.) that any remembered event has meaning only in the light of what comes later. This 'dizzying word' 'thief' (SG 26), in itself insignificant, became a nucleus for a crystallization of meaning only because of the subsequent pattern of Genet's life. Also out of place are questions about why – for what reasons and motives – the 'choice' was made; we can't ask why Monet painted in the style he did, what his reasons were. (We can perhaps ask why he painted 'in the impressionist style', but not why he created impressionist paintings in his own unique style, a style which distinguishes him from every other impressionist painter.) Yet insofar as the notion of choice is connected to that of responsibility, it still has something of a foothold here: do we not, in a sense, hold people responsible for their styles, do we not praise and blame them?

This analogy with style can be pushed a bit further to help us make sense of why a change of fundamental project is difficult; it is not easy to change one's style, as long as we don't take the word 'style' too superficially. This might in part be explicated via Merleau-Ponty's notion of 'sedimentation': the way in which my 'habitual being in the world' (PP 441), through being sedimented in the body, brings it about that my past has a *weight*.[13] A type of action (e.g., smoking) or a way of being (e.g., having an inferiority complex), if repeated many times, acquires a kind of weight which makes it difficult – though not impossible – to do otherwise. We must

> recognize a sort of sedimentation of our life: an attitude towards the world, when it has received frequent confirmation, acquires a favoured status for us . . . [H]aving built our life upon an inferiority complex which has been operative for twenty years, it is not *probable* that we shall change. (PP 441–2)[14]

This is not the only thing which makes changing a fundamental project difficult, however; one problem is that most people are not explicitly aware of what their fundamental project is, any more than they are explicitly aware of their own individual style. The sissy is unlikely to recognize sissyness as a *pattern* in his life – much less that 'initial stiffening against my body and the inanimate in-itself' – and may be unable to do so without existential psychoanalysis.[15] Moreover, the global nature of a fundamental project, 'the project which can no longer be interpreted in terms of any other and which is total' (BN 479), makes it difficult both to recognize and to change: '[m]y clothing (a uniform or a lounge suit, a soft or a starched shirt) whether neglected or cared for, carefully chosen or ordinary, my furniture, the street on which I live, the city in which I reside, the books with which I surround myself, the recreation which I enjoy' are all unified by my fundamental project (BN 463). But most importantly of all, the original fundamental project is a project in bad faith; and to change this pattern I must acknowledge my responsibility for the pattern of my life. That means that, again with the help of existential psychoanalysis, I must reflect *purely*. I must acknowledge my responsibility not just for my style of clothing, my housekeeping skills and my preference for dry toast but for my character traits such as sissyness or cowardice.

These considerations only skim the surface; there are many further issues to be explored *vis-à-vis* this notion of a fundamental project. Nonetheless it does, it seems to me, illuminate in a phenomenologically convincing way both the hiker's sense that he could not but have stopped when he did and his friend's sense that he could have done otherwise.

Freedom and Facticity

Sartre is well aware of the objections which common sense will make to the conception of freedom he has developed:

> Much more than he appears 'to make himself', man seems 'to be made' by climate and the earth, race and class, language, the history of the collectivity of which he is a part, heredity, the individual circumstances of his childhood, acquired habits, the great and small events of his life. (BN 482)

Sartre begins by returning to the notion of the coefficient of adversity: the fact that things within our instrumental complexes may resist our efforts. This cannot be an argument against our freedom, however, because the notions of 'resistance' and 'obstacle' make sense 'only within an instrumental-complex which is already established' by a free project:

> A particular crag, which manifests a profound resistance if I wish to displace it, will be on the contrary a valuable aid if I want to climb upon it in order to look over the countryside . . . Even if the crag is revealed as 'too difficult to climb' . . . [it] is revealed as such only because it was originally grasped as 'climbable'; it is therefore our freedom which constitutes the limits which it will subsequently encounter. (BN 482)

He adds that there remains a 'residue' belonging to the in-itself 'which is responsible for the fact that in a world illuminated by our freedom, this particular crag will be more favorable for scaling and that one not' (BN 482; cf. BN 488; PP 439). This makes it clear that obstacles are the joint product of freedom and the brute in-itself. It also indicates that, although Sartre is focusing on obstacles and the coefficient of adversity in things because it is these that might look like objections to freedom, exactly the same points apply to aids or means, to what he sometimes calls the coefficient of utility in things. These too are the joint product of freedom and the brute in-itself. Monasterio (1980) adds here a point that Sartre does not sufficiently stress: that things can be aids or obstacles to our free projects only if the body is, *inter alia*, a thing among things, and, we might add, only because it is a thing which has the particular properties that it does have. The granite of the prison wall resists my efforts to escape in part because my body is a solid physical object that cannot penetrate granite; it is, in part, that same property of my body that allows me to pick up the granite block in pursuit of my project of building my house. If our bodies were gaseous, we might not be hemmed in by the prison wall, but at the same time we would not be able to pick up the granite block. (Cartoons featuring ghosts tend to treat this point inconsistently.)

So there are obstacles, and means, only through freedom; but equally, there is freedom only through obstacles and means: 'this *residue* is far from being originally a limit for freedom'; on the contrary, 'it is thanks to this residue . . . that freedom arises as freedom' (BN 482). This is not to say that they do not *restrict* freedom, i.e., they really are obstacles. But 'freedom can exist only as restricted since freedom is choice' and every choice 'supposes elimination and selection' (BN 495). But a restriction is not a limit.[16] The very idea of action, i.e., of realizing one's projects, implies a distinction between the projection of an end and its realization; otherwise 'I am plunged in a world like that of a dream in which the possible is no longer in any way distinguished from the real' (BN 482). So '[t]here can be a free for-itself only as engaged in a resisting world' (BN 483). And it also follows that

> success is not important to freedom . . . Thus we shall not say that a prisoner is always free to go out of prison, which would be absurd, nor that he is always free to long for release, which would be an irrelevant truism, but that he is always free to try to escape . . . he can project his escape and learn the value of his project by undertaking some action. (BN 483–4)

If 'situation' is defined as the world of things revealed 'as already illuminated by the end which freedom chooses' (BN 487), we can conclude that 'there is freedom only in a situation, and there is a situation only through freedom' (BN 489). Although Sartre refers to this as 'the paradox of freedom', it is not a paradox in the logical sense: the notion of situation expresses the *internal relation* between freedom and facticity. Sartre goes on to look in detail at a series of 'structures of the situation' – themselves internally related (cf. BN 489) – to explore this interplay between freedom and the situation: my place, my past, my environment, my fellowman, and my death. He does not claim that these structures exhaust the situation. Indeed he suggests that unchangeable physical features of my body – my being short or having only one arm (BN 489) – could equally figure in this list. But his comments on these other structures are sufficiently rich to enable us to imagine what he might have said about these features of the body.

Sartre's remarks on 'my place', 'my past' and 'my environment', and indeed on 'my fellowman' insofar as this refers to the Other-as-*object*, are variations on this same theme: these things do not limit freedom but are on the contrary its condition; at the same time, they would not exist as structures of my situation but for my choice of ends. These remarks do nonetheless contribute a richness of detail and bring out implications that might not be obvious. His remarks on 'my fellowman' *qua* Other-as-*subject* and on 'my death', however, introduce some new concepts; these are shown to be limits on my freedom, but limits which I never encounter because they involve, in his term, 'unrealizables'.

My place, my past, my environment, my fellowman (Other-as-object)

My place, my past, my environment (life-space). Each of these things may look as if it presents an argument against freedom: the absurdity and painfulness of my living at Mont-de-Marsan; the irremediability of my past decision to resign my post; the unpredictability of the puncture which curtails my plans.[17] In each case Sartre makes the general point that freedom and the situation are internally related: 'facticity is . . . the only thing in terms of which it is meaningful to posit an end. For if the end can illuminate the situation, this is because the end is constituted as a projected modification of this situation.' So living at Mont-de-Marsan is only painful 'in relation to my dream of seeing New York' (BN 494); the irremediability of the past expresses the fact that choices have consequences: 'in order for the future to be realizable, it is necessary that the past be irremediable' (BN 497);[18] freedom 'implies the existence of an environment to be changed' (BN 506). But one or two new points emerge: with respect to my past, the distinction between this 'unchangeable element in the past' and its meaning, 'which is eminently variable' (BN 497) in a way which is 'strictly dependent on my present project' (BN 498).[19] Thus if my fundamental project last year emphasized the importance of taking a principled stand against the forces of encroaching managerialism, but since then I have come to recognize the desirability of a steady income, the meaning of my past act may change from 'a courageous act' to 'a stupid and empty gesture'. And in regard to my environment, '[e]very free project in projecting itself anticipates a margin of unpredictability due to the independence of things precisely because this independence is that in terms of which a freedom is constituted': hence 'I have never ceased to expect [the unexpected puncture] as unexpected' (BN 507). Sartre makes a strong case that none of these things *limits* my freedom.

My fellowman (Other-as-object). This bears closer scrutiny. I 'find myself engaged in a world in which instrumental-complexes can have a meaning which my free project has not first given them', 'an already meaningful world which reflects to me meanings which I have not put into it' (BN 509–10). Sartre's focus here is on what he calls 'collective techniques' which 'determine my belonging to collectivities'. For example, belonging to the human race is defined, *inter alia*, by knowing how to speak; of course we never just 'know how to speak', we 'know how to speak a certain language' (BN 512). The concern is that my speech – my free expression of my thoughts, 'the free project of the sentence' (BN 518) – is 'subordinated to the speech of others and ultimately to the national speech' (BN 519). At first sight this may seem more threatening to freedom than the issues raised earlier, since such collective techniques affect not just my surroundings, not just my ability to succeed in my projects, but the very way in which I execute my free projects – as if the collectivity has entered me, penetrated my own citadel of subjectivity. Yet Sartre argues, first, that '[b]y employing a technique, the For-itself surpasses the technique toward its own end' – I surpass my native language towards my end of expressing my thoughts about Sartre's philosophy – and moreover that without these techniques I could not express those thoughts; thus these collective techniques do not limit my freedom. Secondly, these techniques owe their continuing existence to the 'free surpassing of the given toward ends' by individuals; a language which is not living is not a language, and it is the use of these collective techniques for free projects that 'sustains' and 'founds' them, that gives them life. My free projects need collective techniques, and collective techniques need my free projects (BN 523). Thus individuals and the collectivities to which they belong, defined by such shared techniques, are internally related; my subjectivity never was a citadel.

My fellowman (Other-as-subject) and my death

Sartre's observations about these two apparently totally dissimilar structures of the situation are remarkably similar; indeed he sees them as fundamentally connected. Death is 'the triumph of the point of view of the Other over the point of view *which I am* toward myself' (BN 540); I can no longer look back at him (BN 544); hence the motto of *Huis Clos* (*No Exit*): 'Hell is other people.'[20] They both *limit* freedom;[21] but as 'unrealizables', they are not limits which we encounter, so that Sartre can say that '[f]reedom is total and infinite, which does not mean that it has no limits but that it never *encounters* them' (BN 531). Can we make sense of this?

Although death is one of those topics most closely associated in the public consciousness with existentialist writings, I will concentrate on *my fellowman* here.[22] We know already that my being-for-others is 'a meaning which is *mine* and which I have not given to myself' (BN 509): 'Jew, or Aryan, handsome or ugly' (BN 523). Here we have to do with 'a *real* limit to our freedom', purely and simply because 'an Other apprehends me as the Other-as-object and . . . [hence] that my situation ceases for the Other to be a situation and becomes an objective form in which I exist as an objective structure' (BN 524–5). But, as we have already seen, my being-for-others is unrealizable or inapprehensible: I can apply the word 'Jew' to myself, but 'I can not join the meaning of this word to my person' (BN 527). My being-for-others, like my death (BN 547), is not only an unrealizable, it is an unrealizable–to-be-realized (BN 528ff.). That is, I have to take a stand – even if it be a stand of indifference – on my being-for-others, I *cannot but* give it 'a meaning in the light of the ends which I have chosen' (BN 527): my being-for-others as a Jew is revealed to me in my pride, my shame, or my indifference at 'being-a-Jew' (BN 529). (It goes without saying that Sartre's choice of example is deliberate; he is alluding here to the ontological structures underlying the anti-Semitic oppression he analysed in AS.) Such a meaning is an attempt to grasp or 'assume' my being-for-others, but because it is by its very nature ungraspable, I do not *encounter* the limit on my freedom which it constitutes. To encounter these limits would be to be able to step outside the situation, which is precisely what we cannot do. Rather as Wittgenstein suggests that 'in order to be able to draw a limit to thought, we should have to find both sides of the limit thinkable (i.e., we should have to be able to think what cannot be thought)' (TLP, Preface), in order to realize our death or our being-for-others, we should have to be able to look back at our lives from beyond death, or to *be* the Other in his subjectivity.

Sartre is often understood as having undergone his own 'radical conversion' between BN and CDR, and one centre of gravity of this alleged conversion is commonly taken to be a shift from a theory of absolute freedom to a theory of freedom as limited and restricted. The section of BN just reviewed demonstrates that he has always had a nuanced and clear-headed sense both of the dialectical relationship between freedom and the situation and of the limits of freedom.[23] He has simultaneously given obstacles their full weight and shown that they are not limits to freedom because they only appear as obstacles in the light of a free project. And his attempt to analyse those unencounterable limits to freedom which he terms unrealizables is surely moving in vitally important waters, however murky they may be. Again, though his analysis of culture in terms of collective techniques is relatively undeveloped, likewise his analysis of the social structures which may make authenticity for members of oppressed groups all but impossible, his observations on 'my fellowman' go beyond the simplistic individualism and social atomism of which Sartre's earlier thinking is sometimes accused.

notes

1 'Extreme' is Warnock's (1965) and McCulloch's (1994) favoured word, but this sort of language in connection with Sartre's conception of freedom is not uncommon.

2 A surprisingly large number of interpreters of Sartre have in effect interpreted Sartre as holding this absurd view, as Detmer documents (1988: 37–8). Howells is a refreshing contrast: 'I can never quite understand where the idea comes from that Sartre believes we are free to do anything we please' (2002: 224; cf. Howells 1988).

3 This is not to say that there are no important distinctions to be made between different senses of the word 'freedom' in Sartre; e.g., the distinction which Sartre draws between freedom of choice and freedom of obtaining – labelled by Detmer as 'ontological freedom' and 'practical freedom' (1988: 60ff.) – is an important distinction, and indeed depends on the existential ambiguity I bring out here.

4 *Pace* Merleau-Ponty, who interprets Sartre as suggesting that 'the free act can with no difficulty blow [my complexes] sky-high' (PP 442). Cf. Detmer 1988: 90.

5 Barnes translates '*motif*' as 'cause'. Many commentators note the difficulties of translating these two terms and some, understandably, choose to leave them untranslated. These translation difficulties are exacerbated by the fact that Sartre sometimes uses the term '*motif*' to refer to the combination of *motif* and *mobile*, and by the fact that Sartre's initial explanations of *motifs* and *mobiles* are the explanations which a determinist would give and are hence bad-faith explanations.

6 Barnes translates '*partisans de la liberté d'indifference*' as 'proponents of free will'; no doubt this phrase is more familiar to the non-philosophical reader, but that very familiarity is misleading; moreover it disguises the reference to a notion, the liberty of indifference, which was debated by the scholastics and by Descartes in *Meditation IV*.

7 McFee is one of many who make this point. Hume's apparently similar criticism (*First Enquiry* VIII) is arguably closer to Sartre's critique of the liberty of indifference than to the modern critique of a liberty of randomness.

8 In fact, even ordinary randomness or caprice is not in general genuinely motiveless or reasonless: Lafcadio pushed the stranger off the train in order to demonstrate his freedom!

9 This bears comparison to the highly influential analytic account according to which a reason for an action consists of a "pro attitude" of the agent towards actions with a certain property and a belief on the part of the agent that the action in question, under the description under which it is intentional, has that property (Davidson 1980: 3–5). According to Davidson's account, my reason for going to the shops consists of a pro attitude toward actions with the property of acquiring milk and a belief that my action has that property.

10 I have taken the terminology of 'towards-which' and 'for-the-sake-of-which' from Heidegger (BT: esp. §18).

11 The characterization by some commentators of the fundamental project as the 'ideal self' is a little misleading; 'a certain initial stiffening against my

body and the inanimate in-itself' hardly sounds like most people's idea of an ideal self.

12 Granted that Sartre refers to this choice as 'the fundamental act of freedom' (BN 461); but then we would need to say that this use of the word 'act', like this use of the word 'choice', is wholly different from its use in ordinary situations; the very fact that he goes on to refer to '[t]his constantly renewed act' confirms this.

13 Sartre claims that 'the body as facticity is the past as it refers originally to a *birth*' (BN 327). Yet this idea of my body as the concrete realization of my past remains undeveloped.

14 Merleau-Ponty evidently takes Sartre to have failed to recognize such sedimentation; as the sociologist and anthropologist Pierre Bourdieu, a generation younger than Sartre and Merleau-Ponty, puts it, Sartre refuses 'to recognize anything resembling durable dispositions, Sartre makes each action a sort of unprecedented confrontation between the subject and the world' (1977: 73). But that Sartre does not explicitly develop a notion of sedimentation – arguably because he does not develop a notion of habit (see Chapter 5) – does not mean that he could not have, as Bourdieu at least acknowledges. Bourdieu attributes the difficulty of changing a fundamental project to a notion of something like sedimentation, what he calls *habitus* (1977: 215 n. 18).

15 Sartre outlines the parameters of such an existential psychoanalysis in BN IV.2.i; his biographies are efforts to practise existential psychoanalysis on their subjects and thereby to reveal their fundamental projects.

16 Detmer's generally excellent discussion (1988, e.g., 42–3) fails to make this distinction; it seems to me that the only *limits* to freedom (by contrast with *restrictions* on freedom) are those conferred by 'unrealizables'.

17 Wilfrid Desan uses a similar case to argue against Sartre: 'Whatever Sartre may say', he concludes, 'this is a limitation of my choice' (quoted in Detmer 1988: 81). See Detmer's thorough defence of Sartre (1988: 81–5).

18 When Merleau-Ponty writes 'if freedom is doing, it is necessary that what it does should not immediately be undone by a new freedom' (PP 437), he apparently takes this to be contrary to Sartre's conception; the passages in the text clearly show that it is not. See also Detmer 1988: 87f.

19 P. S. Morris (1976: esp. ch. 3) has a particularly good discussion of this point.

20 We should remember that the play takes place in Hell and that the characters are supposed to be dead. The motto is *not*, as it is normally in effect interpreted, 'Other people are hell'.

21 These are *external* limits on freedom, by contrast with the *internal* limit according to which freedom 'can not not-be freedom . . . it is condemned to be free' (BN 525).

22 Much of Sartre's discussion of death is a critique of Heidegger's conception of my death as my 'ownmost possibility' (BT 250) and of his vision of an authentic being-toward-death (BT §53), which Sartre understands as the idea of living one's life in the expectation of death or even as waiting for death, an idea which Sartre regards as absurd. Samuel Beckett's *En attendant Godot* (1953) plays with this insight.

23 Detmer makes this point powerfully (1988: 93ff.).

ethics and beyond

S artre is often thought of as an ethicist – this despite the fact that he never wrote a book on ethics – possibly because his lecture *Existentialism and Humanism*, which does treat of ethics, is so widely read, or because his plays and novels so frequently deal with ethical themes. I want here to say a few words about the ethics of EH, as read through the lens of BN. I also want to give the briefest of indications both of the directions in which Sartre's own thoughts about ethics developed beyond this early statement, and of how the phenomenological enterprise which Sartre began in BN continues to flourish through the sort of critical dialogue he himself so relished.

Ethics . . .

Sartre's view of ethics, like his view of freedom, has been held to be radical. His best-known pronouncements on the topic may seem to confirm this view. He recounts 'the case of a pupil of mine, who sought me out . . . he, at the moment, had the choice between going to England to join the Free French Forces or of staying near his mother and helping her to live . . . I had but one reply to make. You are free, therefore choose – that is to say, invent' (EH 35–8). The idea that *each individual invents his values* certainly sounds like a radical form of subjectivism; it may seem to imply that there is not only no objective but also no intersubjective or society-based value in terms of which to evaluate these individual values. Whatever values the individual invents are as good as any other; if I choose to value kindness to strangers and you to value their torture, there are no grounds on which I can criticize you or vice versa. But, as with his conception of freedom – indeed *because* of it, since Sartre's ethics and his conception of freedom are interwoven – Sartre's conception of ethics is not as radical as this may seem.

Authenticity: the existential virtue

When ethicists speak of 'virtues', they tend to mean excellences of character – courage, generosity, charitableness, magnanimity – which are answers to the question, 'What traits ought we to possess if we are to be the sorts of people we ought to be?' The closest Sartre may be said to come to an answer to this question is: 'authenticity', that is, radical freedom from bad faith (Chapter 4; see BN 70 n. 9). But this seems to invite the question, *Why* should one be authentic? What if anything is *bad* about bad faith? Sartre responds:

> it is not for me to judge him [the self-deceiver] morally, but I define his self-deception as an error . . . it is a dissimulation of man's complete liberty . . . it is also a self-deception if I choose to declare that certain values are incumbent upon me; I am in contradiction with myself if I will these values and at the same time say that they impose themselves upon me. (EH 51)

Sartre's phrase 'I am in contradiction with myself' is commonly read as 'I have committed a self-contradiction', as if to be in bad faith is to be logically inconsistent (Bell 1989: 57; cf. Detmer 1988: 199). But this intellectualist reading doesn't sit comfortably with his developed views on bad faith in BN, since bad-faith beliefs need not be articulate and propositional. The claim might be better read as saying that bad faith is a *lived* contradiction (cf. Flynn's 'practical inconsistency', 1984: 37): the person in bad faith unreflectively chooses his own values but *lives his life as if* he had not chosen them, i.e., as if they are qualities of the world independent of him. To be authentic, by contrast, is in these terms to live consistently.

But does this justify the claim that I *ought* to be authentic? There may appear to be two problems here. First, is not Sartre presupposing that lived contradiction is objectively bad, contrary to his own view that *nothing* has any objective or intrinsic value (cf. Anderson 1979: 48; Bell 1989: 51)? I don't find this worrying: there surely is something existentially problematic about lived contradictions.[1] Second, is this 'ought' really a *moral* 'ought'? It is far from clear what hangs on the answer to this question or on what grounds we could decide it. I am content to say that authenticity is an *existential* virtue and leave it at that.[2]

Freedom: the existential value

Sartre apparently proposes freedom as the ultimate value which we ought to pursue: 'I declare that freedom . . . can have no other end and aim but itself' (EH 51). Existential psychoanalysis, in enabling the individual moral agent to acknowledge his own fundamental project and in giving him the opportunity to choose himself authentically, reveals to him 'that he is *the being by whom values exist*. It is then that his freedom will become conscious of itself and will reveal itself in anguish as the unique source of value.' The authentic person will 'take [freedom] *itself* for a value as the source of all value' (BN 627, italics added).

Various attempts have been made to make sense of the reasoning that will take us from the fact that freedom is the *source* of value to the claim that freedom is itself a (indeed the ultimate) value. But this is not, I think, to the point. If we are to understand Sartre's claim here, it seems better to begin with the explicit contrast Sartre draws between the authentic person's end – freedom – and the inauthentic person's end, which is 'to metamorphose its own For-itself into an In-itself-For-itself' (BN 615, cf. BN 626) – as he also memorably puts it, *to become God* (e.g., BN 576). The person in bad faith has the impossible goal of becoming complete and self-standing, but at the same time conscious; only this would allay the anguish he feels in the face of freedom. But to describe the goal of bad faith as becoming God is not to name a specific value but to allude to the general form of all choices in bad faith: they devalue freedom. By parity of reasoning, to say that the authentic person 'takes freedom as a value' is not to say that he chooses a specific value but to refer to the general form of all authentic choices (cf. EH 51–3): to be authentic is to acknowledge rather than to flee freedom, to value it rather than devaluing it.

Thus there is no distinction to be drawn between being authentic and valuing freedom;[3] to say that we 'ought' to be authentic and to say that we 'ought' to value freedom are one and the same thing. It is moot whether either 'ought' is a *moral* 'ought'; freedom may be said to be an *existential* value.[4]

But, to reiterate: freedom is not a *specific* value. And this means that our worries about radical subjectivism have not yet been allayed. What we really want to know is: are there any *limits* to the values which one can choose authentically?

Capriciousness and license?

Anderson expresses the concern succinctly: 'so long as an individual accepts and values his or her freedom, he or she can do anything and still be authentic . . . Sartre is in effect advocating capriciousness and license' (1993: 64).

It is noteworthy that the pupil whose story is the centrepiece of EH is faced with what *anyone* could regard as a genuine moral dilemma involving a conflict between what *anyone* could regard as values: say, filial devotion on the one hand, patriotism on the other. And whatever he ended up doing, none of us would say that he had made what was *obviously* a bad, i.e., immoral, choice, even if we think that we would have acted differently in his shoes. The issue is: has Sartre cheated with his example? Has he simply helped himself to a ready-made morality to which his philosophical framework does not entitle him? (Cf. Manser 1966: 164; Detmer 1988: 213.) Why, in short, could the pupil not have considered the possibility of torturing his mother instead? As Detmer puts it, 'A torturer who candidly says, "I have freely chosen to kidnap and torture you, and I take full responsibility for my choice", is apparently above criticism' (1988: 163).[5]

The response to this charge is likely to be found, if at all, in two striking claims, the subject of much debate among Sartre commentators: (1) 'in choosing for himself [man] chooses for all men' (EH 29) and (2) that if I am authentic 'I cannot not will the freedom of others' (EH 52).

(1) The first, 'in choosing for himself [man] chooses for all men', has often been viewed as an unjustifiable lapse into Kantianism, an endorsement of Immanuel Kant's categorical imperative: 'Act only on that maxim that you can at the same time will to be a universal law.' Kant, the doyen of deontological ethics, held the categorical imperative to be a dictate of pure reason, and took it to justify a variety of moral duties, for example, the duties not to lie and not to steal. No doubt Kant would include refraining from torture as among our moral duties; but it would indeed be extraordinary if Sartre were adopting a universalizable set of moral duties allegedly grounded in pure reason. His point is rather that one who *chooses himself* creates 'an image of man such as he believes he ought to be' (EH 29). Thus, as Flynn puts it, the moral agent 'is not so much legislating universal statutes as exemplifying an ethical ideal' (1984: 35). Sartre clarifies: 'To choose between this or that is at the same time to affirm the value of that which is chosen.' In other words, to choose is to value and to value something is to see it as valuable wherever and in whomever it may be. This is nothing but a criterion of *coherence*: if I choose myself as a bully or torturer I cannot consistently devalue cowardice or cruelty in another, I cannot repudiate the image of man which I have myself created in myself (EH 29). Of course, many people precisely *live* such inconsistencies ('the pot calling the kettle black'): this is another manifestation of bad faith.

But we are to live consistently. The question then is whether I can *authentically* choose myself as a bully or a torturer. Sartre puts the point slightly misleadingly: 'every man ought to say, "Am I really a man who has the right to act in such a manner that humanity regulates itself by what I do?"' (EH 32). 'Rights' have nothing to do with it; the issue is: can I *consistently* choose that mankind consist of bullies or torturers? At the least such a question ought to give one pause; Sartre certainly means us to feel in anguish the weight of 'complete and profound responsibility' (EH 30) that such a question imposes. It is not yet clear, however, that we *cannot* consistently so choose ourselves.

(2) Sartre also tells us that if I am authentic 'I cannot not will the freedom of others.' Why?[6] We should remind ourselves that one can be in bad faith in respect of others as well as in respect of oneself. The apparently inescapable circles of 'concrete relations with others' – 'Love, language, masochism' and 'Indifference, desire, hate, sadism' (see Chapter 7) – were bad-faith relations. Moreover, Sartre's analyses of anti-Semitism and racism identify the roots of these prejudices as bad faith. If there cannot be an authentic masochist or sadist, if there cannot be an authentic anti-Semite or racist, it seems unlikely in the extreme that there could be an 'authentic torturer'.

If our concerns about the subjectivity of Sartre's early ethics are those we have identified, then he plausibly has the resources to rebut them. And yet the ethics of authenticity may remain somehow unsatisfying, more for *human* than for philosophical reasons: not *wrong*, but somehow peripheral to the concerns of the vast majority of human beings in the world – 'the wretched of the earth' in Fanon's phrase – those very poor, wretched, oppressed human beings for whose causes Sartre battled so hard in his long career of political activism.

. . . and Beyond

Beauvoir articulates this dissatisfaction beautifully; she wrote, years later, regarding her own *The Ethics of Ambiguity*, '[o]f all my books, it is the one that irritates me the most today' (FC 67). And I think her judgement of it must stand as a judgement too of the ethics of the roughly contemporaneous EH. She wrote it in part as a polemic – much as EH was written, and in much the same philosophical framework – to defend existentialism against the contemporary charges of nihilism, pessimism, frivolity and licentiousness. With these polemics and with the overall vision of the ambiguity of human reality, she remained in agreement when she wrote FC (1963). But, she says, 'I went to a great deal of trouble to present inaccurately a problem to which I then offered a solution quite as hollow as the Kantian maxims' (FC 67):

> why did I take this circuitous route through other values besides need to justify the fundamental importance I assigned to need itself? Why did I write *concrete liberty* instead of *bread*, and subordinate the will to live to a search for the meaning of life? . . . I was – like Sartre – insufficiently

liberated from the ideologies of my class . . . I now know, to look for the reasons why one should not stamp on a man's face is to accept stamping on it. (FC 68)

This notion of *need* came to seem to Sartre as well to be 'at the very root of ethics'.[7] He even came to the recognition that 'hunger is an evil, period'.[8] In noting that 'the rich man is delivered from his needs . . . He is never again hungry (he has an appetite)' (NE 61, cf. 547), perhaps he was exhibiting an awareness that he too, as a (relatively) rich man, had been when he wrote EH 'insufficiently liberated from the ideologies of his class'.

There were other concomitant shifts in Sartre's philosophical thinking. Beauvoir wrote that when BN was published, 'Sartre thought that any situation could be transcended by subjective effort; [later he recognised] . . . that circumstances can sometimes steal our transcendence from us; in that case, no individual salvation is possible, only a collective struggle' (FC 242). Combating racism, anti-Semitism, colonialism, slavery and the other major causes of evil in the world was not going to be achieved by individuals undertaking existential psychoanalysis, undergoing radical conversions and becoming authentic. Sartre's early ethics was an ethics for the rich; the aim must *now* be, through 'collective struggle', to bring it about that the poor and oppressed too were 'delivered from their needs' and could have the luxury of seeking 'individual salvation' through striving for authenticity (cf. Detmer 1988: 214).

Some will view these modulations in his understanding of the basis of ethics as radical discontinuities, others – myself included – more as evolution or maturation. In either case, I want to urge, we should admire Sartre's preparedness to 'think against himself' (see FC 261), to tackle residual prejudices in his own earlier thinking.

The magnificent portrait of human reality painted in BN is neither complete nor perfect. We have indicated, just for example, that his description of the lived body, though already richly intricate, misses out some complexities in the interplay between the body-as-object and the body-as-subject; and a complete analysis of the newly foregrounded concept of *need* would demand further enrichment of his conception of the body, as indeed Beauvoir's analysis of women's lived bodies in SS did (see, e.g., Kruks 1998). His analyses of culture and of oppression in his section on 'Freedom and the situation' were rudimentary, though his later work went some distance toward remedying these defects. His neglect of infants and animals creates difficulties for – at least – his distinction between being-in-itself and being-for-itself. Despite all this, as a whole the portrait remains both compelling and liberating. Philosophers continue to 'think against Sartre' – and so we all should, for to do so is to think *with* him.

notes

1 Flynn argues that the person in bad faith is choosing unfreedom, and that this is self-defeating in a way akin to asserting 'I do not exist' (1984: 38); though ingenious, this seems to me still too intellectualistic. Granted that *saying* 'I choose unfreedom' is akin to asserting 'I do not exist', but the man in bad faith does not *say* this; he *lives* it.

2 If the remedy for bad faith is Sartrean *therapy*, we might in any case be uncomfortable about regarding bad faith as a moral *vice*.

3 This also answers the objection that 'since Sartre holds that all humans are free ... it makes no sense to advise them to make freedom their moral goal' (Anderson 1993: 64). Compare this answer to Jeanson's, as epitomized by Stone: the objection has 'overlooked Sartre's distinction between a "natural" or unreflective freedom evinced in our alienations ... and a "freedom-as-valued" in which freedom is recovered and practiced as the explicit objective of a reflective moral attitude' (translator's introduction to Jeanson 1980: xii).

4 These three concepts – authenticity, freedom, and consistency (though this usually understood as logical consistency) – have all been cited by commentators as Sartre's ultimate value. What we see here is that they are internally related and mutually supportive; none is prior to either of the others. This helps to explain the disagreement among commentators as to which is prior.

5 Detmer (1988: 239 n. 76) credits this example to Erazim Kohák.

6 Anderson suggests interpreting 'in choosing for himself [man] chooses for all men' as entailing that '[i]f I choose freedom as the supreme value ... I am in effect affirming freedom as the supreme value or good for *all* men' (1979: 79). I cannot value my own freedom without valuing the freedom of all. Thus understood, the first of our two claims actually implies the second. This ingenious solution, however, seems to view freedom, though the supreme value, as still a value like any other.

7 In a lecture given in Rome 1964; quoted in Anderson 1993: 120.

8 Quoted in Bell 1989: 177. Perhaps he could even come to accept that certain things are 'good, period'; cf. Hazel Barnes's observation that 'if one argues purely abstractly that honesty, consistency, feelings of pleasure, and the sense of being happy with one's life are not self-evident goods which one ought to seek, I agree – abstractly – that there is no external, impersonal proof that they are' (1971: 24). And yet one wants to say that such things are good *without* proof.

bibliography

abbreviations used in this book

Works by Sartre

AS: *Anti-Semite and Jew* (1948) [1946]. Tr. G. J. Becker. New York: Schocken Books.

BN: *Being and Nothingness* (1986) [1943]. Tr. H. E. Barnes. London: Routledge.

BO: 'Black Orpheus'. In *Race* (2001) [1949]. Ed. R. Bernasconi. Oxford: Blackwell.

CDR: *Critique of Dialectical Reason I* (1976) [1960]. Ed. J. Rée. Tr. A. Sheridan-Smith. London: NLB.

CF: 'Cartesian freedom'. In *Literary and Philosophical Essays* (1962). Tr. by A. Michelson of *Situations I, III* (1947, 1949). New York: Collier Books.

EH: *Existentialism and Humanism* (1948) [1946]. Tr. P. Mairet. London: Methuen.

HN: *Hope Now: The 1980 Interviews* (with Benny Lévy) (1996) [1991]. Tr. A. van den Hoven. Chicago and London: University of Chicago Press.

I: *Imagination* (1972) [1936]. Tr. F. Williams. Ann Arbor: University of Michigan Press.

IFI: 'Intentionality: a fundamental idea of Husserl's phenomenology'. *Journal of the British Society for Phenomenology* I/2 (1970): 4–5.

N: *Nausea* (1938). Tr. L. Alexander. New Classics series. Norfolk, CT: New Directions.

NE: *Notebooks for an Ethics* (1992) [1983]. Tr. D. Pellauer. Chicago and London: University of Chicago Press.

PsyI: *The Psychology of the Imagination* (1965) [1940]. New York: Citadel Press.

S: *Situations* (1966) Tr. by B. Eisler of *Situations IV* (1964). Greenwich, CT: Fawcett Crest.

SC: *Sartre on Cuba* (1961). New York: Ballantine Books.

SG: *Saint Genet: Actor and Martyr* (1964) [1952]. Tr. B. Frechtman. New York: Mentor/ New American Library.

STE: *Sketch for a Theory of the Emotions* (1962) [1939]. Tr. P. Mairet. London: Methuen.

TE: *The Transcendence of the Ego* (1957) [1936]. Tr. F. Williams and R. Kirkpatrick. New York: Noonday/Farrar, Straus & Giroux.

W: *Words* (1967) [1964]. Tr. I. Clephane. Harmondsworth: Penguin.

WD: *The War Diaries* (1984) [1983]. Tr. Q. Hoare. New York: Pantheon Books.

Works by others

Beauvoir, S. de
AFS: *Adieux: A Farewell to Sartre* (1984) [1981]. Tr. P. O'Brian. New York: Pantheon Books.
EA: *The Ethics of Ambiguity* (1964) [1948]. Tr. B. Frechtman. New York: Citadel Press.
FC: *Force of Circumstance* (1985) [1963]. Tr. R. Howard. Harmondsworth: Penguin.
PL: *The Prime of Life* (1992) [1960]. Tr. P. Green. London: André Deutsch and Weidenfeld & Nicolson.
SS: *The Second Sex* (1961) [1949]. Tr. and ed. H. M. Parshley. New York: Bantam.

Heidegger, M.
BT: *Being and Time* (1962) [1927]. Tr. J. Macquarrie and E. Robinson. Oxford: Blackwell. (References to this work are to Heidegger's page numbers.)

Husserl, E.
CM: *Cartesian Meditations* (1960) [1929]. Tr. D. Cairns. Dordrecht, Boston and Lancaster: Martinus Nijhoff.
Ideas (1931) [1913]. Tr. W. R. Boyce Gibson. London and New York: George Allen & Unwin/Macmillan.

Merleau-Ponty, M.
PP: *Phenomenology of Perception* (1962) [1945]. Tr. C. Smith. London and Henley: Routledge & Kegan Paul.
PrP: *The Primacy of Perception and Other Essays* (1964). Ed. J. M. Edie. Evanston, IL: Northwestern University Press.
TD: *Texts and Dialogues* (1992). Ed. H. J. Silverman and J. Barry, Jr. Tr. M. B. Smith et al. Atlantic Highlands, NJ: Humanities Press International.

Wittgenstein, L.
CV: *Culture and Value* (1980). Ed. G. H. von Wright with H. Nyman. Tr. P. Winch. Oxford: Blackwell.
PI: *Philosophical Investigations* (1958). Ed. G. E. M. Anscombe and R. Rhees. Tr. G. E. M. Anscombe. Oxford: Blackwell.
RF: 'Remarks on Frazer's *Golden Bough*'. Tr. J. Beversluis. In *Wittgenstein: Sources and Perspectives* (1979). Ed. C. G. Luckhardt. New York: Cornell University Press.
TLP: *Tractatus Logico-Philosophicus* (1974). Tr. D. F. Pears and B. F. McGuinness. London: Routledge.
Z: *Zettel* (1967). Ed. G. E. M. Anscombe and G. H. von Wright. Tr. G. E. M. Anscombe. Oxford: Blackwell.

works on sartre

Anderson, T. C. (1979). *The Foundation and Structure of Sartrean Ethics.* Lawrence: The Regents Press of Kansas.
—— (1993). *Sartre's Two Ethics: From Authenticity to Integral Humanity.* Chicago and La Salle, IL: Open Court.

Aronson, R. (1996). 'Sartre's last words'. Introductory essay of *Hope Now: The 1980 Interviews* (with Benny Lévy) (1996) [1991]. Tr. A. van den Hoven. Chicago and London: University of Chicago Press.

Ayer, A. J. (1945). 'Novelist-philosophers, V: Jean-Paul Sartre'. *Horizon* 12: 12–26.

Barnes, H. E. (1971). *An Existentialist Ethics*. New York: Vintage.

Bell, L. (1989). *Sartre's Ethics of Authenticity*. Tuscaloosa and London: University of Alabama Press.

Boschetti, A. (1985). *Sartre et 'Les Temps modernes': une entreprise intellectuelle*. Paris: Éditions de Minuit.

Cannon, B. (1991). *Sartre and Psychoanalysis*. Lawrence: University Press of Kansas.

Catalano, J. S. (1974). *A Commentary on Jean-Paul Sartre's* Being and Nothingness. Chicago: University of Chicago Press.

—— (1996). *Good Faith and Other Essays*. Lanham, MD: Rowman & Littlefield.

—— (1998). 'The body and the book: reading *Being and Nothingness*'. In J. Stewart (ed.) *The Debate between Sartre and Merleau-Ponty*. Evanston, IL: Northwestern University Press.

Caws, P. (1979). *Sartre*. Boston, London and Henley: Routledge & Kegan Paul.

Charmé, S. L. (1984). *Meaning and Myth in the Study of Lives: A Sartrean Perspective*. Philadelphia: University of Pennsylvania Press.

Cohen-Solal, A. (1987) [1985]. *Sartre: A Life*. Tr. A. Cancogni. New York: Pantheon Books.

Compton, J. J. (1998). 'Sartre, Merleau-Ponty, and human freedom'. In J. Stewart (ed.) *The Debate between Sartre and Merleau-Ponty*. Evanston, IL: Northwestern University Press.

Detmer, D. (1988). *Freedom as a Value: A Critique of the Ethical Theory of Jean-Paul Sartre*. La Salle, IL: Open Court.

Dillon, M. C. (1998). 'Sartre on the phenomenal body and Merleau-Ponty's critique'. In J. Stewart (ed.) *The Debate between Sartre and Merleau-Ponty*. Evanston, IL: Northwestern University Press.

Flynn, T. R. (1984). *Sartre and Marxist Existentialism*. Chicago and London: University of Chicago Press.

Fox, N. F. (2003). *The New Sartre*. New York and London: Continuum.

Goehr, L. (2005). 'Understanding the engaged philosopher'. In T. Carman and M. B. N. Hansen (eds) *The Cambridge Companion to Merleau-Ponty*. Cambridge: Cambridge University Press.

Gordon, L. R. (1995). *Bad Faith and Antiblack Racism*. Atlantic Highlands, NJ: Humanities Press.

Hayman, R. (1987). *Sartre: A Biography*. New York: Simon and Schuster.

Howells, C. (1979). 'Sartre and Freud'. *French Studies* 33/2: 157–76.

—— (1988). *Sartre: The Necessity of Freedom*. Cambridge: Cambridge University Press.

—— (ed.) (1992). *The Cambridge Companion to Sartre*. Cambridge: Cambridge University Press.

—— (2002). 'Sartre's existentialism'. In J. Baggini and J. Stangroom (eds) *New British Philosophy: The Interviews*. London and New York: Routledge.

Jeanson, F. (1980) [1947]. *Sartre and the Problem of Morality*. Tr. R. V. Stone. Bloomington: Indiana University Press.

Leak, A. (2006). *Jean-Paul Sartre*. Critical Lives series. London: Reaktion Books.

Lévy, B.-H. (2003). *Sartre: The Philosopher of the Twentieth Century*. Tr. A. Brown. Cambridge: Polity.

McCulloch, G. (1994) *Using Sartre*. London: Routledge.

Manser, A. (1966). *Sartre: A Philosophic Study*. London: Athlone Press.

Mirvish, A. (1984). 'Sartre, hodological space, and the existence of others'. *Research in Phenomenology* 14: 149–73.

Monasterio, X. (1980). 'The body in *Being and Nothingness*'. In H. J. Silverman and F. A. Elliston (eds) *Jean-Paul Sartre: Contemporary Approaches to his Philosophy*. Pittsburgh: Duquesne University Press.

Morris, K. J. (1988). 'Actions and the body: Hornsby vs. Sartre'. *Philosophy and Phenomenological Research* 68/3: 473–88.

—— (1996a). 'Ambiguity and bad faith'. *American Catholic Philosophical Quarterly*, special Sartre issue, 70/4: 467–84.

—— (1998). 'Sartre on the existence of Others: on "Treating Sartre analytically"'. *Sartre Studies International* IV/1: 271–93.

—— (2003). 'The phenomenology of body dysmorphic disorder'. In K. W. M. Fulford, K. Morris, J. Z. Sadler and G. Stanghellini (eds) *Nature and Narrative*. Oxford: Oxford University Press.

—— (2005). '*Capital sur la honte du corps*'. *Libération*, supplement '*L'empreinte Sartre*', 11 Mars, p. 64.

Morris, P. S. (1976). *Sartre's Concept of a Person*. Amherst: University of Massachusetts Press.

—— (1980). 'Self-deception: Sartre's resolution of the paradox'. In H. J. Silverman and F. A. Elliston (eds) *Jean-Paul Sartre: Contemporary Approaches to his Philosophy*. Pittsburgh: Duquesne University Press.

—— (1985a). 'Mirroring and reflection: some philosophical issues'. *Psychoanalytic Inquiry* 5/2: 325–36.

—— (1985b) 'Sartre on the transcendence of the ego'. *Philosophy and Phenomenological Research* 46/2: 179–98.

Murphy, J. S. (ed.) (1999). *Feminist Interpretations of Jean-Paul Sartre*. University Park: Pennsylvania State University Press.

Santoni, R. E. (1995). *Bad Faith, Good Faith, and Authenticity in Sartre's Early Philosophy*. Philadelphia: Temple University Press.

—— (2003). *Sartre on Violence: Curiously Ambivalent*. University Park: Pennsylvania State University Press.

Schroeder, W. R. (1984). *Sartre and his Predecessors: The Self and the Other*. London: Routledge & Kegan Paul.

Silverman, H. J. and F. A. Elliston (eds) (1980). *Jean-Paul Sartre: Contemporary Approaches to his Philosophy*. Pittsburgh: Duquesne University Press.

Stewart, J. (ed.) (1998a). *The Debate between Sartre and Merleau-Ponty*. Evanston, IL: Northwestern University Press.

—— (1998b). 'Merleau-Ponty's criticisms of Sartre's theory of freedom'. In *The Debate between Sartre and Merleau-Ponty*. Evanston, IL: Northwestern University Press.

Thompson, K. A. and M. (1984). *Sartre: Life and Works*. New York and Bicester: Facts on File.

Warnock, M. (1965). *The Philosophy of Sartre*. London: Hutchinson.

—— (1967). *Existentialist Ethics*. New York: St Martin's Press.

Whitford, M. (1982). *Merleau-Ponty's Critique of Sartre's Philosophy*. Lexington, KY: French Forum.

Wider, K. V. (1997). *The Bodily Nature of Consciousness*. Ithaca, NY: Cornell University Press.

other works cited

Austin, J. L. (1962). *Sense and Sensibilia*. Reconstructed from manuscript notes by G. J. Warnock. Oxford: Clarendon Press.

—— (1970). *Philosophical Papers*, 2nd edn. Ed. J. O. Urmson and G. J. Warnock. Oxford: Oxford University Press.

Baggini, J. and J. Stangroom (eds) (2002). *New British Philosophy: The Interviews*. London and New York: Routledge.

Bair, D. (1990). *Simone de Beauvoir: A Biography*. London: Jonathan Cape.

Baker, G. (2004). *Wittgenstein's Method: Neglected Aspects*. Ed. K. J. Morris. Oxford: Blackwell.

Bermudez, J. L. (1995). 'Ecological perception and the notion of a nonconceptual point of view'. In J. L. Bermudez, A. Marcel and N. Eilan (eds) *The Body and the Self*. London and Cambridge, MA: Bradford/MIT Press.

Bermudez, J. L., A. Marcel and N. Eilan (eds) (1995). *The Body and the Self*. London and Cambridge, MA: Bradford/MIT Press.

Bourdieu, P. (1977) [1972]. *Outline of a Theory of Practice*. Tr. R. Nice. Cambridge: Cambridge University Press.

Campbell, J. (1995). *Past, Space and Self*. Cambridge, MA: MIT Press.

Carman, T. (2005a). 'On the inescapability of phenomenology'. In D. W. Smith and A. L. Thomasson (eds) *Phenomenology and Philosophy of Mind*. Oxford: Oxford University Press.

—— (2005b). 'Sensation, judgment, and the phenomenal field'. In T. Carman and M. B. N. Hansen (eds) *The Cambridge Companion to Merleau-Ponty*. Cambridge: Cambridge University Press.

Carman, T. and M. B. N. Hansen (eds) (2005). *The Cambridge Companion to Merleau-Ponty*. Cambridge: Cambridge University Press.

Carnap, R. (1937). *The Logical Syntax of Language*. Tr. A. Smeaton. London: Routledge & Kegan Paul.

Casey, E. (1998). 'The ghost of embodiment: on bodily habitudes'. In D. Welton (ed.) *Body and Flesh*. Oxford: Blackwell.

Clark, A. (1998). 'Embodiment and the philosophy of mind'. *Royal Institute of Philosophy Supplement* 43. Cambridge: Cambridge University Press.

Cole, J. and J. Paillard (1995). 'Living without touch and peripheral information about body position and movement: studies with deafferented subjects'. In J. L. Bermudez, A. Marcel and N. Eilan (eds) *The Body and the Self*. London and Cambridge, MA: Bradford/MIT Press.

Critchley, S. (2001). *Continental Philosophy: A Very Short Introduction*. Oxford: Oxford University Press.

Crossley, N. (2005). 'Mapping reflexive body techniques: on body modification and maintenance'. *Body and Society* 11/1: 1–35.

Davidson, D. (1980). *Essays on Actions and Events*. Oxford: Oxford University Press.

Dennett, D. C. (1978). *Brainstorms*. Montgomery, VT: Bradford.

—— (1991). *Consciousness Explained*. Harmondsworth: Penguin.

Diamond, C. (1991). *The Realistic Spirit*. Cambridge, MA and London: Bradford/MIT Press.

Dummett, M. (1993). *The Origins of Analytical Philosophy*. London: Duckworth.

Evans, G. (1982). *The Varieties of Reference*. Ed. J. McDowell. Oxford: Clarendon Press.

Fanon, F. (1986) [1952]. *Black Skin, White Masks*. London: Pluto.

—— (1967) [1961]. *The Wretched of the Earth*. Harmondsworth: Penguin.

Fingarette, H. (1969). *Self-Deception*. London: Routledge & Kegan Paul.

Foucault, M. (1975) [1973]. *The Birth of the Clinic*. Tr. A. M. Sheridan Smith. New York: Vintage/Random House.

—— (1979) [1975]. *Discipline and Punish*. Tr. A. Sheridan. New York: Vintage/Random House.

Gallagher, S. (1995). 'Body schema and intentionality.' In J. L. Bermudez, A. Marcel and N. Eilan (eds) *The Body and the Self*. London and Cambridge, MA: Bradford/MIT Press.

Glendinning, S. (2002). 'The analytic and the Continental'. In J. Baggini and J. Stangroom (eds) *New British Philosophy: The Interviews*. London and New York: Routledge.

Good, B. J. (1994). *Medicine, Rationality, and Experience*. Cambridge: Cambridge University Press.

Guillaume, P. (1937). *La Psychologie de la Forme*. Paris: Flammarion. (All translations mine.)

Hare, R. M. (1963). *Freedom and Reason*. Oxford: Clarendon Press.

Haugeland, J. (1995). 'Mind embodied and embedded'. In Y.-H. Houng and J. C. Ho (eds) *Mind and Cognition*. Taipei: Academia Sinica.

Henle, M. (1978). 'Gestalt psychology and Gestalt therapy'. *Journal of the History of the Behavioral Sciences* 14: 23–32.

Kelly, S. D. (2005). 'Seeing things in Merleau-Ponty'. In T. Carman and M. B. N. Hansen (eds) *The Cambridge Companion to Merleau-Ponty*. Cambridge: Cambridge University Press.

Koffka, K. (1935). *Principles of Gestalt Psychology*. London: Routledge & Kegan Paul.

Köhler, W. (1970) [1947]. *Gestalt Psychology*. New York and London: Liveright.

Kruks, S. (1998). 'Beauvoir: the weight of situation'. In E. Fallaize (ed.) *Simone de Beauvoir: A Critical Reader*. London: Routledge.

Leder, D. (1990). *The Absent Body*. Chicago and London: Chicago University Press.

Lewin, K. (1935). *A Dynamic Theory of Personality: Selected Papers*. Tr. D. K. Adams and K. E. Zener, New York: McGraw-Hill.

—— (1936). *Principles of Topological Psychology*. Tr. F. and G. Heider. New York: McGraw-Hill.

Luria, A. R. (1972). *The Man with a Shattered World*. Tr. L. Solotaroff. Harmondsworth: Penguin.

McDowell, J. (1994). *Mind and World*. Cambridge, MA: Harvard University Press.

McFee, G. (2000). *Free Will*. Teddington: Acumen.

McGinn, C. (1997). *The Character of Mind*, 2nd edn. Oxford: Oxford University Press.

Mauss, M. (1935). 'Les techniques du corps'. *Journal de Psychyanalyse* 32: 271–93.

Midgley, M. (2004). *The Myths We Live By*. London and New York: Routledge.

Moi, T. (1990). *Feminist Theory and Simone de Beauvoir*. Oxford: Blackwell.

Monk, R. (1990). *Ludwig Wittgenstein: The Duty of Genius*. London: Vintage.

Moran, D. (2000). *Introduction to Phenomenology*. London and New York: Routledge.

Morris, K. J. (1992). 'Wittgenstein on knowledge of posture'. *Philosophical Investigations* 15/1: 30–50.

—— (1996b). 'Pain, injury and first/third person asymmetry'. *Philosophy and Phenomenological Research* 61/1: 125–36.

—— (2007). 'Wittgenstein's method: ridding people of philosophical prejudices'. In G. Kahane, E. Kanterian and O. Kuusela (eds) *Wittgenstein and his Interpreters*. Oxford: Blackwell.

O'Shaugnessy, B. (1995). 'Proprioception and the body image'. In J. L. Bermudez, A. Marcel and N. Eilan (eds) *The Body and the Self*. London and Cambridge, MA: Bradford/MIT Press.

Peacocke, C. (1983). *Sense and Content*. Oxford: Oxford University Press.

Peirano, M. G. S. (1998). 'When anthropology is at home'. *Annual Review of Anthropology* 27: 105–28.

Phillips, K. A. (1996). *The Broken Mirror*. Oxford: Oxford University Press.

Quine, W. V. O. (1963). *From a Logical Point of View*. New York and Evanston, IL: Harper & Row.

Russell, B. (1956). *Logic and Knowledge*. Ed. R. C. Marsh. London: Allen & Unwin.

—— (1959). *My Philosophical Development*. London: Routledge.

Ryle, G. (1949). *The Concept of Mind*. London: Hutchinson.

Sacks, O. (1985). *The Man who Mistook his Wife for a Hat*. London: Picador.

—— (1990). *A Leg to Stand On*. New York: Harper/Perennial.

—— (1995). *An Anthropologist on Mars*. New York: Vintage/Random House.

Santayana, G. (1922). *Soliloquies in England and Later Soliloquies*. New York: Scribner.

Scheler, M. (1970) [1916]. 'Lived body, environment and ego', extracts from *Der Formalismus in der Ethik und die materiale Wertethik*. Tr. M. S. Frings. In S. Spicker (ed.) *The Philosophy of the Body*. Chicago: Quadrangle Books.

Schusterman, R. (2005). 'The silent, limping body of philosophy'. In T. Carman and M. B. N. Hansen (eds) *The Cambridge Companion to Merleau-Ponty*. Cambridge: Cambridge University Press.

Schwarzer, A. (1984) [1983]. *Simone de Beauvoir Today*. Tr. M. Howarth. London: Chatto & Windus/Hogarth.

Searle, J. (1984). *Minds, Brains and Science*. London: British Broadcasting Corporation.

Spiegelberg, H. (1961-9). *The Phenomenological Movement: A Historical Introduction*, 2nd edn, 2 vols. The Hague: Martinus Nijhoff.

Smith, D. W. and A. L. Thomasson (eds) (2005). *Phenomenology and Philosophy of Mind*. Oxford: Oxford University Press.

Strawson, G. (2005). 'Intentionality and experience: terminological preliminaries.' In D. W. Smith and A. L. Thomasson (eds) *Phenomenology and Philosophy of Mind*. Oxford: Oxford University Press.

Taylor, C. (2005). 'Merleau-Ponty and the epistemological picture'. In T. Carman and M. B. N. Hansen (eds) *The Cambridge Companion to Merleau-Ponty*. Cambridge: Cambridge University Press.

Wang, H. (1966). 'Russell and philosophy'. *Journal of Philosophy* 63/21: 670–3.

Weiskrantz, L. (1988). 'Some contributions of neuropsychology of vision and memory to the problem of consciousness'. In A. J. Marcel and E. Bisiach (eds) *Consciousness in Contemporary Science*. Oxford: Oxford University Press.

Wiggins, D. (1973). 'Towards a reasonable libertarianism'. In T. Honderich (ed.) *Essays on Freedom of Action*. London: Routledge & Kegan Paul.

Williams, B. (1996). 'Contemporary philosophy: a second look'. In N. F. Bunnin (ed.) *The Blackwell Companion to Philosophy*. Oxford: Blackwell.

index